Alexander Strashny

The Ukrainian Mentality
An Ethno-Psychological, Historical and Comparative Exploration

With a foreword by Antonina Lovochkina

Translated from the Ukrainian
by Michael M. Naydan and Olha Tytarenko

UKRAINIAN VOICES

Collected by Andreas Umland

43   Myroslaw Marynowytsch
Das Universum hinter dem Stacheldraht
Memoiren eines sowjet-ukrainischen Dissidenten
Mit einem Vorwort von Timothy Snyder und Nachwort von
Max Hartmann
ISBN 978-3-8382-1806-9

44   Konstantin Sigow
Für Deine und meine Freiheit
Europäische Revolutions- und Kriegserfahrungen im heutigen Kyjiw
Mit einem Vorwort von Karl Schlögel
Herausgegeben von Regula M. Zwahlen
ISBN 978-3-8382-1755-0

45   Kateryna Pylypchuk
The War that Changed Us
Ukrainian Novellas, Poems, and Essays from 2022
With a foreword by Victor Yushchenko
ISBN 978-3-8382-1859-5

46   Kyrylo Tkachenko
Rechte Tür Links
Radikale Linke in Deutschland, die Revolution und der Krieg in der Ukraine, 2013–2018
ISBN 978-3-8382-1711-6

The book series "Ukrainian Voices" publishes English- and German-language monographs, edited volumes, document collections, and anthologies of articles authored and composed by Ukrainian politicians, intellectuals, activists, officials, researchers, and diplomats. The series' aim is to introduce Western and other audiences to Ukrainian explorations, deliberations and interpretations of historic and current, domestic, and international affairs. The purpose of these books is to make non-Ukrainian readers familiar with how some prominent Ukrainians approach, view and assess their country's development and position in the world. The series was founded, and the volumes are collected by Andreas Umland, Dr. phil. (FU Berlin), Ph. D. (Cambridge), Associate Professor of Politics at the Kyiv-Mohyla Academy and an Analyst in the Stockholm Centre for Eastern European Studies at the Swedish Institute of International Affairs.

Alexander Strashny

The Ukrainian Mentality

An Ethno-Psychological, Historical and Comparative Exploration

With a foreword by Antonina Lovochkina

Translated from the Ukrainian
by Michael M. Naydan and Olha Tytarenko

Bibliografische Information der Deutschen Nationalbibliothek
Die Deutsche Nationalbibliothek verzeichnet diese Publikation in der Deutschen Nationalbibliografie; detaillierte bibliografische Daten sind im Internet über http://dnb.d-nb.de abrufbar.

Bibliographic information published by the Deutsche Nationalbibliothek
Die Deutsche Nationalbibliothek lists this publication in the Deutsche Nationalbibliografie; detailed bibliographic data are available in the Internet at http://dnb.d-nb.de.

Cover illustration: "Ancestor Energy", © copyright 2023 by Oleg Shupliak

УКРАЇНСЬКИЙ ІНСТИТУТ ⫽ІІІКНИГИ

Dieses Buch wurde mit Unterstützung des Translate Ukraine Translation Program veröffentlicht.
This book has been published with the support of the Translate Ukraine Translation Program.

ISBN-13: 978-3-8382-1886-1

© *ibidem*-Verlag, Stuttgart 2024

Originally published under the title: "Український менталітет: ілюзії-міфи-реальність" by Dukh i Litera Publishing House, Kyiv, Ukraine, in 2017.

Alle Rechte vorbehalten

Das Werk einschließlich aller seiner Teile ist urheberrechtlich geschützt. Jede Verwertung außerhalb der engen Grenzen des Urheberrechtsgesetzes ist ohne Zustimmung des Verlages unzulässig und strafbar. Dies gilt insbesondere für Vervielfältigungen, Übersetzungen, Mikroverfilmungen und elektronische Speicherformen sowie die Einspeicherung und Verarbeitung in elektronischen Systemen.

All rights reserved. No part of this publication may be reproduced, stored in or introduced into a retrieval system, or transmitted, in any form, or by any means (electronical, mechanical, photocopying, recording or otherwise) without the prior written permission of the publisher. Any person who does any unauthorized act in relation to this publication may be liable to criminal prosecution and civil claims for damages.

Printed in the EU

Contents

Foreword by *Antonia Lovochkina* 11
Preface 15
Acknowledgements 17
What is Mentality? 19
The Genetic Memory of Generations 23
Mentality and Nationality 27
The Roots of Ukrainian Mentality 29
    Prehistoric Times 29

    Trypillian Civilization 31
        Trypillians are the First Ancestors of Ukrainians 32
        Ground in the Millstones of History 33
        Ethnic Features 34

    The Mentality of the People of Trypillia and its Influence
    on Modernity 41

    Pre-Slavic and Proto-Slavic Tribes 44
    Ethnic Features 46
    The Mentality of the Proto-Slavs and its Influence
    on Modernity 48

Peoples that Assimilated with the Ancestors of Ukrainians in
Ancient Times 51

    The Cimmerians 51

    Scythians 52
        Mentality 54

    Sarmatians 59
        Ethnic Features 59
        Sarmatian Mentality and its Influence on Modernity 61

    Ancient Greece of the Northern Black Sea 63
        Greeks and Ancestors of Ukrainians 65
        Ethnic Features 66

Mentality 74
The Influence of Ancient Greek Mentality on the
Ukrainian.. 76
    Interview with Valentyna Krapyvyna 76
Did the Mentality of Ancient Rome Influence the
Ancestors of Ukrainians? 81

Direct Ancestors of Ukrainians 83

    Slavs of the Early Middle Ages 83
        Ethnic Features 83
        The Mentality of the Early Slavs and its Influence on
        Modernity 89

    Kyivan Rus 93
        What does "Rus" mean? 93
        An Excursion into History 94
        Peculiarities of Life and Everyday Life 104
        Mentality 115
        Comparative Analysis of the Mentalities of Kyivan Rus
        and Medieval Europe 120

Ukrainians of the 14th-21st Centuries 123

    Zigzags of History 123
        As the folk saying goes, an uninvited guest is worse
        than a Tatar. 123
        Ukraine as Part of the Grand Duchy of Lithuania 125
        The Ukrainian Cossack State 126
        The Polish Age 127
        Under the Umbrella of Muscovy 129
        Independence 136

    Ethnic Features 138
        Common Features of Ukrainians (Interviews with
        Scholars) 138
        Nationality 152
        Language 153
        Personality vs. Society 154
        Work 155

Religion 155
Authorities 156
Military Matters 157
Education and Science 161
Culture 163
Architecture 164
Theater 164
Painting 165
Music 168
Literature 169
Love 171

Mosaic of the Ukrainian Soul 173

Pearls of a Distinctive Necklace 173
A Tendency for a Settled Lifestyle 173
Business Efficiency 174
Versatility 174
Peacefulness 175
Courage 176
Love of freedom 176
Democracy 178
Spirituality 178
Aptitude 179
Figurative Perception 180
Emotionality 180
Sentimentality 181
Mysticism 181
Sincerity 182
Openness 183
Baroque Thinking 183
Intelligence, Astuteness, Craftiness 184
Self-Will 185
Ability to Self-Organize 186
Optimism 187
Resistance to Stress 187
Joy of Life 188
A Well-Developed Sense of Humor 188

The Reverence of Women 189
Respect for the Family 191
Eroticism 192

Between East and West 193
    Introversion 194
    Moderation 194
    Mercantilism — Unselfishness 195
    Cautiousness — Inertia 196
    Passivity — Initiative 197
    Diligence — Laziness 197
    Unpretentiousness — Striving for Comfort 198
    Sociability — A Closed Nature 200
    Kindness — Unkindness 201
    Patriotism — Tolerance 202
    Politeness — Straightforwardness 203
    "Backwardness" — High Intellectual Capacity 205
    Charisma 206

Echoes of Forgotten Ailments 207
    Provincialism 208
    Conservatism 209
    The Inability for Strategic Planning 209
    Low Self-Esteem 210
    Echoes of Communist Upbringing 212
    Naivety, Infantility 213
    Carelessness 215
    A Closed Nature among One's Group 216
    Lack of Purposefulness 216
    Disrespect for the Law, Anarchy 217
    Inconsistency, a Striving to "Serve Two Masters" 218
    Lack of Curiosity 218
    Lack of Attention to Health 219
    Amorous Adventurism 219

Russian Mentality and How It Differs from the Ukrainian 220
    Nation, Territory, Nature 221
    The Cult of the Tsar 223

The Archetype of an Iron Fist — Aggressiveness and Cruelty ... 224
Statehood — Patriotism — Lack of Individual ... 227
Imperial Thinking — the Breadth of the Soul ... 228
Selflessness vs. Corruption ... 230
Morality and Disrespect for the Law ... 231
Nobility vs. Contempt for Man ... 232
Hospitality vs. Lack of Kindness ... 232
Culture vs. Ignorance ... 233
Entrepreneurial Dexterity vs. Laziness ... 234
Haste — Categorical thinking - Determination ... 235
Unpredictability - Curiosity - Unpretentiousness ... 236
Humor — Camaraderie — Drunkenness ... 237
Love ... 237
Conclusion ... 238

Winds of New Times ... 239
How Ukrainians See Themselves ... 241
The View of Foreigners ... 241

Epilogue ... 249

Foreword

Antonina Lovochkina

Doctor of Psychology,
Professor in the Department of Social Work
at Taras Shevchenko National University of Kyiv

For centuries, the idea has been imposed on the entire world that Ukrainians, Belarusians, and Russians comprise a single people, and therefore the two smaller nations must forever be linked with Russia, which, as underscored in this distortion of history, insists on hegemony. During Soviet times, we were taught in school that the different peoples who come to dwell in the country must form a single nation—the Soviet people, with a single mentality—a Russian one. After the collapse of the USSR, Alexander Strashny was perhaps the first to write a book about the Ukrainian worldview, in which he arguably established that Ukrainians have their own unique mentality that essentially distinguishes them from their neighbors.

This book is exceptional for several reasons. First off, because the study of the Ukrainian mentality was undertaken not by a historian, not by an ethnographer, not by a linguist, but rather by a psychotherapist with many years of experience in the field and who, additionally, is a talented writer. Adhering to all the necessary requirements of scholarly research, Alexander Strashny presented the results of his studies not in the form of a scholarly monograph, but as an interesting, lively work that reflects not just the tip of the iceberg of the Ukrainian worldview, but also what an outside observer fails to notice. In this book there are many strata of little-known, historical facts that Western readers may not expect, but which are conclusively demonstrated.

Based on an analysis of everyday life, customs, culture, language, military matters, and the traditions of Ukrainians, of their ancestors, and of those peoples who joined in the formation of the Ukrainian mentality, the author managed to answer the question of how the Ukrainian worldview was fashioned and why modern

Ukrainians have been shaped precisely the way they are—with all their innate contradictions, shortcomings, as well as merits.

When you read about the ancient history of the lands on which Ukraine is now located, it's as though you're plunging into the actual world of your ancestors. Academic history is mainly the study of the actions of princes, kings, and their retinues. But Dr. Strashny has focused on ordinary people—tillermen, nomads, and warriors. All the author's historical pursuits are directed at explicitly revealing the human factor, the motives for an individual's behavior. As if on the silver screen, the ancient ancestors of Ukrainians appear—the mysterious Trypillians, the ancient Greeks of the northern Black Sea region, the Scythians, the Sarmatians, the Proto-Slavs, the inhabitants of Kyivan Rus, and the Zaporozhian Cossacks. Relying on numerous facts, the author has reconstructed the way of thinking of a person who absorbed Ukrainian history, Ukrainian culture, and Ukrainian traditions, all that ultimately constitutes the cumulative mentality of a modern Ukrainian. Everything is presented so graphically that you feel as if you are participating in events that took place in the ancient past.

This book also offers a captivating exploration of the profound connection between Ukrainians and their land, delving into the deep-rooted beliefs that bind them to Mother Earth. It examines the intricate dynamics between men and women that challenge prevailing patriarchal structures, offering a remarkable source of empowerment for Ukrainian women—an attribute often absent in many traditional societies. It provides a compelling exploration of Ukrainian eroticism, skillfully tracing its origins to the veneration of ancient female deities. The author's refreshing psychological perspective is firmly grounded in socio-cultural and historical analyses. Through these insightful frameworks, it unravels the various contradictions that permeate the Ukrainian mentality. For instance, it sheds light on the perplexing phenomenon of a hardworking and highly skilled man exhibiting extreme laziness. It explores the reconciliation of seemingly opposing traits like collectivism and individualism. It elucidates how sociability and introversion can coexist harmoniously, devoid of conflict. It delves into the reasons behind the curious phenomenon of highly intellectual men being labeled as backward. It explores the intricate nature of human behavior, illustrating how both greed and selflessness can coexist within a single individual. This is merely a glimpse into the myriad examples that the book illuminates. Above all, the book provides a comprehensive understanding of what it means to navigate between the influences of the East and the West. It skillfully uncovers the ways in which Ukrainians assimilate traits from both mentalities, despite their seemingly conflicting nature.

Dr. Strashny's copiously researched material is not only collected into a complete system, but also passed through the author's heart, warmed by humor and emotions. It is no accident that after its release in Ukrainian, this book immediately became a bestseller.

Now, during the war, the Kremlin's propaganda is trying to impose the false narrative on the entire world and on Russians themselves that Ukrainians are unworthy of serious attention, that they are weak and helpless, that they have fallen into a trap that leads them, step by step, to their demise. However, neither the so-called Russian "experts" nor their Kremlin dictator have understood that Ukrainians in peacetime and during war are completely different entities. Few people know what strength and power has awakened in Ukrainians — known for being a kind and peaceful people — during times of danger.

In the 1990s, the leader of the Chechen liberation movement, Dzhokhar Dudayev, uttered what amounts to a prophecy: "The biggest mistake is to disregard the Ukrainians. To consider Ukrainians weak. To offend Ukrainians. Never insult the Ukrainians. They are not as weak as you might think".

This is precisely what writer and psychotherapist Alexander Strashny's book deals with. Yet the author has not only written about the positive aspects of the Ukrainian mentality, but also about the shortcomings that still remain in the Ukrainian worldview.

Recently, a number of fair-minded, interesting publications have appeared on the topic of the Ukrainian mentality. Now, in the 21st century, Ukrainian culture is increasingly etched with the notion of the nature of its national character. But the process is not yet complete. There are still blank spots that require further elucidation.

Alexander Strashny's book answers many questions regarding the Ukrainian worldview, which combines within it seemingly incompatible notions. But mainly the author has answered the question of how a gentle, peace-loving people with a love for singing, who enjoy having numerous, lengthy discussions without making concrete decisions, has managed to constrain the brutal military might from the East in order to protect themselves and the world in the confrontation of Good vs. Evil.

There is a saying about Ukrainians: "My house is on the edge …" Some believe that it speaks to their indifference. But in fact, this saying has a second part that ends like this: "My house is on the outskirts — therefore I am first to meet the enemy".

Starting with the war of aggression in February 2022, Russia cruelly hoped to obliterate Ukraine, to force Ukrainians to abandon their language, their traditions, and their mentality. The wild horde has done considerable damage. Even now, as I'm penning the foreword to this book, an air raid siren is sounding. I'm not in my office, but in a corridor protected only by two walls. And outside the window, exploding enemy missiles can be heard, shot down by the Ukrainian air defense. Unexpectedly for the invaders, at the beginning of the full-scale Russian aggression, positive changes to the Ukrainian mentality began to develop more rapidly than ever before. Ukrainians began to believe in themselves, and the world began to believe in Ukrainians.

Recently, on the eve of the national holiday when Ukrainians wear their national dress — the traditional "vyshyvanky" (embroidered shirts and blouses) — the enemy launched dozens of missiles at Kyiv. The residents of the city did not sleep that night. And how did they feel after a loud and sleepless night? It didn't matter — they put on their fine embroidery and went out to take pictures for the holiday. They were saying: Here we are, the Ukrainians — strong, courageous, and unbreakable!

To anyone who wants to learn more about the Ukrainian mentality and also what is common to and differentiates Ukrainians from Americans, Europeans, and Russians, I recommend that you read this book by Alexander Strashny.

It will give pleasure to everyone, from students to senior citizens.

Kyiv, June 17, 2023

Preface

One can choose a God to worship. One can choose a nationality. One can even choose a history. But no one can choose their mentality.

In 1990, I was invited to give a series of lectures in the U.S. When they asked me where I was from, I answered that I was from Ukraine. No one then knew what country it was or where it was located. When I said that I was from Kyiv, the audience cheered: "Oh, yes, we know, Chicken Kyiv, those cutlets are on the menu of our restaurant". That was it. There was no other information about Ukraine in the civilized world then.

Thirty years have passed. Ukraine has dominated mass media across the world since February 24, 2022. People of the world have turned their attention to Ukraine, and as it turns out, they see Ukrainians as cool people! President Biden mentions Ukraine more often than any other country in his speeches. British Prime Minister Boris Johnson repeatedly addresses journalists in the Ukrainian language. After a twenty-eight-year hiatus, the legendary Pink Floyd band recorded a song in Ukrainian. Paul McCartney unfurled the Ukrainian flag at the first concert of his tour. Parisian high fashion houses adorned their collections in the blue and yellow colors of the Ukrainian flag. Dutch florists produced a new variety of tulips in yellow and blue. The crew of the American SpaceX campaign took the Ukrainian flag into space. Time Magazine has repeatedly featured the President of Ukraine, Volodymyr Zelensky, on its cover.

How did this come to be?

Within the past ten years, two logically impossible things have happened in Ukraine. During the Revolution of Dignity in 2014, Ukrainians singlehandedly overthrew their president-dictator Viktor Yanukovych, who gave the order to fire on them with machine guns. In 2022, Ukrainians repelled the second-largest army in the world, which threw all its sophisticated weapons and might against them. NATO experts shrug their shoulders in surprise: how could this have happened? Ukraine was supposed to surrender three days after the invasion . . . The Russians continually bomb Ukraine — it still stands; they try to level it with tanks — it still stands; they try to destroy it with rockets — it still stands; the

Russian soldiers crawl into Ukraine from every direction and cannot do anything. What steel are these Ukrainians made of?

NATO experts were wrong in their political prognoses. The mad Russian president was also mistaken. Estimating the number of weapons and military equipment, the world did not consider the primary weapon of Ukrainians — their spirit, backbone, and mentality. It is precisely this Ukrainian mentality that will be the topic of my exegesis.

This book was first published in 2008 in Ukrainian and Russian. Preparing the edition for the English-speaking reader, I extensively revised the text to make the content understandable for those who know little about Ukraine but want to learn more about it. Based on an analysis of history, the everyday life of Ukrainians, economy, culture, religion, politics, so forth I singled out fifty dominant Ukrainian mental traits. I compared them with the most common characteristics of Europeans and Russians. Based on my research, I derived conclusions about similarities and differences between Europeans, Ukrainians, and Russians.

The character of a person is revealed in extreme situations. In times of danger, they "take off their mask" and show their best and worst qualities. An entire nation's character can also be exposed in an extreme situation. The events of the Russian war against Ukraine have made me rethink many things. Therefore, this edition includes much material unpublished in previous editions of this book and in English-language nonfiction literature in general.

Looking for an answer to the question "Who is a Ukrainian?" I have tried to be impartial and not to project my own hypotheses; instead, I have tried to describe everything as objectively as possible.

Plato is my friend, but my greatest friend is truth. Even more so when it is the naked truth. I still intend to offer it to my readers.

Acknowledgments

I am grateful to everyone who provided me with invaluable help when I worked on this book: Valeriy Yarovyi, Doctor of History, Professor, and the Head of the Department of History of the Slavs at Taras Shevchenko National University of Kyiv; Kostyantyn Tyshchenko, Professor and Director of the Linguistic Museum of Ukraine; Valentyna Krapyvyna, a senior researcher at the Institute of Archeology of the Academy of Sciences of Ukraine, and head of the Olvia archeological expedition; Yuliy Lifshyts, a researcher of Kyivan Antiquities; Eleonora Solovei, Doctor of Philology and head of the Department of Comparative Studies of Taras Shevchenko Institute of Literature; Olena Kashuba-Volvach, a doctoral candidate of Art History and an employee of the Institute of Art History, Folklore and Ethnology of the National Academy of Sciences of Ukraine; Yaroslav Domanskyi, the head of the archeological expedition of the State Hermitage Museum on Berezan Island; Yuriy Vynohradov, Doctor of History; Professor Kostyantyn Marchenko, Doctor of History; Tetyana and Volodymyr Nazarov, researchers at the Institute of Archeology of the Academy of Sciences of Ukraine; the writers Gustav Vodička and Dmytro Stus; Arkadiy Medvinskyi, the editor of the A.S.K. publishing house; Leonid Finberg, editor-in-chief of the Dukh i Litera publishing house; my wife Tatyana, my daughter Maryna, and my son Denys.

Work on this book continued at a time when bombs were falling on Ukraine. I ended each of my messages to family, colleagues, and friends with the words: "Let's hang in there! We are stronger than the enemy!"

I address these same words to my readers.

What is Mentality?

The collective soul of a people is only a slightly more complex structure than the soul of an individual.
Carl Jung

Mentality as a concept is difficult to understand. It almost does not lend itself to rational interpretation. It is not the same as generally accepted rules and customs, traditions, a language, or a worldview. It is something that can be perceived but not rationalized. However, it embraces generally accepted rules, customs, traditions, language, and worldviews.

There is no precise scientific method to identify certain national traits. There is no concise and explicit definition of the concept of "mentality".

This term is derived from the Latin word *mentalis*, which means *mental*. In the Great Encyclopedic Dictionary, mentality is defined as a set of thoughts, cognitive skills, and spiritual instructions inherent in an individual or a social group. In the Explanatory Dictionary, mentality is defined as a worldview and "mindset". The Dictionary of Foreign Words defines this concept as thinking, a state of mind, a deep level of collective and individual consciousness, which includes the unconscious.

Mentality is a particular set of psychological algorithms that shape the view of an individual or a group of people concerning surrounding reality and, accordingly, determine their behavior.

The concept of mentality first appeared in Alexis de Tocqueville's book *Democracy in America* (1835). Researching the collective consciousness of the U.S., the author discussed the superstitions, habits, and misconceptions characteristic of American society. In his opinion, the American national character embraced all these aspects.

European thinkers of the 20th century engaged in a lively discussion of the concept of mentality. For example, historians of the Annales School viewed mentality as the sum charge of spiritual experience that makes history.

Sigmund Freud made a prominent contribution to developing ideas about the human psyche. He convincingly argued that between the conscious and unconscious, which are intrinsic to mentality as well, the unconscious realm is more important.

In the modern world, the study of mentality is primarily used by special services in training agents for work abroad, in the activities of trade managers, as well as by politicians who seek to impose their values on a particular social group.

An individual is rarely able to objectively evaluate him- or herself and his or her behavior. According to Freud, to comprehend something—an image, feeling or idea, one has to verbalize it and embody it in a verbal shell. Therefore, in this book, we will put into words something that is little understood—Ukrainian mentality; I hope it will become more understandable. I also hope that readers will compare the material of this book with their own life experience, draw from the text, and come to their own conclusions.

Hence, mentality is an asset of every individual. When it is common to some group, formed by an occupation, lifestyle, or ethnicity, we talk about the mentality of a trader, a Christian, a policeman, a fan, a German, a Briton, or a Ukrainian. A family, a generation, inhabitants of an entire continent, or the planet's whole population can be that group. Mentality can have male or female characteristics.

The concept of a group mentality (a collective unconscious) gained recognition thanks to the Swiss psychiatrist Carl Gustav Jung. According to him, the content of the personal unconscious is formed during the entire lifetime of an individual. Still, one lifetime is not enough for the collective unconscious to emerge. The collective unconscious is a kind of instinct that consists of archetypes (archaic types), that is, primary images, ideas, and experiences that arise from the depths of unconscious mental formations.

Jung posited that archetypes are the essence of the psyche, inaccessible through direct experience but formed from the mental imprints of our ancestors' countless experiences. These foundational elements are likened to riverbeds, lying dormant when devoid of life's flow, yet they become vibrant and full when the currents of existence return in force.

Jung emphasized the spontaneity of archetypes. They manifest themselves independently of will or consciousness and emerge unexpectedly. Jung insisted that the extent to which a person remains under their influence is incalculable. Especially a modern rational and pragmatic person is completely unaware of how much his or her life is under the control of irrational forces. Such a person is subject to them no less than a primitive man, who, unlike us, realized that he existed in a realm of otherworldly influences.

The Genetic Memory of Generations

Why do some ancient experiences of *the entire lineage of ancestors* emerge suddenly *from the depths of the unconscious* and affect human behavior? Is it true that if a child from a tribe of Australian aborigines grows up in a European family, then this person and their descendants will "genetically know" how to catch a crocodile? It seems impossible because "how to catch a crocodile" is not encoded in the genes.

Nevertheless, the mechanism of genetic transmission of ancestral memory exists.

We receive genes from our parents, which already record features of our appearance, health, personality, so forth But hereditary traits depend not only on the received genes but also on their functionality. People with a similar set of genes will behave differently in similar situations thanks to epigenetic mechanisms.

This phenomenon has the following mechanism. Each person has a complete set of all psychological traits, including their opposites, encoded in their DNA. The way the ancestor behaved in a particular situation, whether they exhibited courage, cowardice, cruelty, or nobility, is not encoded in DNA. However, due to the chemical reactions that strengthen or weaken the activity of a gene cluster responsible for a certain psychological trait, a *predisposition* to a certain behavior is transmitted from an ancestor. Information from the past alters the activity of genes through chemical modification of DNA: some genes are "turned on", some are "turned off". These changes are transmitted only through the paternal lineage because epigenetic effects on DNA affect sperm and do not affect ova.

Chemical modifications of DNA do not disrupt the sequence of nucleotides that make DNA. The replacement of one nucleotide by another does not constitute a mutation. These external chemical reactions affect a certain gene by weakening or, on the contrary, strengthening the synthesis of the protein included in the chains of the DNA molecule.

Thus, it becomes clear why, if the grandfather had drowned, his grandchildren would be afraid of water; if he had abused alcohol, his descendants would tend to have a similar disposition to the bottle; if he were starving, there would be a tendency to stock up on excess food.

The research of biologists Kerry Ressler and Brian Diaz from the Maury University Medical Center (Georgia, U.S.) have scientifically proved this hypothesis.

The experiment was as follows. Scientists filled a laboratory room containing male mice with the odor of acetophenone, which resembles the scent of bird cherries. The mice did not react to it. Later, using electrodes wired into the floor, the researchers began to use an electric shock every time the scent was released. The mice panicked and tried to run away.

After a series of studies, the mice were no longer electrocuted; only the scent was released. Having smelled bird cherry blossoms, the mice shuddered, jumped up and ran away without being given an electric shock.

The most exciting thing happened later. The mice involved in the experiment produced offspring that were never shocked and were unfamiliar with the scent of bird cherries. When the offspring grew up, the scientists let them sniff acetophenone. The mice reacted the same way as their parents: they froze, jumped up and tried to run away, although they were never given a shock.

The fear of the scent even remained in the third generation — the grandchildren of mice who once dreaded the smell of acetophenone also exhibited a panic reaction.

So, the memory of the danger was transmitted to mice even across generations. But maybe the animals somehow communicated the fear to their descendants?

To determine this, scientists set up an experiment using in vitro fertilization followed by embryo implantation into surrogate mothers. Babies born in this way never saw their "frightened" parents and had no opportunity to learn anything from them. However, they also exhibited stressful behavior in reacting to the scent of acetophenone.

At the beginning of the last century, Nobel laureate Ivan Pavlov observed a similar phenomenon. While developing a conditioned reflex in dogs, he observed that this reflex appears faster and faster in subsequent generations of animals.

In this way, it was scientifically proven that a living being carries an imprint of events that happened to their ancestors: a person usually behaves the same way as their ancestors on the paternal line. Education is not a decisive factor here. Carl Jung plausibly called this "imprint of events" archetypes.

There is an infinite number of archetypes. Jung emphasized they are revealed to their full extent in periods of crisis, like *the channels of dry rivers*, they are filled with a *raging full-water stream* during wars, calamities, reconstruction, and revolutions.

Mentality and Nationality

In the modern world, there are no racially or ethnically "pure" nations. Saxons know well that more than half of the blood that flows in their veins is Polish and Lithuanian. However, this does not prevent them from self-identifying as Germans. Residents of French Normandy are proud that their ancestors were Vikings. However, they will laugh at anyone who would call them Norwegians. France hardly had a better Frenchman than Napoleon, and Poland hardly had a better Pole than Chopin. Yet Napoleon's parents (Carlo Bonaparte and Letizia Ramolino) were not French, and Chopin's father was not Polish.

Therefore, the racial or ethnic factor is not decisive for nationality. This is even more true for mentality.

What nationality were the ancient Romans? Roman? Etruscan? Latin? None of these. They were representatives of a colossal thundering amalgam of the most diverse ethnic groups. And it was precisely the Roman mentality, not the Roman nationality, that made the outstanding achievements of Rome possible.

The taste of a pickle depends not only on its type but also on the barrel into which it was put, and whether it was with or without brine.

A certain part of the population of Ukraine is made up of non-ethnic Ukrainians. Some speak Ukrainian, and some another language. However, all citizens of Ukraine comprise a single entity. Segregating Ukrainians into "pure" and "impure" is a path to nowhere. It is also not uncommon to see citizens who grew up in Ukraine but dislike everything Ukrainian. A stratum of dissidents with different mental superimpositions is typical of any society. Even if a person communicates in another language, they still unconsciously absorb the energy of their ancestors, and the peculiarities of their worldview, values, and superstitions.

The territory of modern Ukraine has been a great road and a giant cauldron of human intermixing since ancient times. The tribes and nations that laid the foundations of the Ukrainian nation at all stages of their development did not prevent the infusion of foreign blood. Everyone who agreed to respect the community and its customs and participated in the military and economic life of society was considered part of the group.

To understand the archetypes of the Ukrainian mentality, we will delve into the history of the peoples who lived on the territory of Ukraine from time immemorial and served to form its Ukrainian hypostasis.

The Roots of Ukrainian Mentality

Prehistoric Times

There are endless disputes about when to start the countdown of Ukrainian history. There is no judge in the polemic about when, in fact, the Ukrainians appeared. But looking for answers to these questions is not that important for our topic. After all, the mentality of a nation comprises a particular set of values, habits, and psychological algorithms of all the past generations that passed on the ancient archetypes "shrouded in darkness to their descendants".

To avoid making a mistake and missing something important, let's start counting down the formation of these archetypes from ancient times.

People settled on the territory of Ukraine approximately a million years ago. In fact, humans were not yet an intelligent species (Homo sapiens). However, at that time, the most stable archetypes of the general human mentality were formed. These were not so much archetypes but rather instincts: survival, procreation, protection against enemies, lust for power, fear of the future, and the desire to pilfer anything that shines brightly. These basic attitudes are common to the mentality of all people and all nations inhabiting planet Earth.

One hundred and fifty thousand years before the birth of Christ, the first global cooling took place. So, what if it did, did life on Earth become worse? Who knows. It became harder, that's for sure. Although perhaps living became somewhat safer. Finally, those pesky saber-toothed cats died out, and lions, crocodiles, and giant spiders fled somewhere. Instead, tasty mammoths and clumsy hairy rhinos appeared. And they could catch fish to their heart's content. True, it was cold. Well, what can you do?

It is probable that during the Ice Age, humanity (Neanderthals, to be precise, who originated 70,000 years ago) began to differ in mentality. Those people who were lucky to be born in Africa lived in warmth and comfort. They rested under palm trees and chewed bananas . . . And their northern relatives had no choice but to master the manufacture of axes, arrows, spears, knives, and skinning devices. They had to learn how to make and maintain fire, sew clothes, and learn hunting strategies. Even then, the tribe was divided into tailors, fishermen, fruit pickers, cooks, healers, so forth And idlers, of whom there were always enough, decorated the walls of caves with art.

In the Paleolithic Age (40–50,000 years ago), humans finally became the human being as we know it. They learned to speak, compose songs, and perhaps even poems, and began to genuflect to the forces on which their life depended—fire, water, earth, the sun. "Communities of professions" appeared—midwives, hunters, warriors, sorcerers. Overall, a person lived then in a sort of "primitive communism": there was neither private property, nor money, nor even a family: the expectations from each person closely matched their abilities; and everyone was provided for according to their needs. Well, it was not exactly like that, of course. What was expected from ordinary tribespeople corresponded to their abilities, but the leader was given according to his needs, as happens under communism.

During the Ice Age, the ice shelf on the territory of Ukraine did not extend below the border on which the cities of Lviv, Zhytomyr, Kyiv, Poltava, and Sumy are located today. In this natural zone, the conditions of a difficult struggle with cold and hunger formed the person. These conditions forced the people, in contrast to the inhabitants of the South, to strain their minds, to live by their wits, and to invent all kinds of tricks. And when the glacier melted (around the fourteenth millennium BC), the "Biblical flood" came. However, it is unlikely that water flooded the entire Earth, as described in the Bible. It fell into the oceans in depressions, turned lakes into seas and formed full-flowing rivers. Here, on the border of the glacier that formed an area with lush vegetation and springs of clean, healing water, the ideal conditions for the physical and spiritual development of the aboriginal peoples emerged. There was neither the exhausting heat of the south nor the merciless cold of the north. Ultimately, the rich *chernozem* (black soil) formed thanks to unique natural conditions. It was on this territory that people found themselves in an area of the rapid flourishing of life.

What were people thinking about then? What did they dream about? What made them rejoice? What did they hate?

Even though spirits and witchcraft determined a person's life, and natural phenomena governed his or her life, the algorithms of thinking of an ancient human, according to researchers, were not much different from ours today. More precisely, our algorithms are not much different from those of that earlier time.

Is it right to count the modern Ukrainian mentality as starting from those distant times?

I addressed this question to Valentyna Krapyvyna, a senior researcher at the Institute of Archeology of the National Academy of Sciences of Ukraine. Her reply was as follows:

For some reason, they believe that our culture begins with Trypillia. It does not. It originated in the Paleolithic Age, about 50,000 years ago. The Kyiv Museum of Archeology stores painted mammoth bones. It was previously believed that these bones were worshiped—there was a certain pattern on them. But Serhiy Bibikov discovered what it actually was. He conducted a traceological analysis and concluded that these were musical instruments. Even now, the northern peoples play very similar instruments. The population of the Paleolithic era was much more developed than we think. They had their own art, in all manifestations—sculpture, painting, and music. And all this directly affected everyday life. People lived by it. Undoubtedly, our culture existed back then.

Trypillian Civilization

The Trypillian civilization is the conventional name for a community of tribes that lived on the territory of modern Ukraine, Moldova, and part of Romania from 5400 to 2750 BC. On the one hand, that seems an incredibly long time ago. On the other hand, if we consider that the duration of a generation is twenty-five years, only 180 to 300 generations have passed since that time.

Trypillia, which means "three fields", is one of the earliest centers of development on the planet. It would be too bold to claim that Trypillians were ahead of the world civilizational process (although many precisely argue that). Still, it is undeniable that they were in its vanguard.

Before discussing Trypillians, we should provide indisputable evidence that the roots of Ukrainians go back to the Trypillian world.

Trypillians are the First Ancestors of Ukrainians

The Ukrainians exhibit specific anthropological differences from the Trypillians. This is noticeable when comparing the Ukrainian type with Trypillian statuettes—neither a sloping forehead nor a large nose is characteristic of Ukrainians.

However, when we say "Trypillians", we do not mean a nation or a single people but a collection of different tribes that created their own civilization on the territory of Ukraine. The inhabitants of this civilization did not belong to any particular ethnic group but were carriers of a common, more or less unified, mentality.

The next argument, which may cast doubt on any connection between Ukrainians and Trypillians, boils down to the fact that during the three and a half millennia—the historical interval between the disappearance of the Trypillian civilization and the appearance of the first "legitimate" Ukrainians—so much had happened on the territory shared by both that there must be nothing left of the "Trypillian spirit".

The following argument defeats that notion. Trypillian people are the earliest settled population on the territory of Ukraine. They chose this region because they found the best land for agriculture here. The fertile *chernozem* had been building up in this area for hundreds of thousands of years. And this exceptional wealth contributed to the fact that since the time of Trypillia, a person who settled on this territory and learned to cultivate the land saw no point in moving anywhere else and remained here forever.

Hence, Ukrainians are a vivid phenomenon of an autochthonous ethnic formation. Not so many nations in the world have taken shape in their own locality, with roots going back thousands of years. Hordes of uninvited guests did not manage to dislodge settled farmers from this territory.

Trypillians, like all great civilizations, ceased to exist at the will of History. However, if we look closely at the artifacts of the local tribes of the next generations—the cultures of the Bronze

Age—we notice that there are Trypillian symbols on their dishes. They are clearly visible later on—on ceramics of the Iron Age (the Scythian-Greek period), and on gray vases of the Chernyakhiv culture. We see the same ornamentation, agricultural technologies, and rituals. Even nowadays, in Ukraine, one can find clay-coated, brightly colored "Trypillian" *mazankas* (clay-walled huts), and the symbolism of Ukrainian patterns on embroidered towels and shirts has prototypes in Trypillian ceramic paintings. Thousands of threads of traditions, shared values, beliefs, and cobwebs of mentality connect 180 generations of Ukrainians with Trypillians.

Ground in the Millstones of History

The area of settlement of the Trypillians covered a large territory — from Transylvania to the Dnipro, from the northern borders of present-day Ukraine to the coast of the Black Sea. The designation of "Trypillia" is a conventional name. This is the name of the town near Kyiv, where in 1897 an archeological expedition under the leadership of Vikentiy Khvoika discovered the first traces of this culture. In Romania it is called Cucuteni.

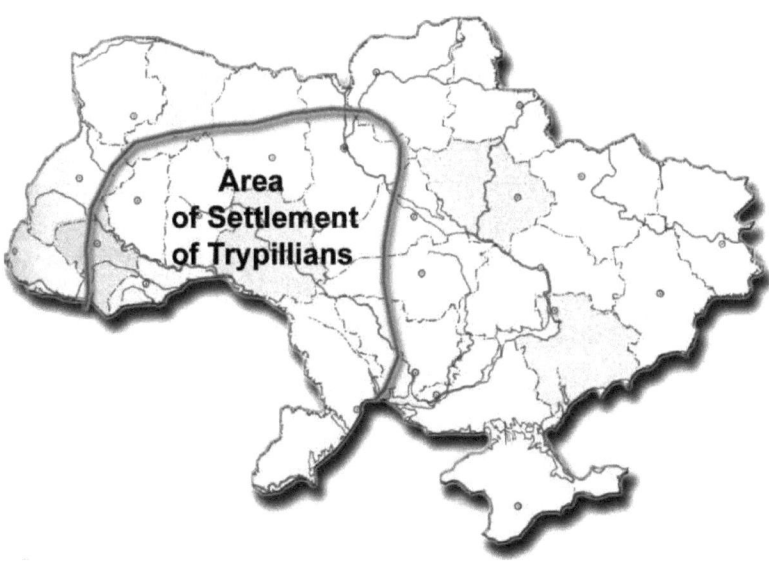

After the appearance of the first Trypillian settlements in the 5400s BC on the territory of present-day Ukraine, a powerful flow of "emigrants" rushed here from Central Europe and Asia in the years 4600–4200. They came here in the hope of finding a better life. The number of settlements increased rapidly; cities arose, iconic architectural structures, works of art, and a proto-writing system appeared; in general, civilization was born. The years 4100 to 3200 mark the heyday of Trypillian culture, crafts, and metalworking. Since the 3200s, for reasons unknown to us, the economy of the Trypillian people began to fade away; the cities declined; the social structure became more rigid; and the pottery craft disappeared. In fact, the civilization disappeared.

Ethnic Features

Nationality

Trypillian culture is strikingly similar to the culture of the Aegean islands. This fact gave grounds for the claim that there was a common cultural space from Crete to the Dnipro River at that time. Perhaps it was not only cultural but also ethnic.

Who came to whom? Did the ancestors of Ukrainians inhabit the Mediterranean, or did the Aegean people come to the Dnipro region? Scientists believe the latter is true. Hence, the first colonists of the Trypillian lands were Mediterranean people.

Studies of the necropolises of later times indicate that the succeeding population of Trypillians was heterogeneous. It was an amalgam of different peoples, tribes, and sub-ethnic groups. They brought their customs, language, knowledge, technologies, and beliefs to the Trypillian culture for over two thousand years. However, Mediterranean and proto-European skull types have been found more frequently than any others.

Society

Trypillians were mostly peasants. The most common type of settlement was a *khutir* (a single homestead settlement), which consisted of 7–15 small families, most likely close relatives. This way of life was not much different from the social structure of other developed societies of that time, such as the Biennials, North Africans, and Central Americans.

However, Trypillians lived not only in *khutirs*, but also in what one could consider huge cities for the time. They knew how to organize and manage the lives of thousands in communities. Undoubtedly, they had a mayor, bureaucracy, and a police force. Probably, they also had a "tax inspectorate", hospitals, and prisons. It is possible that the Trypillian "megalopolis" was a kind of prototype of the ancient city-state.

We can assume with a high degree of probability that life in Trypillian society was almost heavenly — quiet, peaceful, and calm. After all, they had no enemies! The bow and arrow were their favorite weapons. But there were no signs of armed conflicts. Only traces of minor conflicts have been found — a few dozen arrowheads in some places. It seems that wild steppe tribes exerted no pressure on the Trypillians — the former simply did not exist at that time. Although their horses were tame, judging by the type of harness, it seems they were not used for military purposes.

Women played a special role in Trypillian society. Their time passed in daily concerns: they ground grain, carried water, fed cattle, painted bowls and jugs, wove canvas, sewed clothes, and made shoes from leather. Judging by the incredible number of female clay figurines, women in Trypillian society enjoyed great authority.

Economy

From 5500 to 4000 BC, the so-called agricultural revolution took place on Earth — it was the transition from gathering wild plants to cultivation, from hunting animals to breeding them. The tribes of Trypillian culture were among the first to switch to agricultural production; they did it much earlier than the inhabitants of other regions of the planet. After all, the conditions were most favorable for them.

Cultivating the land, Trypillians lived in one place for 50–70 years. Once the soil was exhausted, they moved to a neighboring territory. Researchers claim (and there is every reason to believe this) that Trypillian agriculture was highly developed and that there was a surplus of produce. Trypillian civilization was one of the first societies with no food supply problem. The crops exceeded the needs. Similar to the current situation in Ukraine, foodstuffs were exported to the Caucasus, Africa, Mesopotamia, Asia, and the Balkans in large quantities.

Trypillians were not only skilled farmers but also gifted artisans. In the early stages, their tools were made of stone, but in 3600–3150 BC, they already had workshops for processing flint, the primary Neolithic raw material.[1] They used it to manufacture arrowheads, sickles, scrapers, axes, and other things that were necessary for the household.

The world began to master bronze at the end of the third millennium BC. Trypillian bronze artifacts date back to the fifth millennium BC. Even at that time, the Trypillians used a large number of high-quality copper tools, which had no gas porosity or cracks.

There are probably hardly any people who would not want to claim the invention of the wheel. However, while the world believes that the first image of the wheel was found on Sumerian frescoes in southern Mesopotamia (3200 BC), it is present on Trypillian ceramic figurines in the 5000s BC (if the dating is correct).[2] And the image of a horse, like figures of other domesticated animals, such as cows, bulls, pigs, cats, and dogs, is found much more often in the archeological materials of Trypillia than of other cultures of that time.

Culture

There are many conflicting points of view regarding Trypillia. But when it comes to the culture of these tribes, even the most ardent skeptics are forced to admit that Trypillian culture is undoubtedly a world phenomenon.

Archeologists have found thirty to 200 highly artistic ceramic artifacts in almost every Trypillian dwelling. These include saucers, bowls, jugs, mugs, amphorae, and crater-shaped fruit bowls. The quality of the tableware is impeccable — it is thin, smooth, and skillfully painted in white, black, red, and dark chestnut colors. The patterning of the ornament is perfect; it abounds with symbols and

---

1   The Neolithic is the New Stone Age.
2   Sumer is a historical region in the Near East. It was located between the Tigris and Euphrates rivers, on the territory of modern Iraq.

signs. Most likely, these signs related to primordial magic, an appeal to otherworldly forces, a request for patronage and protection, and an attempt to control these forces. Possibly, the Aegean-Trypillian art ceramics gave an impetus to the emergence of the ancient ceramics of Ancient Greece, the first samples of which appeared in the years 2000–1850 BC.

Every Trypillian household had a loom; sometimes, there were even two of them. Trypillian housewives were gifted artisans who manufactured shirts, dresses, and skirts. They decorated their work with original, colored ornamentation. Over their clothes, Trypillian fashion sophisticates wore necklaces made of copper, stone, glass (yes, even at that time, they had glass jewelry!), beads, and sea and river shells. They also had exquisite taste in gold and silver jewelry.

Architecture

Besides the culture, Trypillia had huge cities with clean rows of two-story cottages, well-planned streets, and spacious squares, which comprised another world phenomenon. Trypillians could not have replicated all this from somewhere else because the size of European cities of that time was ten times smaller, with a population of 500 considered a large number! Trypillians had their own ideas about population density. Their cities had more than 10,000 inhabitants! Many respected researchers do not doubt that the people of Trypillia created the first urban civilization in world history.

Why did they need these "megalopolises"? No one knows for sure. Some historians claim that they were necessary to protect themselves against the steppe people. Others insist that there were no steppe people at that time, and cities were the centers of social, economic, and religious development. Or maybe big Trypillian cities, like Tokyo, London, or New York, emerged and spread out? In seven thousand years, our descendants may also wonder why we needed huge cities such as New York.

Of course, Trypillians also had one-story houses. Once you entered, the oven was on the right, a bench with dishes on the left, and the altar in the most prominent place.

Religion

Trypillians always had clay figurines of the higher powers they worshiped displayed on their home altars. The Mother Goddess symbolized motherhood and fertility; a bull was a symbol of land cultivation and wealth; a snake was a symbol of dexterity; a dove symbolized the sky. The sacred ideals of the Trypillians were embodied in clay figurines and various patterns on ceramics. One could see images of the sun, a spiral, a cross, a circle, waves, and the "all-seeing eye of Destiny". These ideals were similar to the worldview of later peoples such as the ancient Greeks, Scythians, Celts, and Slavs. In fact, the entire pagan worldview is alike: a three-tier division of the world—the worship of Heaven, Earth, and Water, forces of nature, and the cult of the Great Mother. On Trypillian figurines, the Mother Earth sometimes appears with raised hands/arms, like the Slavic goddess of fertility Mokosh, and Oranta. The latter is depicted in the Kyiv Cathedral of St. Sophia, the main Christian religious temple of Ukraine. The cult of the Mother Goddess, shared by the Trypillian civilization and the related civilization of Crete, passed into antiquity and was revived in the worship of Cybele, the mother of gods and mortals, one of the most revered goddesses of Rome and Greece.

However, despite all the similar characteristics in ancient sacred views, Trypillian society followed its own path and created and developed its own religious ideals and rituals. For example, the famous "Chinese" symbol of yin and yang, portrayed as two snakes merging in an endless circle of harmony and movement, first appeared not in China but among the people of Trypillia.

Language

Unfortunately, scholars do not have records of Trypillian orators at their disposal. There is also a lack of written sources, both in symbols and ornaments. How, then, can one draw conclusions about the "Trypillian language"?

Here's how. After analyzing Slavic languages, linguists singled out words that do not have analogues in related Indo-European languages, such as the Germanic, Romance, Indian, Iranian, so forth branches. Similar research was conducted with reference to ancient Greek. As a result, scholars collected a layer of vocabulary that seemed to be of unknown origin. And since this vocabulary could not have appeared out of nowhere, it is believed that the "unknown" words were inherited from the language of a more ancient society that lived on this territory, that is, from Trypillia.

So, what kind of language was it?

Scholars believe that the central characteristic of the Trypillian language was mainly words with open syllables. Imprints of a similar language structure were found in Crete and Asia Minor. This suggests that the language of Trypillian culture most likely belonged to the group of ancient Black Sea-Mediterranean languages.

In the ancient Slavic language, open syllables also prevailed, with a tendency toward an even alternation of vowels and consonants. The Ukrainian language preserved this more than any other Slavic language. It also inherited the most significant number of words, some pagan gods' names, and some geographical locations from the "Trypillian" language.

According to Yuriy Mosenkis, the author of the book *The Language of Trypillian Culture*, it is due to its connection to Trypillia that the Ukrainian language, unlike Bulgarian, Russian, or Polish, belongs to the Mediterranean group.

The Writing System

Did Trypillians have a writing system? This is one of the favorite topics of debate among Ukrainian intellectuals. One can often find the following statement: "Research on deciphering the inscriptions of Trypillian culture proves that the Phoenicians were not the inventors of the letter-sound alphabet. The tribes who lived on the territory of modern Ukraine and who are known as Trypillians invented it many centuries before the discovery of the most ancient examples of the Phoenician script".[3]

How did literacy actually originate on Earth?

In the ninth millennium BC, there was already a means of storing and transmitting information in the territory of the Middle East.

---

3   M. Susloparov "'Deciphering the Ancient Writing from the Banks of the Dnipro River,'" *Kyiv* (1986).

It was a system of clay balls, where each ball marked one object (a cow, ram, etc.). In the fifth millennium BC, balls were stored in special containers, on the surface of which symbols were applied as a concise description of what was inside. But writing as we know it appeared around 3300 BC among the Sumerians. Their cuneiform symbols revealed administrative records and literary works, such as the *Epic of Gilgamesh*.

Starting from the second millennium BC, literacy appeared among the Phoenicians.[4] The appearance of hieroglyphs among the Egyptians and Babylonians dates to approximately the same period. After twelve hundred years, the Greeks adapted the Phoenician alphabet; notably, it happened as late as the 8th century BC. Even Homer's epic poems *The Iliad* and *The Odyssey* were disseminated orally during the author's lifetime and were written down only in the 6th century BC.[5] Homer did not write down his poems because of his blindness but because of the lack of literacy in Greece. The oldest Greek inscriptions known to humanity, which immortalized the name of the winner of the Olympic Games, date back to 776 BC. How much Ukrainians would like to believe that the Trypillians had literacy long before the Phoenicians, Egyptians, and Greeks! However, reputable scholars draw a disappointing conclusion: the people of Trypillia had no writing system.

"Excuse me", the optimists object, "but they definitely used signs! There were 239 of them found on household kitchenware alone!"

"Correct", the skeptics answer. "But these signs have not been deciphered yet. The Trypillian symbols are only ornaments".

The skeptics might be right. However, there were no random signs on ornaments at that time. Dots, spirals, circles, rhombuses, and triangles could have been used instead of writing. Two waves denoted water; a rhombus stood for land; a rhombus with a cross for cultivated land; and a rhombus with a cross and dots for a sown field. We still use similar symbols, for example, on road signs.

---

4   Phoenicia was an ancient country on the eastern coast of the Mediterranean Sea, on the coastline of modern Lebanon and Syria.
5   There is a theory that Homer is a collective image. In this case, that doesn't matter.

This was from this standpoint that the Sumerian scholar Anatoliy Kifishyn approached deciphering Trypillian written symbols. In his study, "The Experience of Deciphering the Proto-Sumerian Archive of the 12th-3rd millennium BC", he claims that he managed to decipher several Trypillian pictograms and concluded that the Trypillian Shakespeares did not yet know how to write down their poems on clay tablets. Still, careful heads of the households used pictograms like "grain", "barley", "hoe", "plow", and "wheel" to keep records of material values and note the amount of manufactured agricultural and handicraft products on special tokens.

Not all scholars agree with this hypothesis. And yet, we are here undoubtedly dealing with a historical phenomenon of the initial phase of the emergence of writing. Unlike Sumer, the only difference is that this phase did not evolve into a complex sign system but remained at the level of information transmission through pictographs, drawings, and patterns. After all, one doesn't have to scratch I LOVE YOU on a pottery shard! You can draw something instead. It's less trouble, and a completely illiterate young woman will immediately understand the message.

The Mentality of the People of Trypillia and Its Influence on Modernity

It is not easy to understand the mentality of the country you visit as a tourist. It is difficult to understand the mentality even of your own country, where, it would seem, you know everything inside and out. This author, you see, is ambitious enough to draw conclusions about the mentality of the Trypillians. Isn't he too self-confident? Isn't he taking too much upon himself?

Yes, maybe, indeed, this is too ambitious. But my choice is this: either I take on too much or nothing at all, in which case I should turn off the computer and go have a beer. The latter, of course, is more attractive. Especially since no one commissioned this book, and who knows if it will be published. But if you are holding it in your hands, it means it has come out. So, let's be self-confident and choose the first path.

The archetype of the land shapes the mentality of any agrarian society. This archetype was also decisive in the mindset of the Trypillians. As befits farmers, they were open, pragmatic, and hardworking. And given their Mediterranean roots and southern abode, they were sociable, cheerful, and friendly. The gamut of colors on their ceramics can be attributed to the cheerful nature of Trypillians. A Trypillian exhibit can be recognized from afar in the halls of historical museums. It is bright, spectacular, and sunny, standing out like Renoir's paintings among the sad paintings of other artists.

All evidence suggests that the mentality of Trypillians did not contain the aggressiveness and unjustified cruelty common in that time. In the "yin-yang" system, they were a "yin" nation: soft, romantic, and feminine. It is not known if they even had an army.

Trypillian society created a high level of comfort in everyday life. Their dwellings were 70–140 square meters in size. How many people in the 21st century live in their own two-story cottages? For the Trypillians, this was the norm. They painted their tidy dwellings with colorful patterns and framed them with flowers; these traditions are still alive in modern Ukraine, unlike Europe, where houses are more massive and pragmatic, and unlike the monotonous settlements of Russia.

The lands of Trypillia, like Western Europe now, were flooded with "emigrants"; the Trypillian quality of life was much better than the European one, and life itself was more attractive.

Only a wealthy society can attain high achievements in culture and art. And the rapid development of Trypillian arts and crafts was possible precisely thanks to the incredible economic prosperity of the Trypillian proto-state, whose citizens had the opportunity to purchase expensive tableware and thereby financially support the artisans. Confident in the future, rich people had elegant clothes, gold and silver jewelry, rings, and necklaces.

Trypillians had developed both urban and rural cultures. However, only an urban environment can produce creative personalities: thinkers, artists, and architects; rural areas are indifferent to such "indolent" people. The presence of a unique urban infrastructure, prototypes of written signs, artistic values, indigenous craft technologies, and the early development of bronze allows us to argue that Trypillian society was one of the most intellectually developed of its time.

However, to live well, one needs more than high intelligence. It is also necessary to work hard. The quality and quantity of the products produced by Trypillians attest to their lofty work ethic.

No Trypillian settlement existed in one place for more than three generations. During this time, its inhabitants cut down the surrounding forests, killed the game, and exhausted the soil under their crops. But it is surprising that when they left the old city, they burned it to the ground. Why? Did they sacrifice houses to the gods? Or maybe they didn't want homeless people to come to their family nest? The reason remains unclear. We can only conclude that their readiness to start a new chapter of their lives was part of their nature.

Before concluding, let's talk about the role of women in Trypillian society. No doubt, women were respected. And they certainly loved them! Their female figurines are incredibly erotic, exhibiting all the female body's detailed nuances! Can a cheerful southern society not be erotic? Their statuettes suggest that in the early stages of their development, Trypillians considered stout young women with small breasts and large hips to be the ideal of female beauty. Later, long legs and a slender athletic body shape came into fashion.

And yet, is it appropriate to tie the Trypillian archetypes to the Ukrainian mentality? After all, it is hard to believe, for example, that the Ukrainian and Trypillian languages are similar.

Well, I will give an example from my own "Trypillian" life.

Once, the medical director of the Ukrainian branch of the Sanofi pharmaceutical company, Volodymyr Moshchych, and I had dinner in the same Parisian restaurant. In France, it is considered impolite to approach those sitting at neighboring tables and ask them something. However, hearing our conversation, a certain gentleman could not contain his curiosity and came over to ask us: "Excuse me, which dialect of the Italian language do you speak?" We answered that we were speaking Ukrainian. Like Ukrainian, the Italian language is a dialect of the Trypillian language.

After all, where did many autochthonous common words in the Ukrainian and Italian languages come from? In both languages, vowels and consonants are equally distributed, which gives them both an exceptional melodic quality. This distribution is shifted toward consonants in many other languages. I believe that, if my colleague and I spoke Russian, Polish, Bulgarian, Hungarian, so forth the gentleman would not have approached us and asked about our "Italian dialect".

Language and mentality survive under any conditions. In texts from thousands of years ago, ancient German or ancient Slavic languages are intelligible even now.

The people we know nowadays as Hungarians moved to Europe from Western Siberia more than a thousand years ago. In the 1990s, when Hungarian specialists took part in constructing a gas pipeline in Siberia, the local Khanty-Mansi people interpreted for them. They had never been to Hungary, yet they understood their "relatives" without any difficulty.

And that's how it is: it is impossible that the Ukrainian language would have no trace of the Trypillian language. And it is implausible that Ukrainians do not have some features of the Trypillian mentality. Ukrainians are descendants of the Trypillian people. They absorbed Trypillian genes and inherited their basic archetypes. As they say—like father like son!

Pre-Slavic and Proto-Slavic Tribes

What happened to the current Ukrainian territory's population after the Trypillian civilization's disappearance?

Although the civilization disappeared, the best lands for agricultural production remained. Therefore, the people who lived on these lands had no need to look for something better and also stayed.

But uninvited guests appeared in this region.

Since the second half of the third millennium BC, tribal communities of the Yamna culture appeared on the territory between the Danube and the Don. This was a mixture of aggressive semi-nomadic communities that stayed here for about a thousand years. Their settlements had the appearance of both small villages consisting of dugouts and fortified homesteads.

For the next 1000 years, the entire second millennium BC (the Bronze Age), tribes of different cultures lived on the territory of present-day Ukraine. Specialists have noted about twenty of them: Corded Ware Culture, the Catacomb Culture, the Timber-Grave Culture, and others. These tribes existed separately, were engaged in their own economies, and were at different stages of development; they probably all believed in their own gods. Still, archeologists have found a lot in common among them, which points to the continuity of values typical for this territory.

The most diverse tribes gradually gave rise to the Proto-Slavic tribes — a group of nationalities united by a common territory, similar values, and a similarity in vernacular language.

It is possible that the so-called Proto-Slavic tribes have only an indirect relation with the current Slavs. But we are interested not in the ethnic composition of different tribes but in the mentality of the ancient inhabitants of the proto-Ukrainian lands, regardless of their nationality. These tribes lived on the territory of present-day

Ukraine for thousands of years, passing on their archetypes from generation to generation.

Based on archeological data and on Herodotus's *The Histories Book 4: Melpomene*, we will single out some features that will help us draw a conclusion about the mentality of the Proto-Slavic tribes and the psychological archetypes that modern Ukrainians inherited from them.

Ethnic Features

According to many historians, the Slavic people did not arise as a result of a development of any single tribe, but rather because of the spontaneous integration of related Indo-European tribes. If this is true, then the Slavic nation is racially mixed.

The Proto-Slavs did not have a writing system. Archeological excavations do not offer any data about their language. The only certain thing is that their languages belonged to the Indo-European language group. We assume that the Proto-Slavs spoke in similar Indo-European dialects, and, most likely, could easily understand the language of related tribes.

The Proto-Slavs lived mainly in large and small villages that were not fenced in. Settlements were located in clusters at different distances from each other or stretched along riverbanks, reminiscent of Ukrainian villages with their "Trypillian" *mazankas* and the free planning of settlements. Along with ordinary dwellings, they built larger buildings, presumably for economic purposes.

In everyday life, the ancient Slav farmers used a ritual calendar associated with agrarian magic, which, in particular, singled out the days of pagan prayers for rain. The texts of these, which are most common in the Kyiv region, coincide with texts in modern Ukrainian agronomic manuals.

In general, the economic life of the Proto-Slavic tribes was unambitious. They did not overburden themselves with work. Everything they grew or gathered and which they could hide from the raids by nomads, they consumed. Although there were periods when they exported grain to the Roman Empire. Many treasures of Roman coins were found on the territory of Ukraine. The quadrantal, the grain accounting measure borrowed from the Romans that was used in Ukrainian metrology until 1924, also attests to trade with the Roman Empire.

Regarding the culture of the Proto-Slavic peoples, I will offer two opposing points of view.

Here is what Herodotus wrote: "This country has nothing worthy of attention, except for many and very large rivers".

And here is what Valentyna Krapyvyna, Doctor of History, claims: "Ukrainian culture comprises all the cultures that have ever been on this territory. At the same time, of course, you cannot equate all of them with Ukrainians. I always adopt a different point of view and ask my colleagues: why do you like agricultural Trypillia, with its stunning cosmogonic ideas, so much, and why do you not like the tribes that appeared soon after that (Pit-Grave Culture, the Catacomb culture, Timber-Grave Culture)? They are just as interesting! These were Indo-Europeans, who were also a part of us. The representatives of the Pit-Grave culture already had stone tombstones. This culture left behind amazing ceramics. They were not painted; instead, they were decorated with chiseled cord ornamentation, which sometimes reflected their calendar. Representatives of the Catacomb culture and Timber-Grave Culture had the rudiments of writing. Which is to say, all this is in no way inferior to Trypillia".

What was the Proto-Slavic religion? Since long ago, the ancestors of the Slavs venerated the forces of nature, which occupied a central place in their beliefs. They considered land, groves, lakes, and rivers sacred. Each clan honored a mystical ancestor, the founder of the clan. Interestingly, since the 7th century BC, the Proto-Slavs, at least a certain part of them, worshiped the ancient Greek gods. Herodotus describes how the Hyperboreans repeatedly sent sacred gifts to Delos, the spiritual center of ancient Greece (an island in the Aegean Sea, the "ancient Greek Vatican", so to speak). These were ritual offerings to Artemis, one of the twelve supreme deities of Olympus. Her main sanctuary was located on Delos.

Artemis was the goddess of hunting, forests, and chastity. She was considered a symbol of the restoration of nature, the flowering of life, and an abundant harvest. This is why Proto-Slavic farmers worshiped her and sent her sacred gifts.

Herodotus's mention of a certain Hyperborean Abarius, who traveled with the symbol of Apollo—an arrow—and supposedly did not consume anything, that is to say, "lived on thin air" and preached, provides another example that the ancestors of the Slavs worshiped the ancient Greek gods.

Herodotus also recognizes the influence of the Proto-Slavs on Ancient Greece. He wrote that the inhabitants of Delos included two Hyperborean women, Arga and Opida, among their saints. They collected gifts for them, composed hymns in their honor, and buried them near the sanctuary of Artemis after their death.

Of course, ancient Greeks and Slavs honored Dionysus, the god of wine and merriment. How could they not?

The Mentality of the Proto-Slavs and its Influence on Modernity

So, what was the Proto-Slavic and, accordingly, the Proto-Ukrainian mentality? What was the core perception of the surrounding world?

It was the same as for the Trypillians—land. It could not be otherwise. Grain growers are neither nomadic nor warlike people. They are simple, soft, and "agricultural". They grew wheat, fed hogs, fished, hunted, rested, and praised Dionysus. They did not engage in "silly" kinds of things, like culture: their ceramics, although with bas relief ornamentation, were gray, far from the sophistication of the Trypillians.

Do we have evidence that the Proto-Slavic mentality was soft, "feminine", and sincere? We certainly do. According to Herodotus, the ancestors of the Slavs did not really fight with anyone. They wore many gold ornaments, and they were not monogamous (the Agathyrsis) so that thus they would be brothers and relatives to each other and have neither envy nor hatred. Proto-Slavs always willingly gave shelter to relatives who left their country due to an invasion of snakes. They were unsurpassed sorcerers and healers. Herodotus mentions that women used beaver testicles to treat uterine diseases. Nowadays, beaver castoreum, a product of a special gland of beavers, is also used to treat uterine diseases, skin ulcers, thrombosis, and disorders of the gastrointestinal tract.

The ancestors of the Slavs lived in open fields. This took courage. Economically, the Proto-Slavic ethnic group was poor. Only because of poverty could a gentle people survive surrounded by aggressive nomads. This is a defense mechanism. Rich people are robbed. But what can you take from the poor? Perhaps that is why Slavs have much less desire for painstaking quality work than, for example, Europeans: if you do something to the best of your abilities, most likely it will be taken away. And even now, no matter what a Slav does, it is not of good quality. There are exceptions, of course. The desire to preserve something and pass it on to descendants also failed to develop among the Slavs. This might be why Ukraine ranks last in Europe regarding welfare to this day.

So, the economic, cultural, and social life of people we consider Proto-Slavs was primitive. However, it was not much different from the life of the ancestors of the Germans, the British, or the French: survival at that time was the only goal of all Indo-European tribes.

Before I conclude this chapter, I will cite the book *Ancient Greece*, published by the Italian Institute De Agostini. This quote gives an idea of how the ancient Greeks perceived the Proto-Slavs, particularly the Hyperboreans.

"The Hyperboreans were a happy people who enjoyed harmony, did not know enmity, or diseases, had no need for anything, lived in a surprisingly mild climate and died only from being full of life. The Hyperborean land is a Greek utopia, a dream of a better world. Every year, Apollo necessarily visited the country of the Hyperboreans, whom he never forgot; he felt gratitude to these people and protected them for saving his mother, the goddess Leto, from the wrath of Zeus's wife, Hera".

There you have it! The ancient Greeks, with all their snobbery, it turns out, were envious of the Proto-Slavs! And for some reason, it is believed that the ancient Eastern European peoples, and therefore the proto-Ukrainian peoples, were not respected at that time. It's not true! They were greatly respected!

In this chapter, we have brought together the disparate Proto-Slavic tribes. This is, of course, all relative. One person differs from another person, and one tribe differs from another tribe.

It is appropriate to say in relation to a person, but also in relation to a whole nation: "A man is known for the company he keeps".

Peoples that Assimilated with the Ancestors of Ukrainians in Ancient Times

The Cimmerians

The Cimmerians ruled in the territory of Ukraine for about 500 years — from the eleventh to the sixth centuries BC. What did the ancestors of Ukrainians acquire from them? Did they get anything at all? If so, has any of it remained in the mentality of a modern Ukrainian?

The Cimmerians were an Eastern European people whose name became known thanks to Homer. According to modern historians, they occupied the entire territory of present-day Ukraine — from the Carpathians to the Donetsk region. These tribes arrived, apparently, from Iran. In the ancient Iranian language, "Cimmerians" means "a mobile unit of a nomadic population".

Theft was the main occupation of this "mobile unit". The Cimmerians were a highly aggressive ethnic group. Without giving it too much thought, they went into battle with their enemy, who was more numerous than they, defeated it, and plundered its settlement. In the struggle with the Cimmerians, Phrygia, Lydia, and Bithynia were defeated. The Greek cities of Asia Minor fell prey to their daring raids for a long time. In 714 BC, the Cimmerians became far too arrogant — they invaded Urartu, the most powerful state in Eastern Asia, which controlled Northern Mesopotamia, Syria, the Transcaucasia, the current Turkish and Iranian territories. A vast army from all over Asia gathered against them. However, military units from the "proto-Ukrainian" lands inflicted a crushing defeat on this mighty force.

What accounted for the Cimmerians' victory? I dare to assume, not least their mentality. While training and discipline defined the military art of their neighbors, anarchism, audacity, and a lack of manners characterized the mentality and, therefore, the military tactics of the Cimmerians. Cimmerian warriors behaved so defiantly and unpredictably that they drove even the most barbaric brutes into a dead end. They also were victorious thanks to tactics unusual for their time, which depended on mobility. Their troops did not have infantry; instead, they comprised only mounted units of archers. Such an army was highly maneuverable, and their small arms were distinguished by an unprecedented long range and penetrating power. They carried out their assaults at a gallop, not shooting over their horses' heads, but behind them in the opposite direction. Such was the signature style of the Cimmerians: the horses, rushing headlong from danger, did not need stirrups; their flight was directed only by the legs of the riders — a unit flew past the enemy in a whirlwind, and a shower of arrows mowed them down.

That is why bulky, well-equipped troops could not defeat them. The Scythians adopted this tactic from the Cimmerians and eventually pushed the latter out of the "proto-Ukrainian" lands. A segment of the Cimmerian tribes went to work for their former enemies; some migrated to the forest-steppe regions, where they assimilated with the settled agricultural population and formed one of the links in the formation of the Slavs.

We will return to the Cimmerians later in this book. For now, I will note that their battle tactics entered the arsenal of the subsequent generations that lived in these territories. In addition to the Scythians, these included the Venedi, Sclaveni, and Antae. This tactic also marked Ukrainian Zaporozhian Cossacks, whose raids were always characterized by swiftness, boldness, and unpredictability. The Ukrainian troops adopted this style under the command of the "elusive avenger" Nestor Makhno during the Russo-Ukrainian war of 1917–1921. Thanks to its mobility, maneuverability and unpredictability, the Ukrainian army drove back the current Russian offensive and pushed the powerful Russian army away from Kyiv back to the territory of Belarus in 2022.

Scythians

The Scythians, nomadic Iranian tribes, invaded the Black Sea steppes at the turn of the 6th century BC. Did they come as intruders or in peace? It doesn't much matter now; they just appeared.

And without much difficulty, they occupied almost the entire territory of modern Ukraine.

The Scythians ruled the "proto-Ukrainian" lands from the sixth to the third centuries BC.[6] And what a commotion they made! Whether you like it or not, they powerfully influenced the locals' minds. In any case, there is no doubt that some Scythian blood flows in the veins of modern Ukrainians and Eastern Slavs in general. Conquering new territories, the Scythians did not intend to kill or displace settled farmers. It was not in their interest. Moreover, analysis of archeological artifacts indicates that the Scythians actively involved representatives of autochthonous communities in their political and socio-economic structure. And after their alleged "disappearance", they did not go anywhere — they settled and remained on this land, adding their link to the formation of the Ukrainian nation.

Let's turn to the influence of the Scythians on the mentality of the ancestors of Ukrainians. But first, we must come to an understanding of the Scythians' mentality.

According to some scholars, the Scythians were a highly cultured, wise people; according to others, they were rude and international terrorists. Even Herodotus either cites them as a model people or emphasizes their barbarism.

Scythia was a heterogeneous community consisting of different ethnic tribes. Animal husbandry determined their social structure. But first, the Scythian state proved itself as a well-established military organization. The tsar was at the head of a strong and disciplined army. His power was unlimited and "divine" — he was subject only to Papias (Zeus) and Tabitha, the queen of the gods. The highest caste consisted of the royal Scythians, who considered everyone else enslaved to them.

The Scythians controlled the trade routes that connected the ancient world with the agricultural regions of the forest steppe. They were not the only ones who claimed it. The Macedonians, for example, had similar claims. In 339 BC, Philip II, the father of Alexander the Great, invaded the Black Sea steppes. The Scythians did not submit their lands to his control. In 335 BC, the army of

---

6 The Crimean Scythians survived longer.

Alexander marched to Scythia—reaching the Danube, but the commander did not dare go farther. In 331 BC, the Macedonian army besieged Olbia, an old Greek city located 30 kilometers from modern Mykolaiv in Ukraine. However, it suffered a devastating defeat, and its surviving soldiers fled.

So, having brought half the world to its knees, the troops of Alexander the Great could not defeat the Scythians. The Romans could not either. By resisting the invaders, the Scythians respected their good neighbors—the northern Black Sea Greeks. They adopted their customs, culture, and religion. The closeness of the Scythians to the ancient world connected them to an advanced civilization and allowed them to enrich world culture with their masterpieces—jewelry made of gold and silver.

In the 3rd century BC, several aggressive ethnic groups, Sarmatians, Goths, Thracians, and Celts, invaded the southern Ukrainian steppes. They destroyed Scythia as a state. Eastern Scythians submitted to the Sarmatians and assimilated with them; others dissolved among the settled autochthonous population of the "Ukrainian" forest-steppe.

Mentality

What can we conclude about the Scythian mentality?

The mentality of a king differs from that of an enslaved person. A farmer's mentality differs from that of a soldier. However, their common territory and specific historical processes formed a relatively homogeneous worldview among the Scythians.

Let's start with "nationality". It is believed that the Scythians were Iranians. Correct, their "Iranian nature" affected their way of life, language, and culture. After all, it was manifest in the complete obedience to the leader typical of the East. But for some reason, the Scythians themselves renounced their Iranian roots. Among all their legends, it isn't easy to find those connecting their worldview with the values of the East. In addition, they believed that they originated either from Zeus and the daughter of the river Borysthenes or from Scythes, the son of Hercules. Therefore, it is difficult to call their worldview Eastern.

And what kind of Iranians were they, after all? Perhaps they were Iranians before 623 BC; they initiated a long campaign against the Median Kingdom. And when they returned, during this time, an entire generation arose from Scythian wives and the enslaved (it is logical to assume that most of them were Proto-Slavs). Since then, the term "Scythian" indicated belonging to the Scythian state rather than to the Scythian ethnic group. In general, the logic is as follows: being Scythian, Roman, or American is not about nationality but primarily a mentality. Is that not so?

Let's return to the Scythians. What determined their way of life? Pilfering and war. They were brave warriors and talented commanders; they defeated those who stood in their way, not only by force, but also by cunning. However, the term "organized bandits" can also be applied to them. According to Herodotus, the Scythians ruled Asia for twenty-eight years and turned everything upside down with their arrogance and arbitrariness. And it wasn't only in Asia. In the proto-Ukrainian steppes, didn't they upend everything? They demanded tribute from everyone and seized everything they could. This way of life only strengthened the archetype of poverty in the mentality of settled agricultural tribes who shared this territory.

Wealthy Scythian kings owned herds of cattle and had numerous slaves. But ordinary Scythians did not seek wealth. Their way of life can be called "moderate asceticism" — they limited themselves to a minimum of things necessary for life.

In ancient Greek, the word Scythian means "gloomy, unfriendly". They probably were this way. Scythian ceramics create a depressing impression; they are dull and colorless. It is unlikely that you would want to have some on your table. And that's why rich Scythians preferred Greek dishes instead.

Let's be honest: "unfriendly" is a polite definition. The Scythian is a symbol of cruelty. The Roman poet Ovid writes about the Scythians: "They hardly deserve to be called people; they are angrier than wild wolves. They are not afraid of the law, their law is inferior to force, and the sword wins over justice". You can also understand the Scythian who, having killed an enemy, drinks his blood, in this way "absorbing his power". It is also possible to justify the Scythian warrior bringing the heads of enemies killed in battle to the king; otherwise, he would not receive his share of the loot. But even despite the cruel customs of that time, it is disgusting to imagine how a Scythian rubs himself with human skin, makes cloaks out of it or, while peeling it off together with nails, makes a cover for his quiver. Their habit of collecting the skulls of relatives killed by their own hands is also beyond human comprehension.

Although we judge them by our standards, I wonder what the Scythians would say if they saw how we live. Maybe they would have a long laugh.

Did the Scythians like to drink? To some extent, yes. Every Scythian ruler held a wine festival once a year in his region. However, not everyone had the right to drink, only respected people—murderers. And serial killers who distinguished themselves were given the privilege of drinking two whole cups. These cups would satisfy Ukrainians only as a light aperitif. In general, the Scythians were not drunkards and condemned the Hellenes for their bacchanalian frenzy. But the Scythians loved to indulge in drugs. As Herodotus said, they threw hemp seeds on hot stones and, enjoying its smoke, screamed with pleasure.

The religious views of the Scythians are reflected in the famous pectoral jewelry from the burial mound of Tovsta Mohyla, the pride of the National Jewelry Museum of Ukraine. It has three levels: the first is the absolute, below it lie the "roots of life", and the third is the darkness of demons. In fact, the three-tier division of the world is present in all Indo-European religions. It also appears in the pre-Indo-European worldview, for example, that of Trypillia.

According to Herodotus, the Scythians respected the ancient Greek gods. In reality, they had their own gods. Herodotus drew an analogy that was understandable to his compatriots. Probably, the Scythian Papai was a relative of Zeus, and maybe also of the Persian Ormuzd; the goddess of love Argimpas was an analogue of Aphrodite, and possibly her more ancient eastern predecessor Astarte (Ishtar), whose cult the Scythians encountered in Syria. In addition, it is not very credible that the main goddess of the Scythians was Tabithi-Hestia—the patroness of the hearth, family happiness, and hospitality: the Scythians did not have houses, and we know how they "valued" hospitality from the story about the son of the Median king, whom the Scythians killed and served to his father for dinner.

Still, the enormous influence of antiquity on the Scythians is evident. Actually, they appeared in the Black Sea steppes only when the Greeks arrived there. And, living side by side with them, they maintained not only trade but also family relations, creating Hellenistic-Scythian settlements. The Scythians adopted from the Greeks their experience, their traditions, and character; and, without a doubt, their mentality as well. After all, not only ordinary citizens but also kings (Scyles), and even tribes (Kallipids), seduced by the attractive aura of Hellas, absorbed the magic of a superior civilization, its values, and archetypes.

The Scythians recognized many gods but built sanctuaries only for Areus, the patron of war. He was their main idol. He was the only god to whom they offered the most honorable sacrifices, including humans, worshiping their sole fetish—the sword.

The Scythians had no theaters, no libraries, no art galleries. Why would they carry all that behind them on carts? But the "gold of the Scythians" is an indisputable world phenomenon. People with refined artistic taste, great erudition, and wisdom could order such masterpieces from Greek masters.

Against the background of the absolute supremacy of Areus's sword in the Scythian religious view, an exciting nuance comes to our attention: Argimpasa, the goddess of love, is most often depicted on Scythian gold artifacts. It turns out Scythian kings and their subjects respected her the most.

Lastly, to outline the Scythian mentality's main components, let's consider their burial rite. They buried a concubine, a cook, a groom, a bodyguard, a messenger, and other desperately needed helpers in that world along with the king. The Scythians carried the dead for forty days so that all their relatives could say goodbye to them. What, forty days . . . in the sun? Well, the Scythians were not fastidious people.

In general, what does this imply: was there nothing else attractive in the Scythian mentality apart from military discipline, bravery, intelligence, unpretentiousness, and the high artistic taste of their kings? Were there only bad traits: cruelty, arbitrariness, brutality, insolence, gloom, unkindness, and a passion for collecting skulls?

In addition, there was something else worthy of the highest respect in the Scythian mentality.

Scythians were a symbol of freedom, independence, and defiance against foreigners. The Scythian mentality is the mentality of an eagle, a strong, ruthless, and free bird.

A Scythian never left a wounded comrade on the battlefield and freed one who was captured at the cost of his own life. A Scythian never left his family, people, or country in trouble. By his nature, he could not be a traitor.

A Scythian would not let an insolent person go unpunished and would ensure that the offender remembered his punishment for the rest of his life.

And judging by the massive number of golden images of Aphrodite-Artimpasa, the Scythians had no issues whatsoever regarding sexuality.

Is the mentality of Ukrainians similar to That of the Scythians?

The Scythian worldview was fully manifest in the mentality of the Ukrainian Zaporozhian Cossacks, who won many victories in the European Thirty Years' War of 1618–1648, and, on their own territory, ensured the triumph of sedentary society over the nomads (this will be discussed in another section of this book). In essence, the Zaporozhian Cossack and the Scythian share the same archetype—a cruel, proud warrior with a highly developed sense of self-worth. He didn't care about the law—he was free, independent, undemanding, did not obey other people's authority, and was not afraid to do battle with an opponent who was superior in strength and numbers. He was a mercenary, a member of a proto-state military formation. His main job was to be on guard, to be at war, and to make trips to foreign lands, including distant ones. He won not so much by strength as by tactics and cleverness. He was a faithful companion, who was not used to getting sick, who got rich after raids, yet who did not appreciate his wealth and wasted his gains. He was merciless, "wild", and cruel; he gained fame and honor in battle and believed shame awaited the coward.

He performed bacchanalian mysteries, and after their performance was gripped by a bacchanalian frenzy. And finally, he was very fond of women, but he considered showing his romantic nature unworthy of a warrior.

And didn't the Scythian mentality, to the surprise of the whole world, provide Ukrainian soldiers during the Russo-Ukrainian war of 2022 with the opportunity to face the eastern Russian barbarians with dignity?

Sarmatians

Sarmatian tribes (Roksolani, Iazyges, Alani, etc.) prevailed on the territory of Ukraine from the 3rd century BC to the 3rd century AD. They came from the South Ural steppes and settled to the northeast of the Scythians. In the middle of the 3rd century AD., they were swept away by Germanic tribes, the Goths. Some Sarmatians became part of the Gothic state of Ermanaric, some assimilated with the Proto-Slavs of the Chernyakhiv culture, and others settled beyond the Don. The Huns finally crushed the Sarmatians: they exterminated those they could and assimilated the rest.

For 600 years, the Sarmatians greatly influenced the peoples' worldview in the locality where they lived.

Ethnic Features

Sarmatians were "relatives" of the Scythians. They both had a similar anthropological type. Herodotus writes, "the Sarmatians speak the Scythian language, but it has been distorted since ancient times".

Like the Scythians, the Sarmatians were a military nation where the entire male population was conscripted. Ancient authors always emphasized the Sarmatians' aggressiveness and their belligerent character.

The Sarmatians fought with the Scythians both as enemies and as allies. In peacetime, they divided the zones of influence and made raids on Proto-Slavic villages, the Pontic king Mithridates' lands, and ancient poleis (Pontic Olbia, Tyras, Nikonion). The Roman Empire waged war on the Sarmatians.

Even though cavalry prevailed in the Sarmatian army, their military tactics differed somewhat from their predecessors. Cimmerians and Scythians had light cavalry, but Sarmatians had a heavy one: their horses were not fast but extremely strong. While the Cimmerians would dash past the enemy and shower him with arrows, the Sarmatians would launch a frontal attack. They also used a sword of about 70–110 cm long.

The basis of the social organization of the Sarmatians was a clan community formed by a group of related families. They lived in a camp, in tents that resembled Mongolian yurts. They did not have cities, at least not on the territory of Ukraine. In winter, they insulated the tents; they did not build dugouts or other stationary facilities. They were nomadic people and stayed in one place until the livestock ate all the grass. Then they moved to another location. At the same time, each tribe had its own territory, going beyond the boundaries of which caused intertribal military clashes. The Sarmatians ate meat, cheese, and milk. They bred horses and other animals, which, despite the continuous movement, did not lose weight. When burying the dead, they put things that they used during their lives next to them: weapons and cups with wine for men, jewelry, mirrors, and needles for women.

War and robbery constituted the basis of the Sarmatian "economy". Attacking the steppe peasants and residents of the Greek poleis, they robbed them and enslaved healthy, muscular men.

The Sarmatians did not shy away from crafts either: they sewed clothes from leather, they knew how to extract and process metals, and jewelers made jewelry from gold and silver. The Sarmatians actively traded skins and handicrafts. But their main article of export consisted of slaves who were traded in Greece, Rome, the Middle East, and even in India and China.

Since an animal was an integral part of the life of these nomads, it affected their culture; Sarmatian gold and silver artifacts were made in animalistic shapes. They included many images of leopards, panthers, wolves, bears, deer, goats, boars, eagles, rams, and horses on weapons, household items, and horse harnesses. Wild animal fights were a common motif. Eros and his wife Psyche were also often depicted on Sarmatian gold wares.

The Sarmatians had neither their own writing system nor a borrowed one.

Gynecocracy, a high position of women in society, a kind of matriarchy, characterized the Sarmatian social system. Sarmatian women deserve a separate discussion. Their duties extended beyond maintaining order in the household and raising children. In the *Periplus* by Scylax of Caryanda, there is information that Sarmatian women often held the reins of power. The records of Polyaenus (2nd century AD) also confirm this, describing the queens Tirgatao and Amagi as the leaders of the Sarmatian tribes.

Sarmatian women were warriors on a par with men. In addition to jewelry, they placed weapons in the grave of a dead woman or even a girl. And family burials were formed around the tomb of the woman who was considered the progenitor.

Ancient authors reported that the Sarmatians were excellent horsewomen who skillfully threw darts and shot arrows. They were emancipated, independent, and participated in military "showdowns" as equals. They loved hunting; sometimes, they went boar hunting along with men, and sometimes even without them.

All this seemed incredible to their Greek neighbors, who perceived a woman as a servant, so they made up legends about Sarmatian women, particularly about the mysterious Amazons.

Sarmatian women differed from the "weaker sex" of the neighboring nations not only in their warlike behavior and lust for power, but also in their passion for beautiful clothes. A noble Sarmatian woman's wardrobe was impressive! One could find a gold diadem, earrings, a necklace, and all kinds of jewelry with precious and semi-precious stones such as rubies, garnets, carnelians, and turquoise. Not even Greek women had such rich and tastefully selected clothes! And the Greeks did not have such amazing women.

Sarmatian Mentality and its Influence on Modernity

So, who were they, the Sarmatians, are they direct participants in the formation of the Ukrainian nation and Ukrainian mentality?

Like the Scythians, they were robbers and disrupters. Their constant raids and demands for payment of excessive tribute had a detrimental effect on the development of agricultural tribes. Sarmatian unpredictability made the life of farmers so unbearable that a significant part of them went farther north to Desna, so to speak, to the Chernihiv region.

The Romans described the appearance of the Sarmatians as follows: "An angry face, a rough voice, his hair is not cut nor is his beard shaven". The historian Arrian, one of the procurators of the Roman Empire, who often fought with them and therefore knew them directly, makes an interesting observation that will help to understand the psychology of the Sarmatians: "It is difficult to get their horses galloping at first, but they can bear any load, and then you can see how a lively, stocky, and stout horse gets tired, and this little scabby nag first overtakes it, and then leaves it far behind".

But this was said about horses. What does it have to do with the Sarmatians?

A person gets a dog similar to themselves in character. The Sarmatians bred horses "similar to themselves in character". We can assume that "they were slow to get moving at first", but later, they pushed forward so hard that it made them unstoppable. Slowness at the beginning and mayhem at the end comprises a typical Sarmatian trait.

Sarmatian women are their most significant treasure. The very word "Sarmatian" means "subject to a woman." Women fought side by side with men and did not really strive for the primordial women's dream — settledness and stability. That is why they didn't leave behind settlements or other evidence of a quiet family life.

There could be a Sarmatian influence in the belief of the Ukrainians that "a man is the head of the family, and a woman is the neck, and she turns the head whichever way she wants". Ukrainian women's traits, such as obstinacy, rebelliousness, and the ability to put both a man and a conqueror in his place, might come from Sarmatian Amazons. Ukrainian women's refined taste in clothes might also come from the Sarmatian fashionistas. After all, European women, even more so American women, with all their means, dress more simply than Ukrainian women.

The distinctive traditions of the Sarmatians, both "good" and "bad", not only significantly influenced Ukrainians' customs and traditions but also those of other peoples who lived close to them. In particular, Polish aristocrats proudly emphasized that their roots were Sarmatian and wanted artists to depict them "à la Sarmatian". In art history, there is even a special term called the "Sarmatian portrait". By the way, Bohdan Khmelnytsky, the most famous Ukrainian hetman, also modestly called himself a "Sarmatian prince".

According to linguists, many Ukrainian words, including the names of settlements and rivers, are survivals from the Sarmatians. The unique Ukrainian pharyngeal "h", which doesn't exist in Russian or other Slavic languages, is hypothetically also Sarmatian.

The Ancient Greece of the Northern Black Sea

The cover of this book bears the title: *Ukrainian Mentality*. What does Ancient Greece have to do with it? Yes, there were Greek settlements on the shores of the Black Sea. You might wonder what the connection between those settlements and Ukrainians is. Does the author want to say that the ancient Hellenes also took part in the formation of the Ukrainian nation? He has brought up the Trypillians, Scythians, Sarmatians, and all kinds of Hyperboreans. Now what, the Greeks too?!

The close connection of the ancient Black Sea Greeks with the settled and nomadic population of the territories of present-day Ukraine existed for about 1,000 years, from the archaic period of Hellenism to the general decline of antiquity in the third-quarter of the 4th century AD. After the defeat of Pontic Olbia, the inhabitants of the city and the surrounding territories moved to the north, assimilated with the steppe communities, adding their link to the ancestors of Ukrainians, and undoubtedly influenced the mentality of the inhabitants of this region.

What was the ancient Greek mentality in general, and what specific features did the Greeks who lived in the Northern Black Sea region have?

The ancient world is such a fascinating topic that it is difficult to return once you set out on a journey there. Therefore, we will only spend a little time on our tour of the ancient Hellenes; we will just briefly get acquainted with their life principles, customs, religion, culture, and, of course, their mentality. In this pursuit, our reliable guides will be the sources of archeological research on Greek settlements.

Greeks and Ancestors of Ukrainians

The first ancient Greeks appeared on the lands of the Northern Black Sea in the second half of the 7th century BC. They came from the Ionian city of Miletus.

Why did they come here? Were they so badly off where they lived?

The reason is fairly clear: the harvestless metropolis needed grain, leather, and other agricultural products. And did they have a high living standard in their historical homeland? Probably not. Don't get me wrong, life in Ionia at that time was wonderful. But those owning land and slaves in Miletus, winning a good name and respect in the state, did not venture to the territory controlled by the Proto-Slavic tribes. The lowest echelons of society flocked to the Proto-Slavs; these were losers, homeless people, and prisoners whom it was cheaper to put on a ship and expel from the country than to feed. Political exiles, aggrieved paupers, bankrupt people, pirates, swindlers, hetaera, thieves, and fugitive slaves arrived in the proto-Ukrainian lands . . . Nice company, wasn't it? However, these were the bravest, most fearless adventurers! Those who were not afraid to cross three seas and end up the devil knows where at the edge of the world to start life with a clean slate. Just this way, the "scum of society" once moved from Europe to North America and turned the continent into a model of high civilization in just a few centuries. Britain dumped its "trash" in Australia, and Australia turned into a prosperous country. Similar "outlaws", but, in fact, people of strong will and powerful inner energy appeared in the southern Ukrainian steppes and began to establish antiquity here; priests, philosophers, architects, craftsmen, and strategists arrived with the immigrants.

How did the local, autochthonous settled population welcome the uninvited guests? Peacefully. Traces of significant military clashes between them and the newcomers have not been found in archeological excavations.

In the initial phase of the development of the coast, the Greeks suffered an acute labor shortage and were forced to introduce the autochthonous population into their economic and cultural orbit. The desire of young immigrants, mostly men, to obtain wives from among the local beauties also facilitated this process.

While laying out Borysthenes, the first city they founded in the Northern Black Sea region, the Greeks lived in primitive dugouts. But soon, they learned from the experience of the "locals" and built simple houses that were quite suitable for life, uncharacteristic of Greece, but similar to the *mazankas*, the clay-walled huts of the forest-steppe zone of the Dnipro River region. At first, the Greek colonists had to closely study the life of the autochthonous "barbarians", whose dwellings had apparent advantages over the Greek variety: they were better equipped, provided with convenient trinkets, and had a permanent hearth.

Analyzing the names of the inhabitants of ancient cities — Borysthenes, Olbia, Chersonesus, archeologists concluded that a significant portion of the local population was present in the Greek settlements of the Northern Black Sea region. The fact of friendly relations between the Greeks and the inhabitants of the steppe zone of Ukraine is obvious: when the Greeks arrived, they integrated a significant part of the "locals" into new economic and social conditions of existence.

This was most notable during the heyday of antiquity from the fifth to the third centuries BC. At that time, records indicate a robust growth of the economy, culture, and well-being of both the Greek and the local population; in most of the territories of the agricultural and pastoral tribes of the Middle Dnipro region (in the present regions of Kyiv, Donetsk, Cherkasy, and Kirovohrad) a large amount of expensive Hellenic pottery, gold products, and other evidence of a "sweet" life were found. The Greeks also had strong ties with the inhabitants of the Carpathian-Danube basin.

Ethnic Features

The Individual and Society

In the era of antiquity, as in all other times, people wanted to live happily and well. And individual well-being depended on social status, on whether people were aristocrats, free citizens, or slaves.

In "individual vs. society" relations, ancient ideas rested on the principle that humanity consisted of those who conquer and those who are conquered. Equality contradicts harmony, and therefore there are people of a "superior" species, such as Hellenes, men, and citizens, and other "inferior individuals", namely, all women (regardless of origin), all slaves (regardless of intelligence), and all barbarians (regardless of "nationality"). The Greeks equated slaves with domestic animals and treated them well; unlike Roman slaves, Greek slaves did not stage uprisings except on rare occasions. Women were not much different from slaves. A wife was not a "soulmate" for a man. She was instead a hired hand, a free hetaera, and a bearer of children. After all, her body was weak and imperfect. And the "eternally feminine" traits — the inability to study, lust, and the inability to take responsibility for their actions — forced the poor Greeks to keep their wives in submission. Women did not always obey; Sappho's feminist love lyrics and the description of mass demonstrations of women for their rights (admittedly, presented as an amusing incident) in one of Aristophanes' comedies attest to this. The Greeks also considered children to be weak and, therefore, inferior creatures. When a girl was born in the family, the parents, at least the men, perceived it almost as a punishment from the gods: not only was there one more inferior creature in the family, but also one of an inferior gender. However, this attitude toward a woman did not prevent the Hellenes from deifying her. This was, allegedly, the dichotomy in their mentality.

A man is better than a woman! From the point of view of the Greeks, this was unquestionable, like the fact that a Greek was better than everyone else. After all, a Greek (and who else?) was wise, courageous, and just. And a non-Greek was, of course, a barbarian, a small, worthless person, a coward, a greedy, undisciplined, and lazy individual. That is to say, those who belong to our group are good, and those who don't are bad.

However, despite the discriminatory attitude toward "foreigners", at least compared with the Romans, xenophobia didn't bother the Greeks: a characteristic feature of their society was openness. This once again reveals the ambiguity of their mentality: believing that each separate polis should exist autonomously and not depend on anyone, the Hellenes never isolated themselves from the surrounding world. They actively communicated with the "barbarians" and willingly shared their cultural heritage, religion, craft skills, knowledge, and traditions with them; in return, they borrowed technological and economic know-how, methods of land cultivation, and construction techniques from them.

In the dilemma of the individual vs. society, the Greeks placed society above the individual. They believed that no personal interests could be higher than the state's. Even children, in their opinion, were born not to the family but to society. And the concept of "family" in the ancient Greek mentality did not mean "father—mother—children" but a particular community formed by a large number of relatives: if someone offended someone, curses fell not only on their head but also on their entire family. Any person was inseparably identified with the city where they lived. The Greeks did not have "passport" surnames. In their locality, the father's name was added to the name (e.g., Mastor, son of Bert), and outside of it, the name was followed by "registration": Philina of Olbia, Heraclitus of Ephesus, so forth

Curiosity was a characteristic feature of the Greek worldview. Formulaic answers did not satisfy the Greeks. This feature of theirs became the primary basis for the robust development of ancient philosophy.

A shared meal with friends was integral to a Greek's life. At social gatherings, men enjoyed wine, discussions, music, and erotic entertainment with enslaved women, male slaves, and hetaeras. All in all, they had a good time hanging out and getting it on.

Authorities

The concentration of power in one pair of hands marked the vast majority of peoples of that time. The king received "carte blanche" "from the gods" and had unlimited power. However, the Greeks changed this tradition: having invalidated the power of the ruler, they switched to democracy, and the previously innocent words "despot" or "tyrant" became swear words. As early as the 7th century BC, each polis was founded as a free city-state; its rulers obtained power through general voting at popular assemblies, where any citizen (women and slaves, of course, did not take part) had the opportunity to express their opinion freely. These assemblies functioned as the state's legislative body, similar to a permanent council, elected by citizens. State decrees usually began as follows: "The Council and the People have decided ...". The nobility of a claimant's family to power, its wealth, of course, was significant, but much less than, say, in Rome. The Greeks' organizational abilities came to the fore. And while the world was under the rule of tyrants, emigrants from Hellas built democracy in the lands of the Northern Black Sea. Democracy is one of the most significant phenomena introduced by the ancient Greeks both in world history and on the land that is now Ukraine. The Greeks never had either all-powerful kings or lavish courts. Their freedom of choice, speech, humanism, morale, and ethics amazed many generations of foreigners. The Greek citizens' participation in their city-state's political life was simply extraordinary in those days. Other peoples could not comprehend it (and, in fact, still cannot): how is it that the ruler can be controlled? Why can't he make his own decisions? Or be obliged to adhere to some ethical principles or rules of conduct? Or justify himself to society? No way! It's the same as a captain handing the ship over to the sailors!

The Greeks didn't care about such reasoning. However, despite their democracy, they did not create a common constitution or a standard set of laws — each polis had its own laws. Unwritten rules supplemented the written ones; judges made decisions not according to law, but according to reason, according to their inner sense of justice. This feeling was based on the fact that if the gods wanted the world to have poor and rich, masters and slaves, men and women, then there was no need to measure everyone by the same scale — general equality before the law was considered a dangerous and utopian illusion. In general, unlike the Romans, the Greeks did not have much respect for jurisprudence and "authority". The

Greeks despised even their guardians of order and mocked them in every way. They perceived this profession as not worthy of a citizen, and Scythians or slaves ultimately performed this function.

The Greeks also disliked private entrepreneurs and considered it shameful to work for them. Their citizens preferred working in their own workshop and wanted to work for something other than a wealthy owner, even if in a managerial position.

Work

In all honestly, the ancient Greeks treated work without much enthusiasm. Of course, they understood that to live, one must work. But they didn't believe that work was the meaning of life; after all, they had slaves and mercenaries for that purpose. And a sophisticated man should have plenty of free time so his life would be pleasant and worthwhile. In Greek legends (by the way, similar to the Slavic ones), no one works. Well, Hephaestus is doing something, and Hercules cleaned some stables . . . And, after listening to the myths, the ancient Greek citizens adhered to the slogan "we are not slaves, and slaves are not us". They did not exert themselves in work; instead, savoring diluted wine, they plunged into discussions.

So, the citizens were wasting time. And what did the hired workers, among whom there were many Proto-Slavs, do in the city-states of the Northern Black Sea region? First of all, they worked in construction. However, this occupation was not considered honorable.

Despite the snobbery of the townspeople toward the rural population, the most organic activity in ancient Greece was considered to be close to nature: farming, growing flowers, and fishing. But artisans did not enjoy particular respect. Especially shopkeepers — they were generally regarded as swindlers. It is not for nothing that they prayed to the god of swindlers, Plutus.

However, no matter how much the Greeks of the proto-Ukrainian lands shunned work, they were good at working. Their architects, artists, potters, and jewelers were excellent masters of their craft and significantly contributed to the development of both ancient society and the surrounding ethnic groups.

Military Matters

In military matters, the Greeks of the Northern Black Sea region lagged far behind their neighbors and fellow citizens from metropolises. Wars continued in Sparta and Athens. However, the Hellenes, who lived next to the ancestors of the Ukrainians, were peaceful people and never attacked anyone first. As a result, they did not have a strong army and didn't honor Ares, the god of war.

What did the Northern Black Sea Greeks do when they were captured by marauders—Sarmatians, Huns, Getae, Thracians, and Macedonians? They still had to go into battle. When they were desperate, they turned to the Scythians or the Romans for help. But that depended on the situation, since the Greeks also had to fight against the Scythians and against Rome. But first of all, they tried to negotiate with invaders. Barbarians repeatedly destroyed Olbia, but no traces of significant military cataclysms have been recorded in any of the rural settlements of this region.

Culture

In ancient times, poetry, theater, philosophy, rhetoric, and ethics enjoyed great popularity in Hellas. Settlers in the cities of the Northern Black Sea region actively developed the achievements of ancient Greek culture. Many works of art, highly artistic ceramics, and masterpieces of sculpture went there from Miletus, Athens, and other cultural centers. The general cultural level of the inhabitants of Olbia, Chersonesus, Thira, and especially rich Panticapaeum was high and contributed to the rapid development of local architecture, sculpture, painting, ceramic, and jewelry-making industries. Thanks to close ties with Athens, the best artisans and architects willingly went to the shores of the Euxine Pontus from the capital.

The construction of temples in the Northern Black Sea region's Greek polis was fundamental. Blue and yellow as well as red were the primary colors that the Black Sea Greeks used to paint their buildings.

The excavations of the cities of the Northern Black Sea region led to the discoveries of many different sculptures. In those times, marble, limestone, and bronze statues of gods, heroes, and noble citizens decorated squares, crossroads, and necropolises.

Many talented sculptors belonged to the local artistic bohemians. Although they were inferior in technique to the best Athenian masters, they had their own style peculiar to this region: they depicted gods and people more distinctly, more realistically, and less ascetically, although somewhat carelessly.

Under the influence of the best samples of tableware brought from other parts of the ancient world, local ceramists created an infinite number of products painted with scenes from the lives of gods and mortals. Not only Greeks but all nationalities on both sides of the Dnipro River used these products with pleasure.

It is impossible to think about ancient civilization without the distinctive culture of the Northern Black Sea region. Despite lying on the periphery of European civilization, this culture entered the treasury of world values. Many works of art, made by both visiting and local masters, testify to the developed artistic tastes of the inhabitants of this region. They were produced not only by the Hellenes but also by seemingly "wild" peoples such as the Scythians, Sarmatians, and such "agricultural" people as the Proto-Slavic tribes. This territory gave the world at least three outstanding philosophers—Sphaerus of Bosphorus, Bion of Borysthenes, and the Scythian Anacharsis. The latter is included among the famous ancient "seven sages".

Medicine

Naturally, the ancient Greeks perceived diseases as misfortunes and curses of the gods. However, following the teachings of Hippocrates (460–370 BC), they were the first to treat these curses effectively. Hippocrates used diets, emetic and laxative mixtures, and recommended a healthy lifestyle. The "Father of Medicine" introduced the concept of psychological types and called for taking care of not only the body but also the soul. He believed that philosophy, rhetoric, and poetry are no less important for good health than drugs, enemas or physical exercises. These views of Hippocrates were well known to the doctors of the Northern Black Sea region.

And what if, despite poems, surgery or gymnastics, the disease still did not abate? In this matter, the ambiguity of the ancient Greek mentality shows itself once again. Or, maybe, on the contrary, its lack of ambiguity: in the Greek imagination, a frail person was a burden to society, and if the disease did not go away for a long time, it was pointless to bother with that person. Asclepius, the god of healing, did not treat the chronically ill and did not advise his priests, the Asclepiades, to deal with them. Greek philosophers, including Plato, also condemned treatment that "sustained disease only to delay death". The ancient Greeks believed that if a sick person had a conscience, then they would not long trouble the doctors but would call on the gods, give final directives regarding property, and would duly take poison. The arrangement of a final banquet was a phenomenon, if not usual, then at least not strange. After all, the Greeks treated death philosophically. As Epicurus noted, "while we live, there is no death, and when it comes, we are gone". The Greeks also did not cure feeble children and left the seriously wounded on the battlefield.

Religion

The pantheon of ancient Greek gods is well known, and it makes no sense to describe it in this book. It is only necessary to emphasize that the old gods instructed but did not order how mortals should arrange their lives. In Hellas, there was no single constitution but there was a single religion. On the way to democracy, the Greeks went so far that they elected both rulers and gods. Each polis had its protectors from among the celestial beings, whose cults, respectively, were dominant, and determined the content of religious mysteries. They chose, in addition to the main deity, others as well, even those who were not "registered" on Olympus.

Zeus, Demeter, Dionysus, and Apollo were revered in the Olbian polis, which was closest to the steppe farmers. In their honor, the Olbians organized celebrations and sacrificed domestic animals, which they ate during the holidays. Cults of Cybele, Athena, Hermes, Achilles, Hercules, and Aphrodite were also widespread.

Why did they choose these gods from the entire pantheon?

Zeus is, of course, the main deity. Demeter is the goddess of fertility. That makes sense since people occupied with agriculture lived there. Among their neighbors, the Proto-Slavs, one of the main divinities was also the goddess of fertility, Mokosha, an analogue of Demeter. Dionysus is the god of wine, carelessness, fun, pranks, and freedom from rules and prohibitions. Who else would the adventurers-settlers venerate?

But above all, Apollo was held in high esteem in Olbia. Two temples were built in his honor in the city. Even the temple of Zeus was inferior to them in size. Herodotus remarked that the Hyperboreans, the ancestors of the Slavs, also revered Apollo. This coincidence was certainly not accidental.

The divine forces of nature, such as the Titans, Helios, Selene, Oceanids, the gods of winds, the Erinyes, Maenads, Charites, and nymphs, also occupied an important place in the ancient Greek religion of the Northern Black Sea region, as well as in the beliefs of the local autochthonous population. The Greeks joked that, when going to the forest or the river, one would rather meet a nymph than a man.

The ancient Black Sea Greeks liked to practice magic, sorcery, and astrology. They often used flowers in their mysteries. By the way, the traditional Ukrainian women's wreath is a relic of that time: in ancient written sources, a flower wreath is first mentioned in 600 BC. However, it is unknown who borrowed it from whom — the Greeks from the Proto-Slavs, or the Proto-Slavs from the Greeks.

And in conclusion, the religion of the Greeks is totally eroto-centric. In their legends and myths, exciting romantic adventures are the main occupation of gods, heroes and mortals. The main troublemaker, as befits the leader, was Zeus: his harem contained almost the entire female divine pantheon and every mortal who accidentally or deliberately caught his eye. The thunder-bearer achieved his sacred goal in various ways — by force, cunning, or persuasion. Other "gods" followed his example. There were also "nuns", such as Hestia, Artemis, and Athena among the celestial beings of Olympus. But exceptions, as we know, only reinforce the rule. And the rule is this: in the beginning, there was Chaos. Out of Chaos arose what took over the Universe — Eros. Eros rules over everything — over the gods, nature, and mortals, and is the main force of the Cosmos. According to the ancient Greeks, Eros awakens all the best in a person and contributes to the enrichment of the soul.

Love

So, the ancient Greeks reduced their religion to the slogan "Love, Sex and Rock-n-Roll". That is, "God is Love". They built their lives on the same principle. Erotic scenes were depicted even on household dishes. Representatives of the male sex enjoyed unlimited freedom and frivolously entered various intimate relationships: with a wife, a female slave, a male slave, a concubine, or a hetaera. Confined to the four walls of the gynaeceum (female half of the house), the women had to be content with erotic play among themselves. Moreover, there was no need to hide it: not only ancient Greek religion but also the ancient Greek mentality was totally erotocentric. This was especially the case in the lands of present-day Ukraine.

"And why specifically there?", you might ask.

Various world cultures have traditionally associated the cult of Love with fertility: the fertilization of the earth, the appearance of seedlings, and a rich harvest. In agricultural communities, there has always been a belief that there is a magical connection between Love and the Earth. Therefore, erotic cults were especially revered in such societies. But both Greek and non-Greek settlements of the Northern Black Sea region were primarily agricultural.

Greek immigrants dedicated the first temple they built on the lands of present-day Ukraine neither to the supreme god Zeus, nor to the mother of the gods Cybele, nor to the protector of travelers Hermes, nor to the lord of the seas Poseidon, but to the most charming of the immortals, the goddess of love, Aphrodite.[7] Accordingly, it is easy to conclude that the cult of Aphrodite among the Greeks of the Northern Black Sea region was one of the main ones.

Mentality

In ancient Greece, there was no single worldview. However, we can single out some general features.

---

7   This temple was built in the sixth century BC. in Borysthenes. It was discovered in 1997 by an expedition of the Institute of Archeology of the National Academy of Sciences of Ukraine under the leadership of Volodymyr Nazarov.

The psychological portrait of the ancient Greeks of the Northern Black Sea region is as follows. One way or another, we find many of their traits in the mentality of a modern Ukrainian.

The ancient Greek who lived on the northern coast of the Black Sea was sociable and belonged to a large family, a city. He respected the state, but he treated representatives of the authorities dispassionately. As a proud and freedom-loving person, he did not tolerate dictatorship and regularly took part in public assemblies, where he told the naked truth about everything that came to his mind. He was above the law; he observed order but without fanaticism.

At the same time, he was peaceful and non-aggressive; he was kind to foreigners (if they did not intend to conquer him), he did not wage war against anyone, and as a rule, he knew how to negotiate with the steppe people. He willingly passed on his knowledge and culture to his neighbors, and also took over their business secrets from them. He could happily marry a local girl and give his children non-Greek names.

The Greek citizen looked down on the peasant. Although he himself had a connection with the land or the sea, he enjoyed spending time in the garden, growing flowers, and fishing. Possessing features characteristic of a resident of the South (kindness, sincerity, directness), his thinking was marked by lightness, frankness, and a developed sense of humor, but also provincial frugality and a desire for petty profit. However, pragmatism occupied an insignificant place in his world outlook: he did not respect private entrepreneurs and shopkeepers and did not equate happiness with wealth. Happiness, in his view, primarily depended on such factors as freedom, being carefree, beauty, health, and last but not least—a cheerful mood.

Therefore, the Black Sea Hellene did not enjoy working for money or to accumulate great property; he neglected monotonous work and, as a rule, did everything carelessly and hastily. Although his products were not of high quality, they were attractive with their own style, cheerful colors and soulfulness. His region did not contribute world-famous painters, sculptors, architects, and playwrights, but its citizens' general cultural and intellectual level was high.

The ancient Greek of the Northern Black Sea region bowed to the divine forces of nature and the wildest, most unruly gods. This choice was not accidental since he himself was of the same disposition.

Healing and medicine reached a high level of development in his area, but the ancient Greeks did not want to be treated by healers.

But he adored sharing meals with friends and gladly participated in festivals honoring Dionysus, the god of wine and fun. Archeological excavations confirm that the Greeks of the Northern Black Sea region lived joyfully: the sites of settlements are completely filled with shards of wine amphorae, kylikes (wine cups), amphora-like vases (in which wine was served at the table), kraters (vessels for mixing wine with water), oenochoai (jugs that could pour wine for three people at once).

After finishing a meal, the ancient Hellene would go to women. Here, to the north of the Pontus Euxinus, where the cult of Aphrodite reigned, local beauties possessed the secret charms of the goddess of love—a friendly disposition, divine beauty, seductive charm, sincerity, carelessness, and an adventurous nature.

The Influence of Ancient Greek Mentality on the Ukrainian

Interview with Valentyna Krapyvyna

Valentyna Krapyvyna is a Candidate of Historical Sciences (Ph.D. equivalent), senior researcher at the Institute of Archeology of the National Academy of Sciences of Ukraine, and head of the Olbia archeological expedition.

"Valentina Volodymyrivna, no one knows better than you the character of the ancient Greeks who lived in the South of present-day Ukraine. In your opinion, did they pass on their psychological traits to the peoples who lived on the same territory?"

"Everything that was on this land, everything that happened here, is present in all of us. And not only in ethnic Ukrainians. This environment

affects you regardless of who you are; this place's magnetism and this land have a very strong impact".

"According to the evidence of scientific research, did the autochthonous population of the Ukrainian steppes remain on the land they cultivated, or were they displaced from time to time? What I mean is, is there continuity? Can the ancient Greeks, who lived in the 'Ukrainian' territories, be considered the ancestors of Ukrainians?"

"Of course, the autochthonous population on the territory of modern Ukraine remained. At the same time, it assimilated with others all the time. Ukraine consists of three geographical zones: forest, steppe, and forest-steppe. The most autochthonous population remained in the forests. After all, it was more protected there. The steppe belonged to nomads; the forest-steppe was a contact zone in which the population changed quite extensively. But at the same time, the forest population was the most backward in terms of development. And look at the culture of the steppe and forest-steppe! Who are we? How do we want to see ourselves? A backward forest population that has hardly experienced outside interventions? Or do we agree that Ukrainians comprise all the nationalities that walked this land?"

"Do you mean nomads?"

"Including nomads. If it did not leave this land, any nomadic society would settle down and merge into the common culture. We have such a mixture here ... Like everywhere else. The Viatichians, Krivichians, Dulibians, Siverianians, Polianians, Derevlianians – how can such diversity be explained? These are various Slavic tribes that were formed depending on relations with other surrounding ethnic groups".

"Is there Scythian ancestry in Ukrainians?"

"I think so. At least on the territory of Ukraine, there are people with specific molars characteristic of the Scythians – there is a study on this by S.P. Seged. However, the traits of the Pechenegs, Polovtsians, and other nomads are also in Ukrainians. Around thirty years ago, I traveled by bus from Kyiv to Ochakiv.[8] There were many stops at bus stations, and I noticed that the Kyiv and Cherkasy regions comprise one type of population and one kind of food. And in the Kyrovohrad region, the population is entirely different, let's say, more related to the nomadic ethnic group: thin,

---

8 Ochakiv is a city in the south of Ukraine, 30 kilometers from ancient Olbia.

squat, with flat facial features, and with somewhat slanted eyes. And they ate completely different food: buns with poppy seeds, jam, and all kinds of pies, characteristic of the Kyiv and Cherkasy regions, completely disappeared; instead, they had more meat products, fruits, and some Central Asian sweets. This is, in fact, among other things, the influence of nomads. And after so many centuries!"

"Interesting, very interesting...."

"At that time, I watched this gradual change in the population with great interest. It was indeed a revelation for me. And then I was in the Mykolaiv region. There, there was a complete mixture. However, lately, all this has been a little obscured".

"What can you say about the ancient Greeks? Did they have a significant influence on the locals?"

"Definitely. However, the process of Hellenization took place in several stages, and the degree of influence on different regions varied. Some settlements belonged to the settled agricultural population of the forest and forest-steppe. These are our famous settlements of Khotivske, Sharpivske, Nemyrivske, Bielske, and others. Here, Greek ceramics appeared very early on, as early as the seventh century BC. So, the first stage of Hellenization is the penetration of Greek goods into the life of the forest-steppe population. Gradual accustomization to these products marks the second stage. I would not even call this a process Hellenization, rather, the penetration of Greek culture initially through goods".

"Did traditions, cults, and rituals follow the merchandise?"

"Listen, listen, I will tell you about this as well. So, merchandise appears, its quantity grows, and people get accustomed to it. Moreover, these are remote areas – just look where we have forest-steppe, and where the Greeks are. Then the nomadic Scythians come to the steppe. But among the Scythians, Greek ceramics appeared much later than in hill forts, no earlier than the fifth century BC, because the Scythians themselves appeared here only at the end of the sixth century. However, the most interesting thing is that the Scythians have less Greek ceramics than the inhabitants of hill forts – the Scythians were just beginning to get accustomed to Greek goods, they were just taking a liking to them. In contrast, the population of the forest-steppe and even the forest had long been accustomed to them and uses them, one might say, on a daily basis. Now let's address the question of Hellenization. There is one nuance here.

THE ANCESTORS OF UKRAINIANS 79

The forest-steppe is far away and not adjacent to Olbia. But the Scythians are close to it. And Greek rites and beliefs, in the first place, penetrate Scythian society – recall, for example, the legend about the Scythian king Scyles, told by Herodotus. And from the Scythians they are transmitted to the inhabitants of the forest-steppe".

"But the Greeks lived not only on the coast of the Black Sea. As far as I know, there were periods when they retreated to the forest-steppe, didn't they?"

"In the middle of the 2nd century BC, due to climatic changes and barbarian invasions, the Olbian chora began to disappear.[9] *At the same time, in Olbia itself at this time there was no significant influx of population. And starting from the end of the second century, there was already an exodus. Where did the residents of Olbia and its choras go? They moved to the Lower Dnipro. At that time, the fortified hill forts arose there on the site of Scythian settlements that existed in the fifth to the fourth centuries BC. A certain Hellenization of the Lower Dnipro population occurs at this time."*

"Valentyna Volodymyrivna, what kind of relations did the Black Sea Greeks have with the 'barbarians'?"

"We know for a fact that in the first centuries AD in Olbia, a significant number of inhabitants had barbarian or mixed names. And these were not just residents -- these were archons, priests, agoranomoi, strategists, that is, people who held the highest positions in the state. Regardless of whether they had Greek or barbarian names, Olbians did not distinguish between themselves; they perceived themselves as a single entity: the father could be Greek, and the son could have a barbarian name. How could this happen in the closed community of the ancient polis?"

"So how could this happen?"

"I tried to comprehend all this based on the following reasoning. Until the first century AD in Olbia, we have a Greek foundation with very few barbarian names recorded. In the middle of the first century BC, Olbia was defeated by the Getae, and life there stopped for a while. And where did the residents go? Where did they go? A decree was preserved in Istria that mentioned the fact that a part of the population left the city after the Getae defeat and migrated to a 'barbarian country'. The same thing happened here – the Olbians went to the 'friendly barbarian country' to

---

9   Chora (χώρα) is a rural area near a city.

the north, where there was peace and mutual understanding, and where a mixed Greek-barbarian population lived. After all, the Olbians, who remained alive after the invasion of the Getae, could not go, for example, to Chersonesus because, as non-citizens of the polis, they simply would not have been given land there. Therefore, they left for free lands, where they had real chances to settle, they joined those with whom they had long-standing friendly contacts and where a certain part of the related population already lived".

"Did they go to the Lower Dnipro hill forts?"

"Yes, to the Nizhny Dnipro hill forts, which, at that time, were quite numerous and where the population was ethnically mixed".

"And what happened then?"

"And then another wave of Sarmatians struck the Lower Dnipro hill forts, and the exodus of this population back to Olbia began. The former Olbians and residents of the Olbian chora brought with them part of the population with whom they had lived in the hill forts. And these newcomers started shaping Olbia in a new way. All those who came here became its citizens. That is why there were so many barbarian names in Olbia. This was a mixed population, but sharing the Greek culture, absolutely Hellenized".

"Thank you very much."

Well, it is nice to know that the ancestors of Ukrainians saved the ancient Greeks during the Getae invasion and then took part directly in the revival of antiquity in the Northern Black Sea region. It turns out that the close interaction of three cultures — that of antiquity, the Scythian-Sarmatian, and the Proto-Slavic — crystallized the general traits that characterized the mentality of this region and later formed the main features of Ukrainian mentality.

Did the Mentality of Ancient Rome Influence the Ancestors of Ukrainians?

Ancient Rome, where the basic principles of politics, economy, military affairs, and jurisprudence were formed, in one way or another, influenced the mentality of all of Europe. Today's Europe is the daughter of Ancient Rome, whose archetypes are fundamental in European mentality.

The history of Ancient Rome dates to the 8th century BC. However, the Roman Empire became the "center of the world" in the 2nd century BC. Then it captured territories from Spain to Syria, from northwest Africa to Britain.

The Northern Black Sea region came into the orbit of Rome's interests in the 1st century BC. At this time, Rome established control over the Crimean Bosporan Kingdom and the Greek city-states, including Tyra, Olbia, and Chersonesus. However, the Northern Black Sea region and other lands of present-day Ukraine were never part of the Roman Empire—despite the latter's military presence. The Roman garrisons did not protect the empire itself but only the approach to it, and Rome did not consider the population of these regions to be its subjects. However, Roman troops encamped on the territory of present-day Ukraine until the middle of the 3rd century AD and turned out to be a real force that protected the region's population from steppe raiders, primarily the Sarmatians. Rome and the peoples who lived on both banks of the Dnipro River had good trade relations—agricultural communities exported grain to Rome, for which they received hard currency: denarii.

This collaboration ended around 260 AD, at a time when nomadic barbarians ravaged the Greek poleis, and the Roman garrisons that guarded them left for the Danube.

In 395, the emperor Diocletian divided the Roman lands into two parts—the Western Roman Empire and the Eastern one, which historians call Byzantium. As for the latter, it was already a state with a different language, a different religion, other traditions, and a different mentality.

There is plenty of scholarly research on ancient Rome. The works of Barbara Feichtinger, Holger Sonnabend, Christian Böhme, Ines Stahlmann, Werner Portman, and other authoritative experts on European mentality provide many answers to many questions.

Having analyzed scholarship on the main features of the Roman mentality, we can conclude that Ancient Rome, unlike ancient Hellas, had a very minor influence on the worldview of the ancestors of Ukrainians: such features as pragmatism, closed-mindedness, snobbery, xenophobia, respect for law, order, and authority, an inclination for painstaking work, strict discipline, and, in the end, control over passions are, finally, not characteristic of Ukrainians and Slavs in general.

Well, it's time we considered the nations that influenced the Ukrainian mentality much more than Ancient Rome.

Direct Ancestors of Ukrainians
The Slavs of the Early Middle Ages

Ethnic Features

> *The Slavs were a very freedom-loving people – they were often taken into slavery, but they still refused to work.*
> *From a school essay*

The community of peoples that made up the indigenous population of the Ukrainian lands in the early Middle Ages is motley and diverse. However, the leading role certainly belonged to the Slavs.

When did the Slavs appear? Where? How did they spread around the world? How long have they lived in the territory of Ukraine? There are no definite answers to these questions. Many opinions, hypotheses, and theories exist, but none can be considered entirely uncontested.

Even though there hasn't been sufficient research on the ancient Slavic tribes, and historical science gives conflicting answers to many questions, it is more or less accepted that the Slavic community is relatively young. Its formation took place in stages, through integration with other ethnocultural groups.

Most researchers date the emergence of the Slavic ethnos, like many other European ethnic cultures, back to the fourth to the fifth centuries AD. This period, called the "Dark Ages" by historians, was the time when the Roman Empire collapsed. However, the death of the giant empire led to the birth of two powerful civilizations — Byzantium and Slavdom. Probably, when the control of both the Germanic (Goths) and the Asian (Huns) conquerors weakened, the Slavs had the opportunity to determine their own destiny. At that time, purely Slavic nationalities began to emerge.

In the 6th century, the Slavs were already a sizeable ethnic group that took an active part in the life of southeastern Europe and influenced its history.

At this time, the Slavs appear in the written sources of the Byzantines for the first time. Although we only have mentions by Herodotus about the pre-Slavic tribes, there is enough material about the Slavs. If we supplement the chronicles and works of Byzantine authors with the conclusions of contemporary historians, we can say the following about the early Slavs.

Nationality, Everyday Life, Economy, Military Affairs, Language, Literacy, Culture, Religion, Sexuality

To which "nationality" do the Slavs belong? Of course, they are Slavic—their names recorded in written sources sound Slavic. However, not everything is that simple.

The Antae were in close contact with the Scythians and Sarmatians. The Venedi were ethnically related to the Germans (Goths). Having flooded into Eastern Europe from Scandinavia, the Goths settled in the southern Ukrainian steppes, created their own state under the Greuthungian king Ermanaric, and, until the 4th century AD, dominated the territory from the Danube to the Don River. The Slavs of the northern Ukrainian regions came in close contact with the Balts and Finns. In the south, the Greeks assimilated with the Slavs.

Many other "visitors" trod over the steppes on both sides of the Dnipro River — the Ugrians, Getae, Huns, Illyrians, Polovtsians, Bulgarians, Obry, Khazars, Alani, Vandals . . . All of them, to one degree or another, assimilated with the Slavs and merged with the settled autochthonous population of the lands of modern Ukraine.

In contrast to the "visitors", who were primarily nomads, settled Slavs lived under their usual conditions. They huddled "in dugouts and pitiful huts without any comforts"; they easily endured "heat, cold, rain, threadbare bodies, and poverty". Every family had an allotment of land; several families made up a farm or a small village. Large settlements were uncommon, especially ones protected by city walls.

Why did the Slavs live in small communities, extremely unsuited to resisting nomads?

Because the land they farmed eventually became depleted, and then a series of disastrous crop failures would follow. They didn't think of sowing the fields with something else: as soon as the yield decreased, they would hasten away from their homes and move to neighboring territories. That is why Slavic farms were small and short-term, and their inhabitants did without Roman extravagances — stone houses and good roads. And sewage systems were of no use to them. Not even a bath — winter was not that long, after all.

Agriculture and animal husbandry comprised the leading spheres of the economy of the Eastern Slavs. They also engaged in handicrafts, leather tanning, weaving, and other household activities.

According to some historians, the level of the economy of the ancient Slavic tribes was relatively high. New tools of production were quickly introduced; methods of land cultivation were improved; and pottery craft was exceptional. However, historical museum exhibits attest to the opposite — before the formation of Kyivan Rus, the Slavs lived in poverty. Their economy was primitive. After all, barbarians were all around, so why produce a lot? They would take it away anyway. Trade was also underdeveloped.

Constantly attacked by nomads, the early Slavs *led a life of reiving* and didn't mind armed robbery as well. Raids on Byzantium were one of their most favorite things to do. Their tactics were purely partisan. But later, they formed combat units, for whom war became a profession. Warriors defeated the enemy and, *returning home from campaigns, brought thousands of prisoners*. The captives became slaves and joined the development of the Slavic economy. The Slavs did not treat slaves in a brutal way like the Romans did, and even better than the Greeks—they accepted them into their families like younger members, and, after a certain amount of time, released them.

According to the Byzantine Emperor Mauritius, the Slavs had *many leaders who disagreed with each other*. And yet, any important decision of the elders had to be approved by the people's assembly—scholars called this tactic "military democracy".

The chronicler Nestor, the supposed author of the *Primary Chronicle*, claimed that "there was one Slavic nation and its language was one". But many modern researchers believe that neither a single Slavic people nor a single Slavic language ever existed. Most likely, in the first millennium of our era, the Ukrainian steppe spoke a distinctive dialect consisting of Slavic, Greek, Scythian, Germanic, Hunnic and, probably, "Trypillian" words.

By the 9th century AD, the Slavs did not have literacy—neither graffiti on ceramics nor any other signs resembling letters. They kept accounts using dashes and notches. Only the Goths, who settled on the lands of the Slavs and later joined them, had Roman-style writing.

Why did the Slavs lag behind the Sumerians by four thousand years in the development of writing? Because the Sumerian, Egyptian, and other cultures were oriented toward the written word, and the Slavic was based on the spoken vernacular. In the Slavic community, writing was generally considered a diabolical occupation, harmful not only for the "writer" but also for his entire tribe: any attempts to scratch something out were punished cruelly, sometimes even with the death penalty. However, legends, tales, and sayings were passed down orally from generation to generation until our time. These stories always feature many fantastic characters—*rusalkas* (mermaids), water spirits, forest spirits, and dragons. And, of course, a whole bunch of demons.

You can't say much about the culture of the ancient Slavs—the excavations of their settlements has not revealed a lot of highly artistic artifacts. Their ceramics were diverse and practical, but somehow too gloomy. But why would it be different? The better the dishes, the more likely nomads will take them away. "Everything they need for life, they bury in the ground in secret hiding places, concealing everything they acquire from the human eye", the Byzantine emperor Maurice testifies in his book *The Strategikon*. And the clothing of the Slavs is unremarkable: "some do not wear shirts or cloaks, but only pants", adds Procopius of Caesarea, the Byzantine historian of the 6th century. Of course, they had festive attire. It was not as rich as the one the Sarmatians had, but it was decorated in a unique way, which is vital for understanding their mentality. Moreover, if the Greeks made "jewelry" for the Scythians and Sarmatians, the Slavs made it for themselves. Moreover, local artisans did not copy anyone but created their own style—their products were inexpensive but original.

Archeological research shows that the ancient Slavs had their own religious system reflecting the world. It corresponded to the established view of a three-tiered structure of the universe, which was typical of many other peoples. According to Procopius of Caesarea, the Slavs also honored rivers, nymphs, and all kinds of other deities.

There is little information about the religion of the ancient Slavs. There is even less evidence of their furtive love life. After all, they did not leave any drawings, memoirs, or romances.

Yet we do know something. Nestor the Chronicler reports: "the Polianians maintained the custom of their ancestors, quiet and gentle, and also a reticence toward their daughters-in-law and sisters ..." Did they give love an insignificant place in their lives? Did they not honor agricultural cults of fertility, connected with erotic mysteries from time immemorial?

They did. The chronicles note: "Slavs used to gather for games and demonic dances and abducted maidens by the water". What the chronicler relates is nothing other than a holiday celebrated in

Ukraine to this day: the Night of Kupala. Fortune-telling, weaving wreaths, merry ritual songs, dancing around a tree of love, jumping over a bonfire, pranks, dressing up as all kinds of evil . . . These rituals are also reminiscent of the ancient Greek mysteries in honor of Aphrodite. On the Night of Kupala, Slavic girls turned into witches and held witches' sabbaths on Lysa Hora (Bald Mountain).

So, it turns out that the Slavs, according to the testimony of Nestor the Chronicler, treated their erotic life eagerly: "they had two or three wives". And they all lived, probably, in perfect harmony. Slavic people are not jealous, oh, not jealous at all! Wives "slept around as much as they wanted, because their husbands did not restrain them at all and were not jealous", and men took women to be their wives not only on the Night of Kupala but also outside of any holidays.

But men also had to endure all kinds of women's nonsense. And why? Because, as Maurice writes, "their women are more intelligent than a person should be by nature".

The Mentality of the Early Slavs and its Influence on Modernity

The desire to briefly define the mentality of any person can be compared with the attempt to stuff them into a box or into a box for a TV, where instead of the marks "top," "bottom," or "sold," "good," "brave," or something else is written. And a drinking glass would be placed in a noticeable spot as a signal. It would mean "do not disturb". Or "do not offer". Or maybe, on the contrary, "likes to pound down a few".

Not a single person but a whole conglomerate of tribes would fit in such a box. And if someone were to say that this is completely pointless, they might be right. Similarly, if someone were to note that every person, as well as every nation, would still have their own peculiarities, which an observant tourist would always be able to notice, they would be right too.

So, before us is a box with the ancient Slavic mentality. Like any other, it has six sides. But we would not be able to single out only six main Slavic archetypes—there are many more.

The formation of the ancient Slavic soul depended on the region. All neighbors left their imprint on the mentality of Ukrainian ancestors. Some of them *had a quiet and gentle way*, others *lived like beasts*, and still, others *kept the Huns' customs*.

But what did the Proto-Ukrainian Slavs have in common? What distinguished them from their neighbors?

First of all, it was **dependence on the land**. A good or a bad harvest year was a matter of life and death for them. Hence their worship of the sun and rain gods, love of nature, and respect for the spirits of darkness—many demons that the proto-Ukrainian Slavs invented for themselves cannot be found in any other mythology.

The archetype of the family was dominant in the ancient Slavic mentality.

The Slavs, of course, valued life. But above all, they valued **freedom**: they settled in an open field, did not recognize anyone above them and did not let anyone enslave or subjugate them—neither a nomad nor their own ruler. Rejection of authority was a primordial ancient Slavic trait.

Living on a small farm, the Slav had to rely only on himself. Hence his **individualism**. But in the mentality of each person, as well as in the mindset of an entire ethnic group, opposite traits can coexist. Collectivism is also characteristic of the Slavs: "they do things as a group, and they share happiness and unhappiness", Procopius of Caesarea claims. Of course, there were conflicts between neighboring houses and neighboring tribes. Such is human nature. However, bloodshed did not often happen: "The Polianians, and Derevlianians, and Siverianians, and Radimichians, and Viatichians, and Croats lived in peace".

Or maybe conflicts were not resolved by force because the Slavs, as Maurice claimed, were cowards?

It is difficult to agree with the Byzantine strategist—life in the open field and the need to master new territories subject to the winds and barbarians clearly testify to a trait like **courage**. Would cowards know how to attack Byzantium repeatedly? But Maurice also records such traits as **cleverness** and **cunning**. Here's what the Slavs came up with: "In case of danger, they plunge into the depths of the water with their heads, holding in their mouths stalks of long hollow reeds". It was difficult for the Byzantine strategist to admit that by forcing the enemy to fight in closed spaces, the

Slavs skillfully lured them and earned victory not by force but by clearly calculated tactics—we see the same thing during the Russo-Ukrainian war of 2022.

Foreigners were also impressed by the **wisdom** of ancient Slavic women.

We will now note some of the less attractive Slavic features. For example, a trait like **sloppiness**: "Their way of life is rough, without any comforts; they are always covered in dirt". Or maybe it's not so much sloppiness as **unpretentiousness**? After all, "they are very hardy; they easily endured heat, cold, rain, threadbare bodies, and poverty".

Byzantine authors also note such characteristic features of the Slavs as **carelessness** ("entering into battle, they never put on armor") and **inconsistency** ("in keeping agreements, they are treacherous and unfaithful to the highest degree"). And the Slavs do not respect order. And where there is no order, there is **a lack of order**, and everything is done God knows how: "in battle, they do not know the correct formation ..."

Slavs did not know the "correct formation", not only in battle, but also in life. Or maybe it's not that bad? Perhaps life in order, even more so in the "correct" one, is not life at all?

I dare to assume that in such a trait of the Slavic mentality as **the habit of poverty**, it makes no sense to look for something positive. But in ancient times, poverty was a kind of protection against nomads—that is to say, we are poor, so there is nothing one can take from us.

Unlike the Romans, who did everything to last for centuries to come, the Slavs were forced to move to new territories from time to time. They nearly settled down properly, and it was time to be on the road again. So why stress in vain? Anyway, we won't be here long. Hence another ancient Slavic trait—**carelessness**. The master's hands are golden, but it seems that the Slav does everything haphazardly. This trait has another equivalent: **purposelessness**, the habit of starting something but not bringing it to an end—that is to say, "somehow, it will work out".

In the same way, the Slavs had a feature typical of the inhabitants of a village—**deliberateness**. They took their time to do things, cooked food without haste, and had no cavalry. They were four thousand years behind in the development of writing and were nearly the last to adopt Christianity. Better late than never, right?

But regarding carelessness, we must note a thing or two.

First: in the conditions of farm life, every master of the house had to be a carpenter, a woodworker, a baker, and his own doctor. And that's why universality is the Slav's characteristic trait.

Secondly: early Slavic art is not exquisite, but the Slavs did not try to copy the Greeks; they followed their own sense of beauty and found their own style — their creativity is original and authentic.

The Slavs themselves were unique — "people of a very tall stature and enormous strength, with hair that was not very white or golden and not quite black", Procopius of Caesarea recalls. They were steadfast optimists. Why be sad?

Another quality characteristic of the Ancient Slavs that was extremely rare at that time was **kindness**. Few would venture to describe their enemies as the Byzantine authors did: "In essence, they are not bad and not at all malicious; with those who come to them and enjoy their hospitality, they are kind in their behavior, as if they were old friends".

A traditional trait of pagan farmers is **eroticism**. Slavic women were noted not only for their love and passion but also for their loyalty: after the death of their husbands, many of them voluntarily agreed to follow them to the next world. And the tradition of polygamy is most likely explained by the fact that there were not enough men in the villages — the nomads took them into slavery. Therefore, women were forced to do more than just women's work. The lack of men and the influence of the Sarmatians, who assimilated with the Slavs, determined the role of women in Slavic society as on a par with men. And sometimes even higher: "women were masters over their husbands and ruled over them".

The psychological traits of the ancient Slavs withstood the pressure of time and were passed on to the next generation of Ukrainian ancestors, to the residents of a powerful Eastern European state called Kyivan Rus.

Kyivan Rus

What does "Rus" mean?

A representative of Ukraine speaks at the UN:
"When Prince Oleh of Rus went to bathe in the river, Muscovites stole his sword, which he left on the bank".
A representative of Russia says:
"What do Muscovites have to do with this? Moscow didn't exist then!"
The Ukrainian representative responds:
"Oh! This is exactly my point".
An anecdote.

Rus was a powerful Eastern European state with its capital in Kyiv. It existed during the ninth to 13th century. The legal successor of this state is Ukraine; it is precisely here that the Ukrainian ethnos arose.

The ancient Rus state had two poles—the northern lands, Novgorod, and the southern, Kyiv. Hundreds of versts of impassable forests separated them; they had a different background, a different ethnic composition of the population, and, undoubtedly, a different mentality. But at that time, only the territories of present-day Ukraine—the Kyiv, Chernihiv, Zhytomyr, Sumy, Vinnytsia, Cherkasy and Poltava regions, and from the 13th century also Western Ukraine—were called "Rus". The chronicles contain many indications that some lands in present-day Russia, under the rule of Kyiv, were not considered Rus as such, and the inhabitants of Ukrainian territories, neither Moscow nor Novgorod, were called Rus, Ruthenians, or Rusians.[10] The Muscovites simply stole and appropriated this name: the renaming of Muscovy as Russia took place by order of Peter I in 1721, and the ethnonym "Russian" was established only at the end of the 18th century, when Catherine II ordered the Muscovite people to consider themselves "Russian" and forbade them to use the term "Muscovites".

---

10 Translating the term into English is tricky due to the confusion and similarity between Rus and Russian. Hereafter, when the author uses "Rus" and "russes" (in his French and Hungarian versions) to refer to the inhabitants of Rus, we will say "people of Rus" to avoid confusion with the state of Kyivan Rus or Russia and Russians.

Ukrainians have never accepted the theft of the name "Rus" from them. The most famous Ukrainian poet Taras Shevchenko never once used the word "Russia" in his works; instead, he always wrote about "Moscow" (Moskovia) or "moskali" (Moskovians).

How did illiterate Slavs, who "lived in miserable huts at a great distance from each other", suddenly "jump ahead of themselves " and build a powerful state? What so unexpectedly changed the mentality of the ancestors of Ukrainians? We are speaking about just thirty to forty-six generations, which is not that long, after all.

To understand what the mentality of the inhabitants of Kyivan Rus was like, let's turn to the materials of archeological research and to medieval authors who knew the inhabitants of Rus personally. Let's try to imagine that person's inner world, to see their "contemporary reality" as they saw it.

An Excursion into History

There are many publications on the history of Kyivan Rus. Therefore, I will not retell material from school textbooks. I will just point out certain key moments that relate to the title of this book.

At the end of the 8th century AD, the Vikings/Scandinavians, called the Varangians during the time of Rus, first attacked the eastern coast of England. "Lord, save us from the plague and the Normans", they prayed in England, Germany, and France. The Vikings reached Spain and Italy, repeatedly besieged Paris and Constantinople, and received immense quantities of ransom. The Norwegians[11] conquered several countries in Western Europe, including the lands of present-day Ukraine, according to the court chaplain of the Frankish state Prudentius, the author of the "The Annals of St. Bertin".

According to Nestor the Chronicler, the author of the *Primary Chronicle*, in 862, the local tribes "drove the Varangians beyond the sea, did not pay them tribute, and began to rule over themselves". But "there was no law among them, and tribe rose against tribe. Discords ensued among them, and they began to war among themselves. And they said to themselves: 'Let us seek a prince who may

---

11 French Normandy remained after them.

rule over us and judge us under the rule of law'. They accordingly went over the sea to the Varangian Rus".

Hence, across the Baltic Sea, there was, so to speak, "Varangian Rus". And from there, as it were, the Slavs invited their ruler, the chieftain Rurik.

According to modern Scandinavian beliefs, Rurik invited himself to rule. But it is not important for our topic whether it was a conquest or an "invitation"; what matters is the fact that the leaders of the Varangian forces brought a large number of Normans with them to the land on both sides of the Dnipro.

Having settled on Slavic lands, they were no longer robbers looking to plunder, but, rather, they were in the role of emigrants, who began to build settlements that were not characteristic of the Slavs but were common for Europe — cities fortified by moats and walls, whose inhabitants were engaged not in agriculture but in crafts.

It was not by chance that the heart of Ancient Rus was formed in the Middle Dnipro region. These lands were far ahead of the northern regions in terms of economic and cultural development.

It is customary to date the beginning of Kyivan Rus as a state to the year 882. At that time, a representative of the Rurik family, Oleh, whom the authors of the Scandinavian sagas call "Odd", seized power in Kyiv. Having united the lands of Kyiv with those of Novgorod, he imposed tribute on the local population and, according to the Norman tradition, conducted raids on Byzantium from time to time.

Niketas Paphlagon (born about 885), author of "The Life of Patriarch Ignatius", says: "At this time, more tainted by murder than any of the Scythians, the people called Ros, through the Pontus Euxinus, came to Stenon (the Bosphorus) and destroyed all the villages, all the monasteries, now raided the islands located near Byzantium (Constantinople), looting all the treasures, and capturing people, killing them all".

It turns out that the Byzantines identified the people of Rus not only with the Normans but also with the Scythians. Constantine Bagryanorodny (905–959), the emperor of Byzantium and author of the treatise "On Empire Management", states: "This is a Scythian tribe, untamed and cruel".

Be that as it may, life went on. After Oleh's death, Rurik's son Ihor (Ingvar) began to rule over Rus. In the 940s, he strengthened the state, grabbed Crimea, and continued raids on Byzantium just as Oleh had done before.

The Byzantine author Pseudo-Simeon describes the events of 941 as follows: "The people of Rus committed many misdeeds: they set fire to the coast, crucified some of the prisoners, nailed others to the ground, or targeted and shot yet others with arrows. They tied the hands of the captives from the priestly ranks behind their backs and drove iron nails into their heads".

In 944, having taken tribute from the Derevlianians, Ihor returned a second time. This time the freedom-loving villagers ran out of patience, and they killed him. Ihor's wife Olha, an energetic and thoughtful woman, rose to power in Kyiv. She took revenge on the villagers three times, but she had to establish the concept of law — from now on, tribute was not collected arbitrarily but in a regulated way. In addition, Olha was the first of the Kyivan rulers who arrived in Byzantium not with war but with peace, thereby making this powerful state not an enemy but an ally. Power passed from Olha to her son Svyatoslav.

Svyatoslav's reign was a series of victorious wars: against the Khazars, Bulgarians, Polovtsians, and the Byzantine Empire. Leo the Deacon, a Byzantine historian, testifies: "The people of Rus, who had gained the fame of being absolute winners in battles among the neighboring nations, believed that a terrible misfortune would befall them if they suffered a shameful defeat from the Romans (Byzantines), and fought with all their might ... Many claim these people are reckless, brave, warlike, and powerful".

The burial rite for fallen soldiers was interesting. Leo the Deacon wrote: "It is said that the Scythians observe the mysteries of the Hellenes, offer sacrifices according to the pagan rite and perform drink-offerings for the dead, having learned this either from their philosophers Anacharsis and Zalmoxis or from the associates of Achilles".

It is a well-known fact that the Scythians observed the mysteries of the Hellenes. But the fact that the "Scythians" of Kyivan Rus also observed these traditions is fascinating. The description of the appearance of Prince Svyatoslav of Kyiv is also crucial for our topic. He looks like a Ukrainian Zaporozhian Cossack! More precisely, the Zaporozhian Cossacks look just like "Svyatoslavs" and Norman Vikings in appearance. Although why, actually, only in appearance? The habits of the Ukrainian Cossacks of the fourteenth to the eighteenth centuries are also Viking-like. Or maybe the Rus-Scythians-Normans-Vikings had a Zaporozhian Sich, just like the Cossacks?

Constantine Bagryanorodny wrote: "In June, moving along the Dnipro River, the people of Rus reach an island called St. Gregory (Khortytsia). They perform their sacrifices on this island: they sacrifice live roosters, according to their custom".

It was just like this. St. Gregory, the island of Khortytsia, became the settlement of the Cossack state in the following centuries.

The historical role of Svyatoslav is ambiguous. At the peak of his power, he conquered huge territories—from the Balkans to the Middle Volga, from the Baltic Sea to the Caucasus. But later, most of the conquests were lost, the wars exhausted the Kyivan state, and the diplomatic relations established by his mother, Princess Olha, with the leading Christian countries, fell apart. Svyatoslav's bravery did not save him from death. In 972 he died in battle against the Pechenegs.

Another civil war began in Rus, caused by conflicts between the princes over the distribution of power. Svyatoslav's illegitimate son Volodymyr by his housekeeper Malusha won this battle. Recruiting a mighty army from friendly Scandinavia, he captured Kyiv.

Taking power, Volodymyr placed twelve of his sons on "regional" thrones. "And he was insatiable in vice, seduced married women and violated young girls. Because he was a libertine", Nestor the Chronicler wrote.

However, married women and girls did not prevent Prince Volodymyr from strengthening his power not only in his "Swedish" family but also in the state. In 988, he introduced Christianity to Rus. And why, for example, not Islam or the Jewish faith, which the Khazar neighbors practiced?

Nestor the Chronicler writes: "Circumcision and abstaining from pork and drinking were disagreeable to him. He said: "Drinking is the joy of the people of Rus, and we cannot exist without this pleasure".

Naturally. Later, Volodymyr began to introduce writing in the Kyivan land.

Prince Volodymyr died in 1015. His illegitimate (again illegitimate!) son Svyatopolk, nicknamed Okayanny (the Damned), took over the Kyivan throne for four years. Fearing the loss of power, he killed his brothers Borys and Hlib. In general, Kyiv's attitude toward this was not anything special, and the history of almost all European countries have examples of such deeds.

Niketas Choniates, a Byzantine rhetorician, writes: "The example of fratricide shown in Tsargrad (Constantinople) became a sample, a model, or even a general rule for every corner of the earth; so that not only Persian, Tauri-Scythian (Kyivan), Dalmatian, and Pannonian (Hungarian) sovereigns, but also powerful rulers of other nations, having drawn swords against blood relatives, filled their homelands with rebellions and murders".

After Svyatopolk, the Kyivan state once again lucked out — the chief throne was seized by Volodymyr's son (now legitimate) Yaroslav, nicknamed the Wise. With the help of the Polish army, he won a victory over his brothers (he executed some, threw others into prison, and sent the remainder to the Pechenegs). He not only rivaled his great father in the organization of the state, but also surpassed him in many ways: he "dealt" with the Khazars, put the Lyakhs, Prussians, Lithuanians, and Finno-Ugric tribes "in their proper place", married his daughters to the rulers and kings of Byzantium, Germany, France, Norway, and Hungary; married Ingegerd, the daughter of the king of Sweden, himself, and founded the Rus-Danish-Swedish union. And while the "Ministry of Foreign Affairs", aided by the efforts of his daughters, took care of the diplomatic field, Yaroslav strengthened the internal life of the state: he built new cities, expanded Kyiv, and built many magnificent cathedrals in it, which have remained to this day. During Yaroslav's reign, the foundations of cultural traditions in architecture, historiography, art, and philosophy were laid, which later developed on the territory of the future Ukraine. During his reign, the culture of the Kyivan state thrived in all its fullness, and Kyiv became a prominent city of Europe. Thanks to a taxation system that imposed low taxes, agriculture, artisanship, and trade developed intensively.

Nestor the Chronicler writes: "And Yaroslav loved religious establishments, and he was devoted to priests ... And he had a penchant for books and read them continually day and night. And he gathered many scribes, translated the Scriptures from Greek into the Slavic language and wrote many books. And he bought books, through which true believers are instructed and are comforted by the teaching of the divine word".

Adam of Bremen, the author of *History of the Archbishops of Hamburg* (the 1070s), confirms Nestor's words: "Kyiv is a worthy rival of the state of Constantinople, the most glorious gem of Greece".

Wow! The Europeans called the Kyivans either Normans or Scythians, and, it turns out, they considered Kyiv to be "the most glorious gem of Greece"!

After Yaroslav the Wise, nature stopped producing genius rulers in the Rurik dynasty for some time: his sons could not strengthen the state. They did not even manage to keep it at the level it was.

The life of the lineage of Rurik reawakened with the birth of Yaroslav's grandson Volodymyr, named after his mother's last name, the daughter of the Byzantine emperor, Monomakh. He once again managed to unite the regional princes, to destroy the Polovtsians, and to revive normal life in the state. Monomakh abolished debt slavery, limited the interest of usurers, allowed servants to complain about their masters, and gave women legal and property rights equal to men. Kyivan Rus regained its lost greatness and power. An unknown European chronicler, the author of *The Life of St. Marian the Irishman*, the founder of St. Jacob's Monastery in Regensburg, describes the generosity of Monomakh: "One of the brothers of this monastery, accompanied only by a boy, led along the road by the mercy of the Holy Spirit, arrived before the king of Rus, received precious furs worth a hundred marks[12] both from this king and from the nobles of the richest city of Kyiv and, putting them on carts, safely reached Regensburg. The monastery's building and the cathedral's roof were completed with this money".

By the way, St. Jacob's Cathedral in Regensburg, built on donations from Monomakh, has survived to this day and is one of Germany's most unique architectural monuments.

Volodymyr Monomakh's "Teachings" — a set of instructions to his sons in which he set out his life principles, also attests to his worldview:

Don't let the sun find you in bed. Thus, my father of blessed memory did, and thus do all good, perfect men.

Above all, do not have pride in your heart or mind.

Beware of lies, drunkenness, and fornication.

Do not envy those who do iniquity. The small wealth of the righteous is better than the great riches of sinners.

As you are deprived — do not take revenge; if hated — love; if persecuted — endure; if insulted — pray.

Do not kill either the righteous or the guilty, and do not command to have him killed; if someone is guilty even of a death sentence, then do not destroy any Christian soul.

Respect your guest, regardless of where he came to you from — whether a commoner, a nobleman, or an ambassador; if you cannot honor him with a gift, then regale him with food and drink.

Pass not by a single person without greeting them with a kind word. Love your wife but let her not rule you.

It is the basis of all things: hold the fear of God above all else. If you start to forget it, reread this counsel frequently: then I will be without shame, and things will be good for you.

Glory to you, lover of mankind!

Monomakh's son Mstyslav must have listened to his father's admonitions. He managed to maintain the unity of Kyivan Rus, to hunt down the Polovtsians on the Don, to drive them across the Volga, and to accomplish many other glorious deeds. And,

---

12   This was approximately about 25 kg of silver.

respecting such a father-in-law, the kings of Norway, Denmark, Hungary, and Byzantium married his daughters. Later, all of Europe had family ties with Kyivan Rus.

After Mstyslav, the power of the Rurik dynasty faded again and forever. There were no more princes like him in Kyiv. Regional rulers took turns capturing the capital and occupying the throne, from where others drove them away. Civil wars continued everywhere. The law was ineffective. The Polovtsians grew brazen again.

The situation worsened catastrophically with the coming to power of Andriy Boholyubsky. He moved the state's capital to Volodymyr, and in 1169 his army captured Kyiv and mercilessly looted it.

In the 13th century, the Old Kyivan state finally fell apart—it was overrun by the Golden Horde. Since that time, Kyiv, Galicia-Volyn and other principalities have developed independently of each other.

Nestor the Chronicler writes: "Suffering from the incursions of the pagans, we come to know God whom we have angered. All the cities and our villages are laid waste. We traverse the fields where horses, sheep, and cattle once grazed in herds, we now see them all desolate".

Why did God suddenly "come to hate" the people of Rus so much? After all, they accepted the Christian faith.

Nestor the Chronicler writes: "We only call ourselves Christians, but we live like pagans ... We behold how places of worship are worn bare by the footsteps of a great multitude, who jostle each other while they make spectacles invented by the devil. And churches stand empty".

Was pagan influence so powerful in Kyivan Rus?

Matthew, Bishop of Krakow, the author of an epistle written in the 1140s, wrote: "The people of Rus do not follow the rules of the Orthodox faith. They worship Christ only in name; but in deeds, they completely renounce him. After all, not wanting to be in agreement with either the Latin or the Greek Church and having separated from both, this people is receiving the sacraments neither according to one nor the other rite".

This is how ordinary people, the ancestors of Ukrainians, lived. I wonder what they looked like.

Ibn Fadlan, secretary of the Baghdad Caliphate, author of the treatise *Mission to the Volga* (921): "I have not seen people with more perfect bodies. They are like palm trees, fair-haired, red in the face, and white in the body. Each has an axe, a sword, and a knife; they don't part with them".

It seems that the inhabitants of the Kyivan state did not suffer from poverty.

Ibn Rustah (end of the ninth/beginning of the 10th century), traveler and author of a geographical compendium *Book of Precious Records*, wrote: "They have many cities, and they are prosperous".

Adam of Bremen wrote: "Rus is called Ostogard[13] by the barbarian Danes because it is located in the east; it is like a watered garden, rich in all kinds of goods".

Abu Hamid al-Gharnati (1080–1169), a Spanish-Arab traveler, wrote: "This country is spacious, abundant in honey and wheat, and barley, and large apples, there is nothing better than these".

How did the inhabitants of Rus treat foreigners?

Ibn Rustah: "They respect guests and treat foreigners who seek their patronage wellv... They [even] treat their slaves well and maintain their slaves' clothes because they trade their slaves".

What did the people of Rus do?

Ibn Rustah: "They make jugs and beehives for bees from wood and store bee honey in the jugs. They mostly sow millet".

Were they engaged in winemaking?

Ibn Rustah: "They don't have vineyards. They make an intoxicating drink from honey".

What musical instruments did they have?

Ibn Rustah: "They have all kinds of lutes, harps, and pipes. Their pipes are two cubits long, and their lute is eight-stringed".

In general, was life in Kyivan Rus expensive or inexpensive?

Abu Hamid: "Life is inexpensive for them".

What was the currency?

Abu Hamid: "They trade among themselves with old squirrel skins. For each of these skins, they give a wonderful round loaf

---

13 Eastern garden.

of bread. They buy all kinds of goods with them: both enslaved females and males, gold, silver, beavers, and other things".

How much did the residents of Kyivan Rus work?

Gervasius Tilburiensis (first third of the 13th century), an Englishman, author of the work *Otia Imperialia:* "The people of Rus languish in idleness, indulge in hunting and excessive gluttony, and almost never cross the borders of their state".

Even after the adoption of Christianity, polygamy still existed among the Slavs for some time. How did the wife behave after the death of her husband? Could she marry again?

Ibn Rustah: "If the deceased had three wives and one of them claims that she loved him, then she brings two poles to his corpse, and they drive them into the ground, then put the third pole across, tie a rope in the middle of this crossbar, she stands on the bench and ties the end of this rope around her neck. When she has done this, the bench is taken from under her, and she remains hanging until she suffocates and dies, and after her death she is thrown into a fire, where she burns".

And what attitudes did the Kyiv Slavs have to magic and sorcery?

The unknown author of *The Saga of Olaf Tryggvason* wrote: "There were soothsayers in the Gardariki,[14] those who knew much about many things".

Nestor the Chronicler wrote: "And they tempt people and bewitch through the word of the devil. More demonic enchantments happen through women; because, first of all, the devil seduced the woman, and the woman seduced the man. So, from generation to generation, many women conjure with sorcery, poison, and other diabolical tricks".

This is indeed true . . . And could a woman be, say, the head of the family?

Danylo Zatochnyk (12th century, author of *Secular Parables*) wrote: "A goshawk is a bird among birds, a hedgehog is a beast among beasts, a crayfish is a fish among fish, a goat is an animal among cattle, a serf among serfs is a serf's serf, a man among men is not a man but he who listens to his wife".

---

14   The term Scandinavians used in the Middle Ages for the Kyivan Rus State.

Well, you can "conduct interviews" with medieval authors to your heart's content. But the length of this book is not unlimited. To understand the mentality of the inhabitants of Kyivan Rus, it is worth turning to the conclusions of modern historians.

Here, briefly, are what they happen to be.

Peculiarities of Life and Everyday Life

Nationality

In Medieval Europe, one cannot find a country whose people did not include different tribes. The same thing happened in Kyivan Rus. The Slavs occupied the majority in the land of this state, but, in addition to them, a large number of various ethnic groups huddled here. During the time of prosperity, an abundant flow of eastern and western emigrants constantly arrived in the state. They considered themselves lucky to join a highly advanced and rich civilization.

Descendants of the ethnic group claiming to have come from "the people of the Swedes" occupied a prominent place among the inhabitants of this country. Not accidentally, foreigners portray the people of Rus ("fair-haired, rosy-faced, white-complexioned") as Scandinavians, although not devoid of Slavic features. At least until the middle of the 12th century, the Normans gave their children both Slavic-Greek and Scandinavian names.

There were no fewer Scythian-Sarmatians descendants in Kyivan Rus than Varangians. It is no accident that the Byzantines constantly confused the people of Rus with the Normans and the Scythians — both had a similar disposition.

Many Greeks lived in Rus — both descendants of the "real" ancient Greeks and Byzantines, who formed the center of the intelligentsia of the Kyivan state. The number of Byzantines in Kyiv increased after the capture of Constantinople by Crusaders in 1204. Residents of the Eastern Roman Empire flocked to Kyiv, where, as Ibn Rustah claims, "guests are respected, and foreigners seeking their patronage are treated well".

But despite the large number of newcomers, autochthonous villagers formed the basis of Kyivan Rus; their roots reached back to past generations of this region's residents, and their descendants formed the Ukrainian nation.

Society

In the Middle Ages, an individual belonged entirely to society. Therefore, the person of that time was "without individual identity". In ancient Rome, there were many portraits of various people. But in the Europe of the following centuries, these are absent. There are only depictions of saints, kings, and bishops. Only in the late Middle Ages did the genre of the self-portrait appear. Since then, self-awareness has become a subject of self-respect and reflection.

The people of Kyivan Rus are also "anonymous". In the chronicles, we do not see anyone except princes. We do not know the names of famous painters, architects, or jewelers. Even the name of Nestor the Chronicler is questionable. Of course, it is not that there was a lack of vivid personalities, strong characters, and outstanding talents apart from the princes in the Kyivan state. There were quite a few such people. But they seemed to be of little interest to anyone.

Women's lot was traditional in Rus. In the village, as in past centuries, a woman had to do all kinds of work. But in cities, primarily in Kyiv, Greco-Byzantine customs prevailed, and the role of women in social life was significant, sometimes even more than in the European countries of the time.

Children in Rus, as in ancient Greece, were not pampered. They had to work hard from an early age, and their knowledge was imparted with a carrot and stick.

However, the attitude toward a man in Kyivan Rus was still better than in Medieval Europe because there was no "Roman xenophobia" here, and neither freethinkers nor "witches" were burned at the stake in the Kyivan state.

Everyday life

Despite its cities, Kyivan Rus remained a rural state. And country life was simple. The furniture was unpretentious: a massive table, not covered with a tablecloth, benches, chests, shelves for dishes. Princes' palaces, although distinguished by a certain elegance, carved armchairs, and oriental carpets, were still inferior to the sophistication of European kings' boudoirs. Kyivan princes rarely even had beds, and had wooden couches instead.

The dishes were just as simple. They were ceramic, wooden, metal, and glass. Brightly painted bowls, jugs, mugs were not often found.

Every house had talismans, such as pagan amulets, that protected the home from evil. Later, Christian icons replaced them, which, in fact, had the same function as pagan talismans.

A characteristic note: in Kyivan Rus, windows had no curtains, and people's lives took place in front of everyone's eyes.

Cities

A large number of cities made Ancient Rus different from previous Slavic proto-state formations. By today's standards, the cities were small, somewhere between ten to twelve thousand inhabitants. The population of Kyiv in its heyday was about 50,000 people. As a rule, cities were built on high riverbanks. The castle of the ruler was in the center, surrounded by wealthy citizens' quarters, with the shacks of craftsmen and the poor behind them. Of course, the bazaar comprised the city's heart. The maidan (city square) had a similar function; it was a place where life teemed, and people gathered.

Cities were of great importance for the security of Kyivan Rus. Even relatively small cities were built like fortresses with ramparts and towers. and differed little from European metropolises. The architecture was somewhat different, and they were not as densely built up. Perhaps this revealed the "rural" feature of the central Slavic mentality, the habit of living in open space.

Economy

The economy of the Kyivan state was in no way inferior to that of Europe. The Slavs, it turns out, knew how to work well.

Significant changes took place in agriculture. This may be explained by the fact that the need to migrate disappeared as the peasants began to use a system of land cultivation, in which they would alternately sow the soil with different crops to avoid soil depletion. Cattle breeding was well-developed; it provided sufficient meat, milk, and hides. Agricultural products not only fed the people to their heart's content but were also exported.

Handicraft-making was one of the most important branches of the economy. Following the example of Western Europeans, craftsmen united in workshops, jointly set up production and found a steady market for their wares. Metallurgy was at a high level.

Construction is the most vulnerable aspect of an economy. It develops only when society is on the rise and is prosperous and confident in its future. The rapid development of urban planning in the Old Kyivan State is eloquent testimony to the high level of the welfare of its citizens.

Trade with Europe, Byzantium, the Caucasus, the Khazar Khaganate, and Arab countries was extensive. Agricultural products, handicrafts, and animal skins were the most profitable export items.

However, it seems that the population of Kyivan Rus had little trust in their own currency as people kept their savings in the dirhams of the Arab Caliphate, the hard currency of that time. And, as the travelers claimed, they used squirrel skins in everyday trade.

Good roads, the "Roman core of European civilization", were lacking in Rus and even in the Ukraine of today. Of course, there were some roadways. But these rain-washed formations could hardly be called roads.

Authorities and Military Affairs

In antiquity, the Middle Ages, and even today, power was in the hands of whoever had military might behind him. Before the formation of Kyivan Rus, Slavic tribes raided Byzantium, but only as poorly organized detachments. Scattered villages, the disparity between tribes, and the lack of a single center prevented them from creating an effective army. And the inhabitants of Kyivan Rus made a wise decision — if you can't create your own army, hire someone else's. That's what they did: they "went across the sea to the Varangians" and invited Prince Rurik with his entire retinue. By the way, at that time, other European countries, in particular the British, similarly had a Scandinavian army.

Hence, the core of Kyivan Rus's army consisted of bold and brazen Vikings, well-trained in military affairs, according to the testimony of Ignatios the Deacon (770–845), the author of *The Life of St.*

George of Amastris, "the people, as everyone knows, are extremely wild and rude with no trace of philanthropy". Does a soldier need any other qualities? One thing is certain, a soldier also needs a bold commander. The Rurik dynasty produced them in surplus. Most of the Kyivan princes were brilliant military leaders. When in 1120, Yaropolk, the son of Monomakh, went with his army to the Don River where the Polovtsians were "huddled", he found them already gone as they had fled across the Volga River upon hearing that the people of Rus were coming.

No matter what, the Rurik dynasty fulfilled its main function of protecting the population of the Kyivan state from the steppe people.

It also performed another function of uniting the Slavic lands. It was the aggressive, authoritarian, and skillful rule of Oleh, Ihor, Olha, Svyatoslav, Volodymyr the Great, Yaroslav the Wise, and Volodymyr Monomakh that made Kyivan Rus quite powerful for a long time.

Of course, the prince held the greatest power in Rus. His relations with those close to him were based, first of all, on personal family ties and his relations with the population were based on robbery — let's call it what it was, that is, on the forcible collection of tribute. Changing the terms does not change the essence of what it was. After all, the prince's armed force, especially in the early days, resembled a band of robbers, and could be compared with a mafia "family" that established control over its territory in showdowns with other "families".

In general, Kyivan Rus, like many European states of that time, was formed through the institutionalization of racketeering, where tribute was a payment to prevent a "raid".

Yet, according to the chronicler, the princely tribute was less than that of the Khazars. The Rurik family's "tax raids" were recognized as legitimate by the people, which provided the family with the opportunity to rule over vast territories. Otherwise, the freedom-loving and armed Slavic tribes could defend their right not to obey their demands. This what members of the Derevlianians did at one time, killing Prince Ihor and forcing Princess Olha to replace racketeering with the law. This undoubtedly contributed to the economic rise of the state. Subsequent rulers supplemented and improved the country's legislative base, bringing it up to the canons of world legal thought of the Byzantine, Roman, German, and Scandinavian kind.

However, the power of Kyivan Rus was not only in their princes. Just as in Ancient Greece, Rus had a popular assembly (*viche*). And if something forced the princes to "tolerate" it, then it was the people who defended the right to independently decide how to live. The *viche* played a significant role in the life of society, and in crises, it took power into its own hands. For example, in 1068, it displaced Prince Izyaslav; and in 1113, contrary to the existing order, it invited Chernihiv Prince Volodymyr Monomakh to Kyiv.

Something similar happened again in Kyiv almost a thousand years later when in 2014, the People's Assembly overthrew the pro-Russian President Viktor Yanukovych and "invited" the pro-European Petro Poroshenko, who later won the democratic elections, to rule.

Religion

The pantheon of pagan gods of Rus was the same as in previous centuries. Gaining power, Prince Volodymyr introduced Christianity as the state religion in 988. The similarity of the Kyivan and Greek mentalities, which had little in common with the mentality of Rome, probably played a significant role in the choice of a Greek-style religion. It is written in the *Primary Chronicle* that when the prince's envoys "came to the Germans and saw them performing ceremonies in their temple", they "beheld no beauty there". But when they came "to the Greeks", while in the temple, "they knew not whether we were in heaven or on earth, for on earth there is no such splendor or such beauty".

The Christian church became an institution that a priori condemned princely quarrels and bloodshed. It did not care whether this or that prince was right or wrong; it strived to preserve the peace desired by God in the state. Rejecting paganism, Kyivan Rus united spiritually and politically with Europe, allowing it to conduct business on an equal footing with Byzantium, Germany, France,

Hungary, and the Holy Roman Empire. Christianity brought literacy to this country and contributed to cultural development.

But common people accepted Christ as God unwillingly. Numerous pagan amulets have been discovered among the archeological finds from the time of Kyivan Rus. Pagan emblems are often interwoven with Christian ones. And sometimes, interestingly, Christian symbols overlap with ancient ones: on some amulets, an image of Christ appeared on one side, and Medusa the Gorgon on the other; Apollo is believed to be depicted on one of the frescoes of St. Sophia Cathedral in Kyiv.

The combination of ancient, pagan, and Christian motifs is a characteristic feature of the ancient Kyivan mentality. In these lands, Orthodoxy coexisted with paganism.

Language

It isn't easy to imagine that the inhabitants of different lands, which had little contact with each other, used a common language. Most likely, the inhabitants of Kyivan Rus communicated in dialects close to each other.

Literacy

With the introduction of Christianity, a writing system finally appeared among the ancestors of Ukrainians. One needed to glorify the princes somehow and carry the word of God to the masses. In 863, the monks Cyril and Methodius compiled an alphabet from Greek and Slavic symbols and translated parts of the Bible as well as other liturgical books into Old Church Slavonic.

In a short period of time, by historical standards, Kyivan Rus turned into one of the most educated states in Europe. The Greek and Latin languages were studied in schools. Chronicles and works of fiction appeared; and libraries were created, the best of which became the pride of Yaroslav the Wise. Yaroslav's daughter, Anna Regina, made an unforgettable impression on the French court by being literate! Unlike her, her husband, King Henry I of France, signed documents with an "x".

However, getting used to writing in the Kyivan state was a challenge. *Mothers mourned their children who went to schools as if they had died.* One can empathize with the grief of mothers: sons sent to study made a break with traditions and adopted a fundamentally new system of values. As Professor Danylevsky remarks, if a person going to war had a chance of return, a child who went "to school" could no longer return to the world of his ancestors.

Literature

The literature of Kyivan Rus was classified as ecclesiastical, historical, legal, and belletristic. The dividing line between these genres was arbitrary as many works preaching Christianity, although written in a lively literary language, provided historical information and contained collections of laws and texts of treaties. The most significant written works that have survived are chronicles compiled by local priests.

The works of Aristotle, Plato, Homer, Socrates, and other ancient thinkers also contributed to forming the reader's worldview. Thanks to the teaching of ancient languages in schools, the literature of Rome and Greece was known in Kyivan lands not only in translations but also in the original. Familiarity with the ideas of philosophers of the West and the East formed a wide-ranging view of the world. It contributed to the emergence of a new class in society—a highly educated intelligentsia.

Works "for the general reader", such as dream books, books on astrology, fortune-telling, so forth enjoyed popularity in Kyivan Rus. The Church forbade them. Even worse for the Church, these books continued to be read, copied, and distributed.

However, there was still a lack of books. The reader rarely received new plots and involuntarily had to reread what they already knew. The peasants remained illiterate; they preserved a vast layer of "alternative" literature, passing down legends, fairy tales, myths, charms, sayings, riddles, and poems from generation to generation. Oral folklore influenced the development of the Ukrainian literary tradition, determining its form, artistic merit, and style.

Philosophy

The philosophical thought of Kyivan Rus was formed under the influence of Byzantium. And the ideas of antiquity, in turn, informed Byzantine thought. Life views of the thinkers of Ancient Greece turned out to be consonant with the views of the ancient Slavic intellectual elite. The ideas about the meaning of life, the conception of the heavens, and ethics corresponded in many respects.

The emphasis on the soul, which found expression in the heart, migrated from the traditions of Ancient Greece, through the Byzantine worldview, to the philosophy of Kyivan Rus. The heart is the center of will, love, the core of dreams, radiant thoughts, and actions. Kyivan philosophers wrote about "carnal matters" with disdain. They emphasized in every possible way the archetype of the suffering martyr who sacrificed his well-being and even his life for the sake of high ideals such as truth, humility, mercy, and, above all, wisdom. Along with the "heart", "wisdom" was one of the main philosophical postulates of Kyivan philosophical thought. This paradigm is embodied in the Cathedral of St. Sophia, Ukraine's main temple.

Handicraft

If Herodotus had visited Kyivan Rus, he would not have claimed that "apart from the multitude of great rivers, there is nothing else interesting in this country". There were a lot of exciting and remarkable things there. Blacksmiths knew unique methods of processing metals, and the masterpieces of Kyivan jewelers were in great demand.

Refined but inexpensive artisan products were omnipresent among Kyivan Rus's inhabitants since childhood. Bright clothes, tiaras, bracelets, hoops, rings, buttons, mirrors, combs, pendants — everything exuded optimism and the affirmation of life. The quality of products often exceeded the quality of similar products from Byzantium, the countries of the East and the West.

Music

Music was an integral part of the culture of Kyivan Rus. We can conventionally distinguish three tendencies of musical life at that time—folk, instrumental, and liturgical music. We can form an idea about folk music based on the archaic chants that are still prominent in Ukrainian folklore. The Ukrainian group "Kalush Orchestra" won the Eurovision Song Contest of 2022, receiving a record number of votes from the audience. The band's song "Stephania" is based on a Kyivan Rus song associated with pagan rites and spells.

Christianity introduced liturgical chants into the culture of ancient Kyiv. The motifs that came from Byzantium were considered sacred and invariable. But later, the influence of Byzantium weakened, and local tendencies in music began to be superimposed onto the canons of liturgical music, which led to the emergence of new forms, in particular, the famous Kyivan chant. The New Year's cycle song "Shchedryk", arranged by the Ukrainian composer Mykola Leontovych, which in an English version is known as "Carol of the Bells", is an example of archaic music that has survived to this day.

Medicine

The medicine of Kyivan Rus was within universal medieval canons. Doctors and healers were very popular and practiced professionally. Princely courts had their own doctors, and monasteries had their own almshouses.

Wars required a large number of wound care specialists. The surgeons had enough work even in peacetime. The annals even mention surgeries to remove tumors. Naturally, obstetrics was an important branch of medicine. Knowledge of phytotherapy was passed down from generation to generation in Kyivan Rus. Not only folk healers but every housewife knew the healing properties of plants and how to prepare decoctions, tinctures, and teas. Home physiotherapy, including baths, compresses, rubbing, massage, wrapping, and enemas, was also popular.

However, what we now know as psychotherapy had an equivalent in Kyivan Rus. If donations to the Church or a pyre where the patient was burned together with their demons were considered necessary "treatment" in Medieval Europe, Kyiv's healing practice was based on pagan traditions—charms. Fortune tellers, whisper enchanters, sorcerers, and conjurers enjoyed popularity among the people. Interestingly, these traditions did not come to the ancestors of Ukrainians from abroad, neither from Byzantium nor from antiquity. They have been preserved in the people's consciousness since time immemorial. Folk "non-traditional" (which does not mean ineffective) healing is successfully used in Ukraine even nowadays.

Love

Written sources sparingly cover the love life of the inhabitants of Kyivan Rus. However, even indirect information allows for interesting conclusions.

Here is one example. Not rushing to accept Christianity, the inhabitants of these lands, according to the *Primary Chronicle*, in line with an ancient tradition, "gathered for games, for dances, and for other devilish amusements, the men on these occasions took any woman with whom they had come to an understanding. In fact, they even had two or three wives each". As was customary since ancient times, *wives were as debauched as they wanted to be because their husbands did not restrain them at all and were not jealous.* The princes of Kyiv, who had Scandinavian roots, did not fight this because Scandinavian customs were similar: polygamy prevailed in Sweden even after the adoption of Christianity until the end of the 11th century. Swedish customs resonated with the Rurik dynasty. In particular, Volodymyr the Great, who, in addition to six wives, according to Nestor the Chronicler, "had three hundred concubines in Vyshhorod, three hundred in Belhorod, and two hundred in Berestov".

Yaroslav the Wise ratified the first law against pagan love traditions. He introduced monetary penalties for polygamy, adultery, incest, unauthorized divorce, the birth of an "illegitimate" child, rape, and a romantic relationship with a priest or nun. For example, for raping a female commoner the fine was thirty hryvnias (seemingly not much) and for raping a noblewoman 1.6 kg of gold. And the fact that the ruler needed to issue this law suggests that this must have been happening in abundance in the lands of Kyivan Rus.

Thanks to this decree, and perhaps because of tradition, a woman's legal status in Kyiv was higher than in Europe: fines were levied even for insulting a woman. A seduced enslaved girl became

DIRECT ANCESTORS OF UKRAINIANS 115

free after the death of her master, and the wife inherited her husband's property.

The church developed a system of marital relations, which was full of prohibitions and restrictions. It was sinful to make love during fasting, on holidays, and for some reason on Friday, Saturday, and Sunday. In fact, according to the Church, it was sinful to make love in general! Just think about it! Sexual relations in marriage, although perceived by the church as less evil than fornication, were also marked as immoral.

Evidently, the population of Kyiv treated church commandments without proper understanding. Influential people had harems not only in pre-Christian times but also later. Preservation of a girl's "purity" and a woman's fidelity was cultivated only in noble families, while ordinary citizens considered extramarital relations to be the norm. And not only young people, but also "married wives" took part in erotic games.

However, wives were boundlessly devoted to men (this is correct, one does not exclude the other): "If the deceased had three wives and one of them confirms that she loved him, then she brings two [impaling] poles to his corpse ..."

You know what followed.

Mentality

Well, now we must do something almost impossible again, that is, to single out the components of the mentality of the inhabitants of Kyivan Rus, a mosaic consisting of the worldviews of several ethnic groups, including the four that dominated: Slavs, Scythian-Sarmatians, Scandinavians, and Byzantines.

Slavic Archetypes of Ancient Kyiv Mentality

Let's recall which psychological features characterized the Slavs of the early Middle Ages. They are the following: dependence on the land, a love for nature, respect for spirits, family, a love of freedom, a love of peace, a hostile attitude to authorities, boldness, intelligence, and cunning. And also: sloppiness, a lack of ambition, inconsistency, a tendency to disorder, carelessness, naivety, and sluggishness. But these also include universality, originality, optimism, kindness, and passion.

Do we find these traits in the people of Kyivan Rus? Most of them are there, undoubtedly. The connection with the land never ended. After all, "this country is spacious, abundant with honey, wheat, and barley".

Reasonable pragmatism characterized the love for nature, and the spirits that inhabited it needed to "cohabit" with Christian saints: *we only call ourselves Christians, but we live like pagans*. The collective had supremacy over the individual; the family was the main "center of the state". The love of freedom of the ancient ancestors of Ukrainians was manifested in the fact that they finally threw off the yoke of the Pechenegs, Polovtsians, and Khazars, and the traditional distrust of the authorities led to the formation of the *viche*.

Residents of the Kyivan state had no xenophobia at all. They treated foreigners and even enslaved people well. They proved their courage in military campaigns. There was a general consensus that this people was "reckless, brave, warlike and powerful", and you can find as many examples of their cleverness and cunning as you want. Open and unpretentious in daily life (modest home decoration, rough furniture, simple dishes), the inhabitants of Kyivan Rus were beautiful people (*I have not seen people with more perfect bodies*), cheerful, true optimists, to whom Volodymyr Monomakh shouted: "Glory to you, lovers of mankind!"

Philanthropy is a trait not characteristic of the Middle Ages. And no matter how soft-hearted the man of Rus was, he still remained a man of his time. However, one cannot call him aggressive—the theme of campaigns of conquest is not central to local *bylinas* (epic poems).

Eroticism is another trait the mentality of the inhabitants of this region inherited from their Slavic ancestors.

However, under the conditions of the identity of the mentality of Kyivan Rus with the previous ancient Slavic mentality, there is little reason to attribute such traits as inconsistency, disorder, and industrial negligence to Kyivans. These qualities were no longer dominant. Everything was done for ages.

Scythian-Sarmatian Features

Earlier, we noted the following psychological features of the Scythians: determination, military astuteness, bravery, cruelty, everyday unpretentiousness, the love of freedom, independence, and, in the elite, high artistic taste.

A Scythian trace is undoubtedly present in both the genotype and the mentality of the Slavic tribes of the "Ukrainian" steppe. And the Byzantines, who equated the people of Rus with the Scythians, were not completely wrong.

And what about the Sarmatians? In them, we noted women's sluggishness, "urgency", obstinacy, and will to power. Like Sarmatian Amazons, the women of Kyivan Rus often dominated men.

And yet, the Normans contributed to the formation of the mentality of Kyivan Rus no less than the Sarmatians.

Scandinavian traits

With the appearance of the Normans, the life of the Eastern Slavs changed radically. The invited guests took power, created a powerful army, and protected farmers from the racketeering of the steppe people. There appeared something that the settled peoples of the Dnipro River region had never had—a state that was determined not by a tribal principle but by a territorial one. Taxes grew moderate and were used for the development of society. Private ownership of land was legalized, professional crafts and an aristocracy were born, the egalitarian principle traditional to the Slavs disappeared—the community now consisted of rich and poor, townspeople and peasants, *smerds* (serfs) and intelligentsia.

The characteristic features of the medieval Scandinavian character make up the archetype of the winner: aggressiveness, decisiveness, uncompromisingness, and purposefulness. In addition, a tendency to order and discipline, conservatism, hard work, frugality in everyday life, and generosity when in power.

Of course, the Scandinavian character was not limited to these features. But they dominated. And it is evident that assimilating with the Normans, the inhabitants of Kyivan Rus became more determined, purposeful and, most importantly, hardworking.

However, the newcomers from the north most likely also introduced something else to the Eastern Slavic mentality: disrespect for the individual, the personification of power, and the administration's brutality toward the *smerds*. Perhaps it was during that time that the idea, which exists in the Ukrainian mentality to this day, appeared in the minds of the population: the government is something alien, the court is always unjust, and there is nothing wrong with stealing something from the state. Finally, wasn't it from that time that dislike of the police—Vikings, who collected tribute rather than protected—took root in Ukrainian society?

So, the Slavs adopted hard work from the Normans. However, this statement contradicts the observation of one English traveler, who noted the following: "The people of Rus languish in idleness, passionately indulge in hunting and excessive gluttony".

Laziness and excessive gluttony . . . We have already met these traits somewhere . . . Was it among the ancient Greeks of the Northern Black Sea region? Just as opposite character traits can be combined in one person, likewise, opposite mentality traits can coexist in the psychology of an entire nation.

Echoes of the Ancient Greek

Medieval authors always emphasized that the "barbarian" world north of the Pontus Euxinus (Black Sea) borrowed much from the Greeks.

What characteristic features did we notice in the mentality of the inhabitants of the ancient Black Sea region? These include cheerfulness, spontaneity, ease of communication, openness, impracticality, a love of peace, collectivism, a dispassionate attitude to work (likewise to order, authorities, and laws), a desire for beauty and for the pleasures of love.

Do we find these features in the inhabitants of Kyivan Rus?

The Slavic tribes, who shared the same territory with the Greeks for a thousand years, absorbed the heritage of Greek culture and Greek civilization even before the formation of the Kyivan state. They encountered the descendants of the Hellenes—the Byzantines, who emigrated en masse to Rus, as close relatives. It is no accident that in the eleventh to the twelfth centuries, Western

Europeans perceived Kyiv as the *most glorious beauty of Greece*. As in the ancient Greece of the Northern Black Sea region, polis-cities were built in Kyivan Rus, which were relatively independent of the capital. Just as in ancient Greece, the *viche* existed in Rus. In Greek and Slavic paganism, the main god was Zeus and Perun, respectively, the God of Thunder. Both the Greeks and the residents of Kyivan Rus treated foreigners well. One cannot enumerate everything! After all, the founders of the Cyrillic alphabet, Cyril and Methodius, rightly concluded that Greek symbols were more compatible with Slavic perception than Latin ones.

Dominant Byzantine Traits

Most Ukrainian historians depict Byzantium, a powerful state that profoundly impacted world history, as a boring bureaucratic society permeated with intrigue and treachery, the dictates of the church, and endless uprisings of slaves. So to speak, a threadbare calque of antiquity.

Indeed, Byzantium gravitated toward authoritarian patterns of thinking, Orthodoxy, and thereby brought the postulate of "the one and only truth" into the mentality of Rus. If in Aristotle's time it was the norm to discuss incendiary topics and to openly express disagreement with the generally accepted point of view, then in Byzantium, and, accordingly, in Kyivan Rus, this was not appreciated, and philosophers, writers, and painters were obliged to promote Orthodoxy. After all, the very concept of Orthodoxy (*pravoslavie* — literally "right glory") suggests something exceptionally legitimate. In the Kyiv-Byzantine educational system, a novel thought was considered absurd as it was believed that everything that needed to be said had already been said. Inviolable canons reigned in literature, music, painting, and architecture. Instead of creating something original, Kyivan creators copied from templates.

On the other hand, having preserved the ancient Greek heritage, Byzantium handed it over to Kyivan Rus. After the fall of Constantinople, Kyiv became the center of culture, education, and art, a powerful transmitter of ancient Greek traditions to world civilization.

Additionally, Christianity came to Russia from Byzantium. Orthodoxy tried to impose the archetype of the eternal sinner, guilty even for his own existence, onto the cheerful Slav. The experience of guilt is an effective mechanism for forming a person's infantile dependence on authorities. However, asceticism did not resonate with the people, and they found a solution: once the Church said, "we must", the people answered, "we obey!" And they pretended to fulfill its will, while continuing to live according to their own rules, not imposed from the outside, and preserving the mental archetypes of previous generations and passing them on to their descendants — Ukrainians.

Protest against official ideology, against the government, against the church, in Kyiv-Byzantine psychological culture, manifested itself in the so-called heroization of the criminal since law-abiding behavior was not respected and was almost considered hypocrisy.

Comparative Analysis of the Mentalities of Kyivan Rus and Medieval Europe

What are the similarities and differences between a Kyivan man's soul and a medieval European's?
Both Medieval Europe and Kyivan Rus were communities of different tribes, ethnic groups, and peoples. Therefore, any comparisons are arbitrary. Still, some conclusions can be drawn. And the conclusions are the following.

Since ancient times, the territories to the west and east of the Carpathians moved along different paths in their development. The Western Roman Empire, the heir of ancient Rome, brought civilization to Medieval Europe. Roman customs reigned, and the Latin language dominated. Kyivan Rus owed its development to Byzantium, the heir of Greek antiquity, which shaped the similarity between the mentality of the inhabitants of Rus and the mentality of the ancient Hellenes.

In Kyivan Rus, people lived in the midst of "heavenly" nature on a fertile, rich land. On the other hand, the Europeans had to earn their living by working an inhospitable landscape and transforming it into a fertile land. Therefore, it so happened that work, one of the central Roman values, was a condition for survival in Europe, and Kyivan Rus traditionally preferred a dispassionate attitude to work since it was possible to survive even without making excessive efforts.

Both in Russia and in Europe, an individual depended on the will of the ruler. But if the will of the king was absolute in Europe, the inhabitants of the Kyivan state proved to be more freedom-loving, established a people's assembly (*viche*), organized insurrections from time to time, and invited a ruler to the throne who pleased them more; the same thing has happened in modern Ukraine.

The vast expanses of the Kyivan state contributed to the breadth and tenacity of the ancient Kyivan soul—insularity is foreign to it. Surrounded by small county-sized regions, impassable swamps and forests, a European man traditionally remained reserved and pragmatic. There was no free thinking among medieval Europeans, as among the Romans, and the general cultural level of the population was not very high.

In Kyivan Rus, the Orthodox Church's influence on the people was much less than that of Catholicism on Europeans. Although there were elements of pre-Christian beliefs in rural Europe, they had much less influence on people than the two belief systems in the lands of Kyiv. Easygoing Orthodoxy, with its attractive churches and majestic liturgies, could not, or perhaps did not want to, sever these people's pagan roots, deprive them of cheerful holidays, their respect for the spirits of nature, their love of life and optimism, all of which were uncharacteristic of Christian doctrine. The Kyivan Church instead pretended to do battle with mystical beliefs, soothsayers, healers, sorcerers, and even witches. All this disappeared from European life as the aggressive and lustful Inquisition forced the medieval European to follow all its ridiculous dogmas, to give up freedom, fun, and even love. Those who were not to its liking, it burned in bonfires; primarily, these were scientists, philosophers, astronomers, and the most beautiful young women.

The family was the center of society in Medieval Europe and Kyivan Rus. But if a man was traditionally the head of the family in Europe, and a woman was considered subservient to the man, it was often the opposite in the Kyivan lands.

"European" moderation, thrift, and contempt for foreigners are concepts alien to the society of Kyivan Rus. European man's isolation in "his home-fortress" contrasted with the openness, hospitality, and generosity of Kyivan Rus's inhabitants. However, a handy feature persisted in the introverted European from Roman antiquity—the habit of working carefully and relying not on God but on himself.

In Kyivan Rus and Europe, the attitude toward order was fundamentally different. In the Kyivan mentality, a criminal was, instead, a semi-romantic character who rebelled against the authorities and conventions of everyday life, while in Europe, such a character was considered a violator of the divine order and culpable for all misfortunes and troubles. From ancient Rome, Europe inherited the habit of the meticulous observance of laws, decrees, and rules, as well as respect for private property, not typical of Kyivans. Fairy tales about Robin Hood only appealed to the lumpenized stratum of European society.

And in conclusion, according to the testimonies of foreigners, the inhabitants of Kyivan Rus were a very handsome people. Women were particularly attractive, emotional, open, and "sinfully passionate". European women who married, as a rule, not according to the dictates of the heart but as a result of a pragmatic agreement, remained restrained in erotic pleasures. This was the demand of the Church.

Well, after the time of Kyivan Rus, having absorbed the best achievements of this state, the progenitors of Ukrainians moved to the next step in the development of their society—the development of their own civilization, their own culture, and their own nation, with their own unique and somewhat contradictory mentality.

Ukrainians of the Fourteenth to the Twenty-first Centuries

Zigzags of History

As the folk saying goes, an uninvited guest is worse than a Tatar[15]

In 1223, hordes of Tatar-Mongols appeared near the outskirts of Kyivan Rus. They defeated the military units of the local princes, who could not unite even in an hour of danger—there is not even a hint of organized resistance to the Tatars in the chronicles. In 1237–1239, the invaders approached Kyiv. On December 6, 1240, they conquered the city.

Having passed through the lands of Kyiv, Poland, and Hungary, plundering these countries' populations and imposing tribute on the captured territories, the Tatars then returned to the Volga.

How did the life of the ancestors of Ukrainians change with the appearance of the Tatars?

It is believed that after destroying the Kyivan state, the invaders brought instability, fear, pessimism, and depression into the life of the Eastern Slavs. Is that so?

Certainly. But only to an extent. According to authoritative historians, in particular, Mykhailo Hrushevsky, with the influx of Tatars, the life of the settled agricultural population of the proto-Ukrainian territories did not change significantly.

A stereotype was formed that the Tatars were a horde of locusts that senselessly destroyed everything in their path. Their community constituted a barbaric, totalitarian, but organized empire that conquered the world from Korea to Croatia, from Muscovy to Palestine. It is surprising how efficiently they carried out everything they planned. But they all needed something to eat. They were pragmatic, capable of clearly calculating their actions, and it was in their interest to ensure that the farmers of

---

15   *Translator's note*: The author does not intend this anecdote as an ethnic slur but instead refers to the notion of the Tatar as invader.

the Ukrainian forest-steppe, the leading suppliers of agricultural products, remained on their lands and produced as much food as possible. This was the only way to feed a huge army. The Tatars destroyed Kyivan Rus as a state. But they left the rural population in peace, if, of course, they did not resist. They robbed them moderately so as not to exhaust the nurturer. That is why little changed for the peasants.

And yet, for the freedom-loving inhabitants of the proto-Ukrainian territories, the Tatar tribute was humiliating. They were not going to leave things as they were for long.

Danylo Halytsky, the ruler of the Galicia-Volyn Principality, was the first to resist the invaders. His military units took control of several cities previously under the indirect rule of the Tatars.

In 1362, the Galician-Lithuanian army led by Prince Olgerd Gedyminovich defeated three Horde khans at Blue Waters, and subsequently, Kyiv Oblast was annexed to the Grand Duchy of Lithuania.

This was the end of the rule of the Golden Horde on Ukrainian lands. "Lithuania, in contrast to Moscow, never submitted to the Horde, even as it was losing individual battles. It did not pay tribute to the Tatar-Mongols, as the Muscovites did for hundreds of years. That is why later, Muscovy hated Lithuania and Ukraine for not genuflecting to the Golden Horde. After expelling the Tatars from Kyiv, the nascent Ukrainian nation rejected the psychology of slavery", writes Volodymyr Bilinsky in the book *The Land of Moksel*.

Therefore, in essence, Ukrainian lands were not occupied by Tatars. Steppe extortionists lived in the neighborhood, only making raids from time to time, and practically did not affect the outlook of the inhabitants of the western lands of the former Kyivan Rus. The population of the eastern proto-Ukrainian territories interacted with the Tatars more often but did not assimilate with them. Coexisting with the Turkic ethnic group only within the framework of paying tribute, the immediate ancestors of Ukrainians were not Tatarized. Many words of Tatar origin have taken root in the Ukrainian military vocabulary, but at an everyday level, they firmly established themselves in the Russian language, not in Ukrainian.

Ukraine as Part of the Grand Duchy of Lithuania

The annexation of Ukrainian lands to Lithuania in the middle of the 14th century was not a foreign invasion but a kind of military-political union that guaranteed Ukrainians protection from the Tatars while preserving the order customary for these t,erritories. "We leave the old be, and we don't introduce a new order" the Lithuanian princes declared.

Even though Ukrainians were part of the Lithuanian principality for about two hundred years, it makes no sense to speak of the influence of the Lithuanian mentality on Ukrainians. In the Lithuania of the time, Lithuanians made up only 5-7% of the population, while a conglomerate of other ethnic groups prevailed.

From the second half of the 15th century, the lands of the former Kyivan Rus were "in the crosshairs" of the principality of Muscovy. As a result of the Muscovite-Lithuanian War of 1500-1508, Lithuania lost its northern territories to Moscow. The lands of the Middle Dnipro region, whose population called themselves "Rus'ian" (rus'kyi) according to ancient custom, remained under Lithuania, and the Northern Black Sea region became the patrimony of the Crimean Khan.

The Ukrainian Cossack State

In the 15th century, runaway peasants, romantics and seekers of knightly glory began to form a peculiar, independent paramilitary formation—the Ukrainian Cossacks.

The first written references to Cossacks date back to the 1490s. In 1552 (1554, according to other sources), Prince Dmytro Vyshnevetsky ("Bayda") founded a fortified fortress on the island of Mala Khortytsia, which at one time was favored by the Vikings, and initiated the Ukrainian Cossack state. Cossacks, well trained in military affairs, led lives of professional soldiers: defending their lands from the Crimean Tatars, they fought as mercenaries under the banners of those rulers who were ready to pay them well. They were part of the armies of Lithuania, Muscovy, Poland, Turkey, Austria-Hungary, Sweden, other European countries, and alternately fought "for" and "against" the same states.

In 1569, Poland and Lithuania united in the Polish-Lithuanian Commonwealth. A universally elected monarch, simultaneously the Polish king and the Grand Duke of Lithuania, ruled it. Later, Lithuania receded into the shadows and lost its influence on Ukrainian territories. The center of power shifted to Krakow. The Ukrainian nobility did not see anything wrong with this since they had to choose between European Poland and backwoods Muscovy in restructuring their territories. Demanding freedom for the Orthodox faith, they recognized the supremacy of Poland over them, a state with a constitutional system, limited monarchical power, guaranteed political freedoms, religious tolerance, and a unique Renaissance culture.

But the autonomous Ukrainian Cossack state remained independent, lived by its own rules, defended Ukrainian lands from enemies, and from time to time, crossing the Black Sea, raided the mighty Ottoman Empire.

In the State Archives of Sweden, there is a letter from 1711 in which the Swedish King Charles XII instructs his ambassador in Constantinople to recognize the Zaporozhian Sich as an independent state.

In Ukrainian history, the 16th century was a period of economic prosperity: crafts, agriculture, and trade developed; a large number of cities were founded, and the Polish kings granted them Magdeburg law, which allowed production independent of the state, free trade, and exempted the population from taxes for thirty years. Ukrainian lands joined the development of the Western economy, and the same processes as in Europe took place in these areas. A bright future seemed to lie ahead; to live and be happy! However, the desire of the Polish nobility to impose their dictates, religion, and mentality on the Ukrainians led to strong national resistance.

The Polish Age

The first Ukrainian-Polish armed confrontation broke out in 1591. At that time, the Cossacks liberated a certain part of the lands that were "under Poland" and restored the Orthodox church hierarchy in these territories. The Polish Sejm had to accept this. The Ukrainians' independent internal and external policy, their disobedience, influence on events in the Crimean Khanate, and daring marches to Istanbul greatly annoyed the Poles. However, they had to tolerate this; otherwise, they would lose some control over the Zaporozhians.

The history of Polish-Ukrainian relations is a series of armed clashes and truces, victories and defeats on one side or the other.

In 1648, an armed uprising broke out led by Bohdan Khmelnytsky, the hetman of the Zaporozhian Army. Having hired 6,000 mercenaries from the Crimean Khan, the hetman demanded that Poland eliminate the rule of the Polish-Lithuanian Commonwealth east of the Dnipro River, withdraw Polish troops from there, transfer power to the Ukrainian chieftain and grant him the right to conduct foreign affairs. This was the first time the idea of autonomous Ukrainian territory was formulated. Poland did not satisfy these demands.

The Ukrainian-Polish war began. Ukrainians massively took up arms, joined the Cossack army, won victory after victory, and in a short period of time, freed both the territory of the Left Bank of the Dnipro River and the entire Right Bank from the Dnipro to the Carpathians from the Poles. The experience of participating in the European Thirty Years' War of 1618–1648 significantly impacted the military training of the Zaporozhians. Slowly, the idea of a complete defeat of the Polish-Lithuanian Commonwealth, the separation of Ukrainian lands, and the creation of their own state began to mature. Khmelnytsky considered Ukraine to be the rightful successor of Kyivan Rus (accurately so) and, during the negotiations, he declared that peace with Poland was possible only if they recognized the independence of Cossack Ukraine on all the lands "previously owned by the Godfearing grand princes".

However, what happened next did not fit into any of the narratives of victorious wars but likely fully corresponded to the Ukrainian mentality. Having at his disposal 100,000 battle-hardened Cossacks, about 40,000 cavalrymen of the Crimean Khan Islam-Giray, pursuing the Poles (the Polish army was in a catastrophic state at the time), Khmelnytsky ordered his troops to retreat. Was it the archetype of Ukrainian non-aggressiveness at work here? Can you imagine Alexander the Great, Hannibal, or Napoleon doing this while defeating the enemy?

But maybe the hetman was right after all. In the end, Islam-Giray, opposing the defeat of the Polish-Lithuanian Commonwealth and the creation of an independent Ukrainian state, refused to participate in the further offensive. And Muscovy eagerly entered the war against Ukraine on the side of Poland.

Be that as it may, the military campaign ended with an agreement recognizing the territories of several voivodeships (local governorships) as Cossack lands, where Bohdan Khmelnytsky began to organize Ukrainian life. He strengthened the Orthodox church, gave peasants plots of land, and established village and city courts. He established diplomatic relations with Turkey, Transylvania, Moldova, Venice, and Sweden. The peasant uprisings in Muscovy at that time were actually nothing more than unsuccessful attempts to accomplish what the Ukrainians had done, that is, putting the government in its place and showing who the master in the house was. "Cossacks want to be Holland or Switzerland", Polish politicians scoffed.

It could not be expected that Poland would give up Ukraine without a fight. In 1651, it resumed military operations, took control of some previously lost territories, and the nobility received the right to return to their estates. However, the peasants continued to resist—they destroyed the estates of the local nobility, tenants, and innkeepers. "Our serfs refuse to perform any duties or remain obedient to Polish nobility", the poor nobles complained.

Even though there was a split in Khmelnytsky's administration, the hetman managed to keep the Cossack army in combat readiness and, in alliance with the Tatars, inflicted subsequent defeats on the Poles. The war, which lasted for six years, with varying success across all the territory of Ukraine, exhausted it economically and morally. There was no end to it, and the population grew weary. The Polish-Lithuanian Commonwealth and Crimea signed an "eternal agreement" of mutual assistance. The threat of a deadly attack by Polish troops from the west and a horde of thousands of Crimean Tatars from the south loomed over Ukraine.

Under the Umbrella of Muscovy

In 1654, the Cossack chief decided to enter into a union with the Muscovite kingdom to preserve political sovereignty in Ukrainian lands.

Muscovy would not allow Ukraine any sovereignty. Khmelnytsky probably had a poor understanding of the mentality of Muscovites—it was never a habit of Moscow not to dictate its will to someone. "Ukraine soon saw that it was in captivity; due to its simplistic understanding, it did not yet know what a tsar was, and the tsar of Moscow was the equivalent of an idol and tormenter", wrote Ukrainian historian Mykola Kostomarov in *The Book of Life of the Ukrainian People*.

Soon, the war between Ukraine and Muscovy began. It lasted from fall 1658 to summer 1659. Because of it, Moscow ceased hostilities on the Swedish front and transferred its troops to Ukraine. In the Battle of Konotop, Ukrainian formations, in a new alliance with former enemies, the Poles and Crimean Tatars, and under the command of Hetman Ivan Vyhovsky, dealt a crushing blow to the 100,000-strong Muscovite army. But then there was another split in the Ukrainian army. Some of the ranks of the Zaporozhians, determined to unite with Moscow, mutinied, and as a result, the enemy troops prevailed. Since then, fourteen generations of Ukrainians were under the umbrella of Muscovy.

However, it did not cover all of them. Ukraine ended up being divided into four parts: the Left (east) Bank of the Dnipro River went to Muscovy, the Right Bank remained under the rule of Poland, the South was ruled by the Crimean Tatars and Turks, and the Zaporozhian Sich continued to exist as an independent state. The border between the Polish-Lithuanian Commonwealth (Poland) and Muscovy stretched along the Dnipro River. Psychologically, the residents of the Ukrainian Left Bank gravitated toward the Muscovites, the Right Bank toward the Poles, and the Zaporozhians remained free and were unconcerned about Warsaw and Moscow.

Year after year, the tsarist regime increasingly restricted Ukrainian autonomy and Ukrainian culture. It constrained the use of the Ukrainian language, reinforced censorship, banned the publication of books in Ukrainian, and enslaved relatively economically independent peasants. Intensive industrial development provoked numerous migrations of rural residents to the cities, where they turned into a Russified, lumpenized mass. Tens of thousands of Ukrainians, a "herd of illiterate cattle", as Peter I called them, were mobilized for the war with Sweden. In this war, the tsar's plans for Ukraine were unacceptable. And in October 1708, Cossack units loyal to Hetman Ivan Mazepa defected to the side of the Swedes. The victory of Peter I's army over Sweden near Poltava on June 27, 1709 led to mass terror against all who called themselves Ukrainians.[16]

A new wave of destruction by the tsarist authorities of the remnants of Ukraine's autonomy intensified from the mid-1760s. Empress Catherine II eliminated Cossack self-government, disbanded the Ukrainian army, and forced its members to join the military of Muscovy, a country which, at that time, began to call itself Russia. Catherine II tried to do everything to make Ukrainians "stop looking like hungry wolves at a forest".

While the process of Russification was gaining momentum on the Left Bank of the Dnipro, Poland sought to establish its customs on the Right Bank. Those who refused to accept Roman Catholicism were forced to move to the Left Bank. However, the nobility's attempts to enslave Ukrainians were met with armed resistance— squads of people's avengers (*haidamaks*) looted the manor estates and did not allow the Polish authorities to tyrannize Ukrainians. However, when popular uprisings escalated, and threatened to bring about the rule of the people, they were brutally suppressed by the joint efforts of Polish and Russian troops. As a result, countless Orthodox churches, books, manuscripts, archives, and paintings were destroyed; many masterpieces of Ukrainian Renaissance culture, the spirit and essence of which were based on the principles of Western European humanist ideas, were lost forever.

In 1793, as a result of the partition of Poland, the lands of Western Ukraine came under the rule of Austria-Hungary. There, Catholicism dominated; cities were granted Magdeburg Law; education was conducted in German and Latin; and the constitution guaranteed personal freedom, private property, and freedom of speech and the press, including publications in the Ukrainian language.

At that time, and during the 19th century, in the Ukrainian territories occupied by Muscovy, the situation was the opposite: Russian imperial rule tried to destroy everything related to Ukraine. Anyone who showed interest in their roots, history, and

---

16 The same thing happened in the Ukrainian territories seized by Russia during the war in 2022.

culture was considered politically suspect. It was forbidden to publish books in Ukrainian, even texts of musical scores. The Gospels translated into Ukrainian were declared dangerous and equated with political propaganda. Petr Valuev, the Minister of Internal Affairs of the Russian Empire, "clarified" that the Ukrainian language "does not exist, never existed and cannot exist". The urban intelligentsia hastened to switch to the Russian language, even as Ukrainian continued to be spoken in rural areas.

However, the Russian minister underestimated the Ukrainians' capacity for cultural resistance. In 1798, even before the birth of Alexandr Pushkin, the father of Russian literary language, the first edition of Ivan Kotlyarevskyi's poem *Aeneid* was published in Ukrainian. In the following decades, many ethnographers and writers dedicated their works to Ukraine, particularly, Taras Shevchenko, whose works both articulated the Ukrainian past and embodied the Ukrainian striving for freedom and independence.

In the 20th century, divided between Russia and Austria-Hungary, Ukraine became unavoidably involved in World War I. The two empires did not conceal the fact that each intended to take possession of its entire territory in the event of victory. At this time, Ukrainians were again forced to be in the trenches on different sides of the front line and shoot at each other. However, both Russia and Austria-Hungary lost the war. And so did Ukraine. Its western territories were divided among Poland, Czechoslovakia, and Romania.

In 1917, under the leadership of Vladimir Lenin, a revolution took place in Russia. The tsarist authorities were overthrown. Ukrainians were indifferent to this event and created their own Ukrainian People's Republic. Finding no support in Petrograd, the leaders of the Ukrainian People's Republic established allied relations with France, Austria-Hungary, and Germany. However, they acted hesitantly, trying (as is characteristic of the Ukrainian mentality!) "to have a foot in both camps". Ukrainians never satisfied Lenin, and he sent troops to Ukraine. A new Russo-Ukrainian war began. Neither the Ukrainian army, which consisted mainly of peasants, nor the people's partisan units, which carried out daring operations behind enemy lines, were able to resist the powerful onslaught of the Bolsheviks.

Independently of Moscow, the Ukrainian People's Republic existed for seven and a half months. With the invasion of Russia in the 1920s, the era of communist schizophrenia began on the territory of Ukraine, which included the uprooting of the best intellectuals—an event that came to be known in history as the "Executed Renaissance" (*Rozstriliane Vdrodzhennia*)—and the most hardworking peasants from society, man-made famines (*holodomors*), the abolition of private property, the development of the economy on utopian communist principles, slave labor, total fear, despair, the destruction of temples of worship, the sale of cultural masterpieces abroad, mass terror, and much more. However, these tests did not break the spirit of the Ukrainian nation, which has experienced many cataclysms in its history. The sense of constant danger is an archetype for Ukrainians.

Without justifying the communists, it is worth noting that they did eliminate illiteracy in the Soviet Union, to which Ukraine belonged; created conditions for studying at universities for people from poor families (because there were no others); provided more space for the development of national culture, and established industry. In Ukraine, hard coal and iron ore production increased by 7–10 times, and the production of cast iron, steel, and electricity grew significantly.

During World War II (1939–1945), Hitler did everything to replace communist schizophrenia with Nazi schizophrenia in German-occupied territories. However, his plans to turn Ukraine into Germany's prosperous and cheap colony failed. Residents of Western Ukraine at first met the German troops with bread and salt as liberators, but, soon realizing that German and Russian fascism were the same in principle, formed their own armed forces known as the Ukrainian Insurgent Army. It fought for an independent Ukraine, both against Hitler's Germany and against Stalin's Soviet Union.

The Soviet Union was victorious in World War II. So was Ukraine. The price paid for victory, though, was excessive. However, Ukrainians gained much from this sacrifice. First, they acquired the mentality of a winner. In addition, many people who survived the occupation came to understand the absurdity of the Stalinist regime. The soldiers who were abroad saw not only death and ruins in Europe but also the European way of life.

After the war, Ukraine (more precisely, the Ukrainian Soviet Socialist Republic) quickly recovered. It received German industrial technologies and regained the territories lost during World War I. The centuries-old process of unification of Ukrainian lands reached a logical conclusion.

Fear of the bacilli of freedom pushed Stalin to implement a new wave of repressions. Once again, train cars moved from Ukraine to Siberia; entire ethnic communities were evicted from their home territories; any display of dissent was suppressed; and the iron curtain was tightly closed. In 1946–1947, Moscow authorities once again created a man-made famine (*holodomor*) in Ukraine, during which more than five million Ukrainians died of hunger, while Ukrainian grain was sent abroad at dumping prices. Ideological censorship tightly controlled writers, composers, directors, and artists. In the mid-1950s, KGB operatives managed to finally suppress the popular armed resistance in Western Ukraine.

Stalin's death stopped the Soviet Union falling into an abyss. Nikita Khrushchev dared to publish data on the atrocities of the Communist Party leadership and the secret police (NKVD) and hence began treating the Soviet people for Stalinist paranoia with shock therapy. He did not manage to completely jettison the communist delusion. Nuclear missiles were transported to Cuba, and the Soviet Union and the USA found themselves on the brink of war, which was avoided as a result of negotiations between Khrushchev and John F. Kennedy.

The eleven years between Stalin's death and the beginning of Brezhnev's rule were called the "Khrushchev Thaw". As time passed, more Ukrainians realized the worthlessness of Soviet rule. In the 1960s, moral resistance to the communist state gained momentum. Many people found it unacceptable to live in ideological mud and rejected the standards of communism. The phenomenon of "The Sixtiers" (*Shestydesiatnyky*) marks the era of the renaissance of Ukrainian culture and mentality. The new generation began to defend the right to their own understanding of life. The popularity of poets, writers, bards, and avant-garde artists increased, and banned works were copied on typewriters and passed from hand to hand (*samvydav-samizdat*).

A period of stagnation marked the 1970s in the Soviet Union; in Ukraine there was a crackdown on Ukrainian dissidents. The people's life was calm and measured. Socialism aimed to impoverish everyone. The economy mainly served the military and space exploration; somewhere, something was being built, something was being launched . . . The Soviet people simulated work, visited theaters, stood in long queues for limited products, visited friends, celebrated both communist and church holidays, waited for decades for an apartment, and dropped a ballot, on which there was only one name, in the ballot box. There was a shortage of everything in the country — sausage, clothes, matches, shoelaces, so forth Even the most famous artists humiliated themselves in front of store managers, imploring them to find a pair of imported shoes, a stick of dry sausage, or a bottle of champagne. Communist leaders ate separately (what a surprise!) and urged the "masses" not to worry about their petty well-being.

The government could not provide welfare to the "masses", and that's why it always promised happiness in a bright future (*svetloe budushchee*). Hypocrisy and lies flourished in all spheres of life. The Soviet bureaucracy neglected human rights and presented an example of a rude and disdainful attitude toward the people.

At school, students were prepared for admission to universities, and those who couldn't get in and went to work were considered losers.

In the 1980s, it finally became clear that the false communist idea had exhausted itself. A grandiose experiment to breed a new man — Homo Sovieticus — failed miserably.

Mikhail Gorbachev stirred up the sleepy villages, and reconstruction began. Non-competitive production stopped; inflated values faded, censorship disappeared; good relations with Western countries were established; and society was divided into the rich and poor.

At that time, a powerful movement for independence from the Soviet Union arose in Ukraine.

Independence

On August 24, 1991, after a failed putsch against Gorbachev in Moscow, the Ukrainian parliament proclaimed the Act of Independence of Ukraine. On December 1, 1991, at a referendum on independence, 90.3% of its residents voted in favor. Russia declared its own independence and officially recognized Ukraine as an independent state.

On December 5, 1994, Ukraine, Russia, Great Britain, and the USA signed the Budapest Memorandum that guaranteed security assurances for Ukraine in exchange for its nuclear weapons arsenal.

A new life for the country began. However, no miracle happened as Ukraine entered the 21st century as an economically devastated country. There was a catastrophic decrease in production; several oligarchic mafia clans took the majority of the country's finances under their control. "Ukraine is not Russia", President Leonid Kuchma declared in his book. But this was not entirely true; at that time, Ukraine remained mentally like Russia.

In the following years, Ukraine was in a state of lethargic sleep. Presidents, party flags, and political slogans changed, but the social and economic nucleus remained the same. The Soviet administrative, tax, judicial, and police systems remained almost unchanged. Despite the declaration of a free market, the country's economy was under the tight control of corrupt government officials. It was impossible to plan the development of entrepreneurship; the procedure for obtaining business permits was a nightmare.

In December 2004, another presidential election was held in Ukraine. The voting results were falsified in favor of the pro-Russian candidate Viktor Yanukovych. Ukrainians refused to tolerate lies and humiliation from the authorities. The Orange Revolution ensued. As a result of massive demonstrations on the Maidan (central square) of Kyiv, a re-election took place, and Viktor Yushchenko became president. Contrary to the plans of pro-Russian manipulators, Ukrainians chose the path of their society's development in the direction of European civilization.

Viktor Yanukovych was later able to return to power, and in November 2013, as President of Ukraine, he was supposed to sign the EU-Ukraine (economic) Association Agreement. Russia began to threaten Ukraine to prevent this from happening. President Yanukovych secretly visited Moscow. What was discussed during the meeting was never revealed to the press. After that, Yanukovych refused to sign the agreement.

However, Ukrainians were ready to defend their future. The worldview "when the people lead, their rulers follow them" has been imprinted in the archetypes of the Ukrainian mentality since ancient times. The Revolution of Dignity occurred, during which unarmed people overthrew the pro-Russia president and once again set their country on the path of development as a civilized European society.

In Moscow, this was perceived by Vladimir Putin as a personal defeat. After all, Ukrainians showed that it was possible to organize the lives of citizens using democratic, social, and simply human values. In 2014, to prevent Ukraine from flourishing and prospering, Russia invaded Ukraine and captured Crimea and Donbas. To eliminate the Ukrainian state, the Russian president tried to create total chaos in Ukraine, which would give him the opportunity to annex Eastern and Southern Ukrainian territories to Russia. However, unexpectedly for Moscow and perhaps for the Ukrainians themselves, the poorly equipped Ukrainian armed forces, led primarily by unprofessional volunteer battalions, decisively rebuffed the Russian military machine. Ukraine persevered in a lengthy military stalemate that cost the lives of over 15,000 Ukrainian soldiers.

Russia struck the next blow to Ukraine on Putin's orders in 2022. On February 24, Russian troops entered Ukraine after intensive shelling from the north, east, and south. Putin expected to win in three days. But everything went against the Kremlin dictator's plan. The outgunned Ukrainian armed forces repelled the invading military juggernaut, which greatly outnumbered them in terms of personnel, and inflicted catastrophic losses on the occupiers.

The Ukrainians survived thanks to the supply of weapons from NATO countries, but primarily thanks to their own mentality, hardened over the ages.

We will draw conclusions about the modern Ukrainian mentality in the section titled "Mosaic of the Ukrainian Soul". But to assemble this mosaic, we must delve into the Ukrainian traditions and customs of the 21st century and several previous generations.

Ethnic Features

Common Features of Ukrainians (Interviews with Scholars)

In this chapter we will conduct "interviews" with experts from different times about the general features of Ukrainians. We could choose from many possibilities. However, we will limit ourselves here to three quite reliable ones.

Our interlocutors include:

Guillaume Levasseur de Beauplan, a French engineer and cartographer who served with the Polish army in 1630–1647 on Ukrainian territory.

Mykola Hohol (1809–1852; aka Nikolai Gogol), the author of famous books about Ukraine, *Evenings on a Farm Near Dykanka*, *Taras Bulba*, and *Myrhorod*.

And Vasyl Myloradovych (1846–1911), ethnographer, researcher of Ukrainian folk life, and author of the publication "The Life and Times of a Lubensk Peasant".

"Gentlemen, let's open with the question about the status of the Ukrainian lands after the Mongol-Tatar invasion in the thirteenth century."

Mykola Hohol:

"In the harsh fifteenth century, the entire ancient south, abandoned by its princes, was devastated and burned to the ground by the incessant attacks of Mongolian predators".

"How did people live then?"

Mykola Hohol:

"Man built neither fortresses nor castles but simply a temporary straw dwelling because everyone thought: why waste labor and money on

a house, if at any given moment the Tatars can come and burn everything to the ground".

"And this probably broke the people's spirit".

Mykola Hohol:

"After losing everything – his home and roof, a man became desperate here".

"Desperate?"

Mykola Hohol:

"Man settled in scorched ruins, in the face of predatory neighbors and constant danger, and got used to looking straight into their eyes, forgetting even if there was anything in the world of which he would be afraid".

"At that time, as we know, the Ukrainian Cossacks emerged".

Mykola Hohol:

"All the riverbanks, fords, and ferries, and every suitable spot in the river country, were scattered with Cossacks, whose numbers no one knew".

"Just on the steppe? Mykola Vasyliovych, you said that the land 'was burned to the ground'. They recovered quickly".

Mykola Hohol:

"Then the entire South, all the space to the Black Sea, was green, virgin wilderness. A plow had never passed through the immeasurable waves of wild plants. Horses alone trampled them, hiding in them as though in a forest. Nothing in nature could be better than the steppe. The entire surface of the earth seemed like a golden-green ocean, on which millions of different flowers were spattered".

"Later, the Cossacks founded Zaporozhian Sich. What was it like?"

Mykola Hohol:

"The whole of the Sich was an extraordinary phenomenon. It was some kind of continuous feast, a ball that began noisily and lost its end. Some people were engaged in trades, others had shops and commercial businesses; but most of them caroused from morning to night".

"Could you tell me more about this?"

Mykola Hohol:

"This general merrymaking had a certain enchanting aspect to it. It was not some gathering of revelers drunken out of grief; it was just the

furious frenzy of merriment. Anyone who came here forgot and gave up everything he had been occupied with until then. One could say he didn't give a damn about the past and with the fervor of a fanatic was committed to the freedom and companionship of those who were the same as he, who had no relatives, no corner to call home, no family, except for the open sky and the eternal feast of his soul. It produced the frantic merriment that could not have been born of any other source".

"Zaporozhian Cossacks were not only carefree and cheerful people, but they also were believed to be good storytellers".

Mykola Hohol:

"The stories and the nonsense that could be heard among the gathered crowd lying on the ground were so ridiculous. They breathed with such profound humor that it took only the entire indifferent external appearance of the Cossack, so as not to laugh wholeheartedly, without even a twitch of a moustache. This striking feature to this day distinguishes the Southern Slav from the rest of their brethren".

"That is, the Cossacks drank and made merry but did not drown their brains in *horilka* (vodka)".

Mykola Hohol:

"It was drunken, boisterous jollity, and yet it was no gloomy joint where a man loses himself".

"But they were constantly in danger".

Mykola Hohol:

"They had unguarded, safe borders, in sight of which the Tatar showed his quick head, and the Turk stared motionlessly and sternly in his green turban".

Guillaume de Beauplan:

"Often, almost every year, Cossacks conducted raids, causing great harm to the Turks. On many occasions they ravaged Crimea, which belonged to the Tatars, and even reached Constantinople, where they destroyed everything with fire and sword; and then returned with much booty and captives, mostly children".

"Why do they bring captive children?

Guillaume de Beauplan:

"They kept them for various services or gifted them to influential people of their region".

"But why did they need adults?"

Guillaume de Beauplan:
"They never kept elderly people with them unless they considered them so rich that they could hope for some ransom".
"Ukrainian Cossacks were believed to be brave sailors".
Guillaume de Beauplan:
"Surprisingly, they would successfully cross the sea in their small self-made boats".
"Why were they highly regarded in Europe?"
Mykola Hohol:
"As we all know from history, the Cossacks' incessant struggle and adventurous spirit saved Europe from the savage incursions that threatened to overwhelm it. The kings of Poland realized their value and the advantages of their warlike, heedful mode of life. They flattered them and sought an agreement with them. Under their remote rule, the Hetmans, chosen from among the Cossacks themselves, transformed the settlements and kurens [Cossack barracks or houses and fighting groups] into regiments and military districts".
"Do you mean officially registered Cossacks?"
Mykola Hohol:
"Besides the registered Cossacks, whose duty was to join the army in case of war, troops of mounted volunteers could always be mustered in times of urgent need. Every man appeared with a mount and armed, and in two weeks such an army could be gathered as no other could have ever banded together so quickly. Once the campaign was over, the warriors went back to their field or pasture, to the Dnipro River ferries, or continued to fish, trade, or brew beer, and were once again free Cossacks".
"What were the military tactics of the Zaporozhians?"
Mykola Hohol:
"All of them knew that it was hard to fight the violent and warlike horde known by the name of the Zaporozhian army, which beneath a self-willed, disorderly exterior, concealed an order exceedingly well-fitted for warfare".
Guillaume de Beauplan:
"They are brave, courageous, or, rather, desperate; they do not value their own lives. They fight most skillfully and masterfully in the camp, under the protection of their wagons. Several times I met Tatars in the steppes. There were more than 500 of them, and they attacked our base,

but they could not do anything, although I had only 50 or 60 Cossacks with me ... They also know how to fight at sea but are not as good as they are in the saddle".

"And you, Mykola Vasyliovych, do you also think that the Cossacks were better as horsemen?"

Mykola Hohol:

"They would mount five thousand horses and go off on a raid".

"In general, were the Zaporozhians cruel?"

Mykola Hohol:

"One's hair would stand on end today at the sight of that horrible trail of atrocities common enough in that half-savage age left by the Zaporozhians wherever they set foot. Murdered children, women's breasts cut away, the skin torn from the legs of those who were set free, the Cossacks were repaying for previous affronts in full".

"Tell me, gentlemen, why was this cruelty necessary? Why did the war with Poland start in the first place?"

Mykola Hohol:

"A Cossack army of a hundred and twenty thousand men appeared on the borders of Ukraine. This was no longer a small party or detachment sallying forth for plunder or in pursuit of the Tatars. No: the whole nation had arisen, for the people's patience was at an end. It had arisen to avenge the violation of its rights; the shameful humiliation of its customs; the profanation of the faith of its fathers and its holy rites; the desecration of its churches; the outrages of the foreign lords; its oppression; all that had so long nourished and embittered the stern hatred of the Cossacks".

"The same thing happened in Ukraine in 2022, Mykola Vasyliovych. How did the Ukrainian popular uprising of the fifteenth-century end: with victory or defeat?"

Mykola Hohol:

"The pages of the chronicles record in detail how the Polish garrisons fled from the towns freed by the Cossacks; how all the rapacious usurer Jews were hanged; how powerless the Royal Hetman Mykolai Potocki was with his numerous army against this invincible force; how, routed and pursued, he lost the best part of his army in a wretchedly small stream; how the dreaded Cossack regiments besieged him in the little town of Polonne; and how, at wits' end, the Polish hetman promised, under *oath, in the name of the king and his ministers, to satisfy all their demands and to restore all their former rights and privileges".*

"Did the Zaporozhians believe him?

Mykola Hohol:

"The Cossacks were not to be taken in by this: they knew the worth of a Polish oath".

"So, does that mean they did not pardon Potocki?"

Mykola Hohol:

"The Russian priests of the town saved his life. When all the priests, in their brilliant gold mantles, went out to meet them, bearing the icons and crosses, led by the bishop himself, crosier in hand and a pastoral miter on his head, all the Cossacks bowed their heads and took off their caps. To no one, not even the king, would they have shown respect at that hour, but they dared not rebel against their own Christian Church".

"So, how did the Cossacks deal with Potocki?

Mykola Hohol:

"The hetman and his colonels agreed to set Potocki free, having made him solemnly vow to leave all the Christian churches unharmed, to let bygones be bygones, and do no harm to the Cossack armies".

"You see, the Zaporozhians were not that aggressive after all. They decided that ..."

Mykola Hohol:

"They would draw the saber on three occasions: when the Polish tax-collectors did not pay due respect to the Cossack elders and stood with covered heads in their presence; when the Orthodox faith was abused or an ancestral custom violated; and lastly when the enemy was Muslim or Turk".

"Gentlemen, please provide a psychological portrait of a Zaporozhian Cossack. The Poles believed that his only occupation was thievery. Is that true? Is it true that, apart from military affairs, he did not know much?"

Mykola Hohol:

"There was no craft the Cossack did not know: he could make wine, build a cart, grind powder, do a blacksmith's and a locksmith's work, and besides all this he could revel in the most riotous manner, could drink and feast as only a Cossack can, all this he could do and more".

"And you, Mr. Beauplan, how do you see Zaporozhians and, in general, Ukrainians?"

Guillaume de Beauplan:

"*In general, there are experts in all crafts among these Cossacks ... All of them are good at tilling the land, sowing, reaping, baking bread, cooking all kinds of meat dishes, brewing beer, mead, homebrew, okovyta [a clear distilled alcoholic beverage], etc.*"

"Well, to brew *okovyta*, of course."

Guillaume de Beauplan:

"*On the other hand, I do not think there is a people on earth who could compete with them in terms of drinking. They are never too drunk not to be able to start drinking again*".

"Even on a military campaign?"

Guillaume de Beauplan:

"*When they are on a military campaign or planning some important matter, they observe extreme sobriety. When a drunkard is found among them on a campaign, the chieftain immediately orders him thrown into the sea*".

"Is that correct, Mykola Vasyliovych?"

Mykola Hohol:

"*If anyone gets drunk on a campaign, he will be given short shrift, whoever he might be. He will be shot on the spot like a dog and left without burial to be torn to shreds by the vultures, for a drunkard on the march does not deserve a Christian burial*".

"The Poles called Cossacks thieves."

Mykola Hohol:

"*A Cossack found guilty of theft was considered a disgrace to all Cossackdom; the ignoble wretch was tied to the 'post of shame', and a club was laid beside him, with which every passer-by was bound to deal him a blow with all his heart. A Cossack who would not pay his debts was chained to a cannon, and he remained there till one of his comrades ransomed him by paying off his debts*".

"Zaporozhians chose hetmans from among themselves. But did the Cossacks obey them?"

Guillaume de Beauplan:

"The Cossacks are very obedient to him and call their chieftain hetman in their language. His power is absolute; he has the right to behead and punish at the stake those who are found guilty".

"How did the proud Cossacks tolerate his arbitrariness?"

Guillaume de Beauplan:

"The hetman must be extremely intelligent, and when meeting with the enemy or in unforeseen situations, he must show flair and courage. When he happens to reveal faintheartedness, he is killed as a traitor and another hetman is elected immediately. In the seventeen years I have spent in this land, all who have held this position have ended their days tragically".

"In this case, you cannot call his rule a dictatorship".

Guillaume de Beauplan:

"The hetmans are very strict, but they do nothing without their military council".

"In general, were the Cossacks mostly peasants?"

Mykola Hohol:

"They abandoned their fathers and mothers and fled from their parents' homes. There were those here who already had a rope around their necks and who, instead of the pallor of death, saw life. There were those here who, according to noble custom, usually could not keep a kopeck coin in their pocket. There were also the seminary school students who could no longer bear the strokes of academic switches and did not retain a single word from school, but at the same time there were those who knew what Horace, Cicero, and the Roman Republic were. There were many officers who later distinguished themselves under the banners of the King of Poland".

"Did those who knew Horace also come to the Sich?"

Mykola Hohol:

"In those times Polish customs had already begun to influence the Ukrainian nobility. Many nobles adopted Polish customs, introducing luxuries, lavish service, falcons, huntsmen, banquets, and courts. All respected men deemed it their duty to provide an education for their children".

"And the father promised his son. . . ."

Mykola Hohol:

"*That he should never lay eyes on the Zaporozhian homebase unless he learned everything taught in the Kyiv Mohyla Academy*".

"The Cossack was, of course, a physically strong person. Otherwise, what kind of warrior was he...."

Mykola Hohol:

"*They were born with a restless, fighting spirit and were known for their blunt and straightforward manner. They were bold and sure marksmen and could swim across the Dnipro River against the current, an exploit for which the novice was triumphantly admitted into Cossack circles*".

"And you, Monsieur Beauplan, what can you say about the Cossacks?"

Guillaume de Beauplan:

"*They are well-hardened and easily tolerate heat and cold, thirst, and hunger. Cossacks are tall, skillful, and energetic. They like to wear nice clothes; they especially flaunt them, having stolen them from their neighbors*".[17]

Mykola Hohol:

"*This strange republic was a child of the epoch. Lovers of war, golden goblets, rich brocades, ducats, and pieces of eight could at all times find employment here. Those who only worshiped women couldn't find anything to do here, for no woman dared show herself even in the outskirts of the Sich*".

"Mykola Vasyliovych, you mentioned that there were many people in the Sich who could not keep a kopeck in their pockets. But something must have been jingling in their pockets after campaigns, right?"

Mykola Hohol:

"*It was rare that they didn't have any valuables, silver goblets, and bangles, hidden among the reeds on the Dnipro River islands so that the Tatars might not discover them, if by some chance they might suddenly find themselves in the Sich. It would be difficult for the Tatars to find them, though, for the owners themselves had begun to forget where they had buried them*".

---

17 By "neighbors", Guillaume de Beauplan implies the Cossacks' enemies. Although stealing from their own was considered a punishable offence, stealing from enemies was acceptable.

"Were the Zaporozhians generous or stingy?"

Mykola Hohol:

"The Zaporozhians hated to bargain and threw down as much money as their hands happened to take out of their pockets. And you wouldn't be able to count what they spent on drinking and feasting, but it would have been enough to keep other men in comfort their whole lives. They had squandered it all in true Cossack fashion, treating one and all and hiring musicians so that all the world might be merry".

"And when they wasted the last of what they had? What then?"

Mykola Hohol:

"They ransacked stores and took things without paying for them".

"It looks like they didn't give a damn about the future".

Guillaume de Beauplan:

"There are no such other people among Christian nations who care so little about tomorrow".

Mykola Hohol:

"What the broad and powerful Slavic nature is alone capable of — for it is to others what the sea is to shallow rivers".

"Gentlemen, we paid a lot of attention to the Zaporozhians. Let's talk about Ukrainians in general. How can you explain their carefree nature?"

Guillaume de Beauplan:

"They collect so much grain from the fertile lands that they often don't know what to do with it ... The lakes are so full of fish that an innumerable number of them, cramped in this stagnant water, die. Hence their laziness; they go to work only when troubles require it".

"That is to say, Ukrainians did not like to work".

Guillaume de Beauplan:

"They are happy when they have something to eat and drink".

"And you, Mr. Myloradovych, what do you think?"

Vasyl Myloradovych:

"Before sunrise, after having breakfast, the landowner and the mowers leave on foot or on carts for the hayfield. The housewife and her daughters retouch the house's white walls after every downpour and, in addition, whitewash the outside of the house three times during the *year: before Easter, the Holy Feast of the Trinity, and the Holy Feast of the Intercession".*

"In your opinion, gentlemen, can Ukrainians be called intellectuals? After all, not all of them could read Horace without a dictionary".

Vasyl Myloradovych:

"The opinions of Ukrainians often exceed his life and education".

Guillaume de Beauplan:

"They are clever and wise, witty, and extremely generous, they do not strive for great wealth, but they love freedom very much, without which they cannot imagine their life. This is why they so often rebel against the nobles. In a word, all of them are fairly clever, but only in matters they consider valuable and necessary, mainly in connection with their peasant life".

"Mr. Beauplan, what, in your opinion, is the worst feature of Ukrainians?"

Guillaume de Beauplan:

"These people are distrustful, treacherous, and insidious, you can trust them only with great caution".

"How often did Ukrainians take ill?"

Guillaume de Beauplan:

"They are distinguished by good health. Few of the Cossacks die of illness, except in old age, because most of them die on the field of glory. I saw sick Cossacks with fever who, instead of taking any medicine, took half a charge of gunpowder, mixed it in half with horilka and drank it all; and then they went to bed only to wake up in the morning completely healthy. I have repeatedly seen how Cossacks, wounded by arrows, being far from doctors, smeared their wounds with earth soaked in their own saliva; it healed their wounds like the best balm. So, as in many others, life generates cleverness in this country".

"Gentlemen, what can you say about the Ukrainian female?"

Guillaume de Beauplan:

"Among them, I happened to see such beautiful faces, which can hardly be found in the whole of Poland".

"Oh yes! How did they find brides? Did they choose them for themselves or did their parents do it for them?"

Vasyl Myloradovych:

"The female's will in choosing a husband is decisive; in case of parental disagreement, the female runs away secretly and gets married anyway. In this case, she risks not receiving a dowry".

"Oh, really? Well, love will find a way."

Mykola Hohol:

"No, brothers, to love as the Cossack soul loves – to love not with the mind or anything else, but with all that God has given you, with all you have! No, no one else can love like that!"

Guillaume de Beauplan:

"Here, unlike the customs and traditions of other countries, a girl is the first to propose to a young man whom she likes ... I saw how girls proposed to young men, and it often worked out".

"Very interesting ... The Amazons behaved the same way. And early Slavic women too."

Vasyl Myloradovych:

"The ancestors of Ukrainians had to experience various family models, starting with the matriarchal one".

"What is the essence of the Ukrainian matriarchal family?"

Vasyl Myloradovych:

"The essence of matriarchy is to establish ancestry through the mother because in a group marriage, paternity can be reliably determined only in some cases, while motherhood is always apparent ... Matriarchy has left quite distinct traces in the Ukrainian family".

"However, for some reason, the groom's parents rarely treated the daughter-in-law in a friendly manner".

Vasyl Myloradovych:

"They try to delegate all the housework to the daughter-in-law: she cooks, bakes, and cleans. In short, she is the real workhorse".

"How can you explain it?"

Vasyl Myloradovych:

"It is possible that distant memories of patriarchy and the adoption and purchase of women typical for this stage of family development influenced the humiliated position of the daughter-in-law in the household".

"Is that so? Yes, people's memory is tenacious. And, in your opinion, what temperament does a Ukrainian woman have?"

Vasyl Myloradovych:

"*Ivan Aksakov says the following about her: 'Natural grace, exquisite taste, artistic thinking, exquisite sophistication in feelings, all this is equally characteristic of all Ukrainian women and compensates for the lack of education'. A Ukrainian woman is an equal; she often dominates in the house. No woman lacks these qualities: she is sweet, friendly, modest, a little dreamy, and likes to sing sad songs*".

"How could a Cossack tolerate a woman's hegemony in the home?"

Vasyl Myloradovych:

"*The relationship between a man and a woman is often quite good, which depends primarily on the people's character polished over the centuries. You see, the Ukrainian character is mental, not emotional. Calmness, restraint, and the ability to think and weigh one's condition dominates it*".

"Yet, there were still divorces".

Vasyl Myloradovych:

"*Almost never did a man and a woman separate for good. She might have love affairs for a year or more, but then the woman returns home*".

"Is that so ... And how did her husband accept her?"

Vasyl Myloradovych:

"*Secrecy and pride force man to nip family troubles in the bud, preventing them from spreading*".

"Almost every Ukrainian man went to the Zaporozhian Sich in the Cossack state from time to time. How did his wife feel about that?"

Mykola Hohol:

"*She saw her husband two or three days per year, and then there was no word from him for several years. In that century, it was shameful and dishonorable for a Cossack to think about a woman and love without having taken part in battle*".

"And what happened when a man would come back home?"

Mykola Hohol:

"*She suffered insults, even beatings; she saw caresses rendered just out of mercy; she was some kind of strange creature in this mob of unmarried knights, on whom the rakish Zaporozhya threw its harsh color. All her love, all her feelings, all that is tender and passionate in a woman, everything changed in her into solitary motherly love. With ardor, with passion, with tears, like a steppe seagull, she fluttered over her children".*

"In a Ukrainian family, was there more joy over the birth of a son or a daughter?"

Vasyl Myloradovych:

"If a father prefers a son as help, then a mother prefers a daughter for the same reason".

"Mykola Vasyliovych, in the end, allow me to ask a personal question. Who do you personally consider yourself to be, a Ukrainian or a Russian?

Mykola Hohol:

"I don't know whether my soul is Ukrainian or Russian. All I know is that I would never prefer a Ukrainian over a Russian or a Russian over a Ukrainian. The natures of both are so lavishly gifted by God. It is as if, on purpose, each of them contains precisely what is absent in the other one".

"You traveled a lot in Europe and met many people. What is your attitude toward Europeans? How do you think they differ from Ukrainians?"

Mykola Hohol:

"You have seen men there too, Godly men like yourselves, and you have talked with them as with your own folk; but when it came to speaking from the heart; then you saw that they were wise men, but not like yourselves at all, that they were and yet were not men like yourselves!"

"Oh, Mykola Vasyliovych, you know how things have changed now! Most likely, you would also say the same about Ukrainians now".

Mykola Hohol:

"I know that knavish ways have taken root in our land. They ape the devil knows what heathen customs; loathe their mother tongue; a countryman speaks not with a countryman; a countryman sells a countryman as soulless brutes are sold in the market. The mean favor of a foreign king, not even of a king, but of a Polish magnate, who kicks them in the snout with his yellow boot, is dearer to them than any brotherhood".

"Is everything so hopeless, in your opinion? Here we are, electing new presidents and prime ministers. Do you think they will take good care of the country?"

Mykola Hohol:

"But even the vilest of these villains, no matter how low he has fallen for all his fawning and groveling in the mud, even he, brothers, has a spark of feeling for his land. And it will rise up one day, and the wretch will wring his hands and tear his hair, loudly cursing his vile life and ready to redeem his shame with suffering".

"Thank you very much, Mykola Vasyliovych, and you, gentlemen, for your insightful answers".[18]

Now it is time to consider other aspects that will help us conclude the actual Ukrainian character.

Nationality

The anthropological makeup of a Ukrainian reflects the ethnogenetic processes that took place on Ukraine's territory during the last millennia. In general, s/he is a typical representative of the Caucasian race, occupying an intermediate link between northern and southern Caucasians, closer to the southern one.

According to morphological studies, the main line of Ukrainians' heredity looks as follows: tribes of the Bronze Age—Scythians—population of Chernyakhiv culture—Kyivan Rus—modern Ukrainian. The presence of the Baltic component is evident in Polissia and Volhynia, while the Celtic one appears in the Carpathian Mountains.

The influence of the Scandinavians is also noticeable. For example, the Nazi breeding program was "disappointed" when it found among the Ukrainians too many, in their opinion, individuals of "Aryan" appearance—fair-haired, blue-eyed, and sensitive-skinned. In all regions of Ukraine, a Mongol admixture is quite insignificant.

Although the genotype of Ukrainians was also influenced by Thracians, Greeks, Hungarians, Jews, Armenians, Khazars, Poles, Russians, and two or three dozen other ethnic groups, scholars believe that in an anthropological sense, Ukrainians are still more

---

18 The answers of Guillaume de Beauplan are taken from his study *A Description of Ukraine* (*Description d'Ukranie*) translated from the French by Iarema Kravets; Mykola Hohol's "answers" are based on the novel *Taras Bulba*, the edition published by Ivan Malkovych and Yevhen Popovych, translated by Mykola Sadovsky.

or less homogeneous and not inferior in their uniformity to, say, the Italians or the French.

The answer to the question of when the starting point of the formation of the Ukrainian nation might be is controversial. Most scholars believe that, most likely, this process began in the fourteenth century AD.

Since the 17th century, Ukrainians have been identified with Cossacks. Written sources of this time record numerous word combinations like "Cossack people", "Cossack language", so forth

In 1650, Guillaume Levasseur de Beauplan produced the first map that mentioned Ukraine. Ninety-eight percent of Ukrainians were believed to live on that land. After Ukraine was integrated into the Russian Empire, a huge number of immigrants were resettled in Ukraine's southeastern regions, and they subsequently Russified Ukrainian cities. Ethnically, the villages there still remained Ukrainian.

Language

The indigenous, autochthonous population lived on the territory of modern Ukraine for thousands of years, passing down their linguistic expressions from generation to generation. Numerous "visitors" added a lot, but the main language structures more or less remained the same.

What is characteristic of the Ukrainian language? It is soft, unhurried, melodious, and easily set to music. No one confuses it with purring French, meowing Chinese, strict German, hissing Polish, harsh Hungarian, sublime and solemn Latin, restrained Finnish or boisterous Russian.

And with what language can a foreigner confuse Ukrainian?

The Belarusian, Czech, and Serbo-Croatian languages are very close to each other. But also, it is similar to Italian in terms of energy, vibrations, emotionality of sound, and in its songlike nature.

The rhythm of the Ukrainian language is much slower than Italian, Spanish, or English. When switching to the Ukrainian language, the tonality of a person's voice slightly decreases, and the volume of the voice also decreases. Deep chest sounds are added, and the timbre of the voice becomes softer and more velvety. The diaphragm works better. As a result, the perception of a said utterance softens, and the overtones of persistence and aggressiveness disappear in the conversation.

"At one time, I switched to Russian in business because it made me tougher", recalls the entrepreneur, Natalya Fedorishyn. And when she was conducting business in Ukrainian, it was "good, no need to pay in advance ... and I can do it for free ... The difference was noticeable". The same can be said about the Ukrainian military: to add aggressiveness to their actions, they switch from Ukrainian to Russian on the battlefield.

In everyday life, some Ukrainian citizens also speak Russian rather than Ukrainian. Almost 350 years of the colonization of Ukraine by Muscovy explain this. However, despite speaking another language, most Russian-speaking residents of Ukraine mentally identify themselves as Ukrainians. Knowledge of the Russian language does not prevent them from fighting against Russia and the population of the occupied territories or from proclaiming "Kherson is Ukraine!" to the invaders.

Personality vs. Society

There has never been a royal court or any particular class of aristocrats in the land of Ukraine. Therefore, in the Ukrainian worldview, the line between the upper, middle, and lower social strata was and remains arbitrary. Society is more or less homogeneous, and relations between people are not based on observing specific hierarchical structures. The hetman was always chosen from among his own, and wealthy landowners did not consider it a shame to go to the Zaporozhian Sich and join the fraternity of those "strapped for money".

A Ukrainian never considered anyone else superior, but also never assumed a position above others as such compensation for an inferiority complex was foreign. Despotism did not characterize the authority of the father, and woman's authority was traditionally great. Children were not severely punished for wrongdoing.

The psychological makeup of a modern Ukrainian is very different from a Russian's. After all, the Ukrainian inherited his or her traits from the Zaporozhian Cossacks, and Muscovy never knew the phenomenon of free Cossacks. This is what the Frenchman C. F. Masson, who was in the service of the Moscow government in 1762–1802 and knew Ukrainians and Muscovites personally, writes in the book *Mémoires secrets sur la Russie*:

"Cossacks have nothing in common with Muscovites, except for the Greek religion and the Slavic language corrupted by Muscovites. Their customs, way of life, housing, food—everything is completely different. Cossacks are beautiful, handsome, tall, agile, active, sincere, honest, brave, and not used to slavery. In short, they are the complete opposite of Muscovites. Unlike Muscovites, their appearance is not uniform; the brand of slavery didn't make them automatons like Muscovites. Cossacks are cruel, but only in battle, and Muscovites have an innate cold-blooded, ruthless, and sadistic cruelty".

Work

A typical representative of Ukrainian society is a peasant who had to work from dawn to dusk. But since he worked for himself, he paid careful attention to the results of his activities. The Russian government sought to instill communal agricultural production on Ukrainian lands. It didn't work out. And until now, individual farms have prevailed in Ukraine.

Ukraine has always produced a significant share of the world's food: about 27% of sunflower seeds, 5% of barley, 3% each of wheat and rapeseed, and 2% of corn.

But the thoroughness of the work of Ukrainians is lower than in Western European countries. The amount of agricultural produce remained high not because of the quality of work but thanks to a large amount of fertile land. Additionally, Ukraine has always lagged behind European countries in the quality of industrial products.

Religion

Religious tolerance characterizes Ukrainians. In past centuries, the hostile attitude toward Roman Catholic Poles or Jews was not based on religious principles. In Ukraine, a Catholic man could easily marry an Orthodox woman, and an Orthodox man a Catholic woman—there was no tension regarding this among the people. Ukrainians even set as an example the Jews' strict fulfillment of their religious commandments to their children.

Ukrainians have never doubted their belonging to Christianity. However, they have always respected supernatural pagan forces outside the canons of the Christian worldview. Pious by nature but not the best parishioner, a Ukrainian did not really distinguish the meaning of certain theological rites, and pagan customs presented no conflict with religious practices. Sorcerers, healers, and born and trained witches enjoyed incomparably greater respect among the people than priests, the main characters of the anecdotes, or even the saints who "are always away" and do not hear the supplications addressed to them.

However, such a seemingly frivolous attitude toward religion did not prevent Ukrainians from learning the general principles of Christian ethics.

In 1685–1686, the Moscow Church absorbed the Kyivan Church. As a result, most Ukrainian churches were under the jurisdiction of the Russian Patriarchate. But the liberation has already begun: in 2019, the Ecumenical Patriarch Bartholomew signed a decree known as a *tomos* granting independence to the Ukrainian Church from the Moscow Church.

Authorities

Throughout their existence, Ukrainians have proven that they do not recognize any authority over themselves and will not long tolerate any power. Ancient Greek democracy and the Kyivan Rus' *viche* became the basis of the popular rule of the Ukrainian Cossack state. Cases of long-term hetman rule were isolated. Attempts to impose a cult of personality led to restrictions or removal of a hetman. Even such a powerful figure as Bohdan Khmelnytsky was obliged to comply with the resolutions of the senior council, which remained the central authority. Ukrainians never identified the concept of "power" with any specific person, be it a tsar, a hetman, or a president.

However, Ukrainians' lack of respect for the authorities also translates into a lack of respect for the law. Violation of the rules is considered the "norm", and the judicial system in current Ukraine is significantly removed from European "Roman" standards.

After the parliamentary elections of 2006, a colossal power crisis arose in Ukraine. The country lived without a parliament or government and, one might say, without a president (he was only seen in the stands of the World Cup) for six months. The Ukrainian economy manifested a strange indifference to politics, and instead of a seemingly inevitable collapse, there was an economic boom: GDP grew by 9.3% (!).

The democratic nature of Ukrainian society reveals itself during presidential elections: the principle of the change of presidents works flawlessly and attempts to falsify voting results incite popular opposition. The president's attempt to go against the people's will in key matters ends in a revolution.

"Ukraine is a democracy. It has a political system that gives birth to unpredictable combinations and leaders. And this unpredictability and the impossibility of knowing what to expect is unbearable for Putin and the Russian regime", argues Timothy Snyder, a professor at Yale University.

Military Matters

After the disintegration of Kyivan Rus, the inhabitants of the present-day Ukrainian territory were defenseless against the raids of nomads. To protect their land from them, courageous men united in the Zaporozhian Sich and created Cossack detachments. These were non-government troops of the people's militia.

These units comprised a brotherhood-like armed force resembling that of the Vikings, or Hellenic Spartan society, or the European chivalric order. Cossacks called themselves "knights" for a reason. Not only did they defend their lands, but they also carried out daring campaigns on enemy territories.

The actions of the Ukrainian Cossacks at sea were no different from the pirate campaigns celebrated in the novels of Robert Louis Stevenson and Raphael Sabatini. Like the swashbucklers of the Caribbean, the Black Sea "gentlemen of fortune" reached the coast of the Ottoman Empire, plundered cities, and deftly evaded prosecution. Cossack detachments sailed across the sea on light boats and thoroughly defeated the Turkish troops, which at that time had no equal in cruelty and military skill. In such a confrontation, courage and adventurism prevailed over drill and blind discipline.

Ukrainian Cossacks are a unique world phenomenon. They have no European analogues. In Europe, there was no border with the Wild Field (Pontic steppe), and military art determined the relations with the enemy. In European wars, different enemies rarely advanced from different sides, but such a situation was common for the Cossacks. Therefore, they had to invent their own rules for conducting battle, strike the enemy with unexpected moves, enter into alliances with one opponent, then with another. Former allies interpreted this as inconsistency and disloyalty. However, this "inconsistency" gained Ukrainians one victory after another and allowed their units to defeat mighty armies.

In 1604, Hetman Semen Skalozub landed on the Black Sea coast of Turkey with a 4,000-strong detachment and thwarted the capture of Austria by the Ottomans.

In 1618, detachments of Cossacks under the leadership of Hetman Konashevych-Sahaidachny, who fought on the side of Poland against Muscovy, reached Moscow.

The Cossack armed forces actively participated in the European Thirty Years' War of 1618–1648. Under the banner of the Austro-Hungarian Emperor Ferdinand II of Habsburg, they defeated the Transylvanian troops and forced them to lift the siege of Vienna. In 1631, two thousand Cossacks on the side of the army of Generalissimo Albrecht von Wallenstein took part in the hostilities against Saxony. The Generalissimo valued the Ukrainians more than the Croats, who were recognized masters of military affairs at that time. In February 1636, a 2,000-strong Zaporozhian cavalry regiment, which fought on the side of Austria, broke into the French province of Champagne, defeated the French troops, and retreated to Luxembourg with much booty. In October 1645, during the hostilities against Spain, the Cossacks stormed the Dunkirk fortress.

Ukrainian Cossacks won many victories. But the main victory was that of settled society over nomadism. The steppe barbarians, who ruled Eurasia for thousands of years, disappeared from world history with the appearance of the Cossacks. The Ukrainians overcame chaos not with order or the sword, and not with a strong hand, but with their spirit, if you will, with their mentality.

If we compare a resident of Europe with a Cossack, we will see the following. At all times, European people acted as the patterns of bourgeois, burgher, and artisan behavior, customs, etiquette dictated. Ukrainians did not fit into any patterns. They lived according to their own will, not someone else's, and this caused quite a stir in Europe. The wary attitude toward the Cossacks stemmed not from the military threat they presented but from another "threat" that menaced Europe—freedom of spirit. The Cossacks' essence was not characteristic of Europeans. Their "Norman" appearance, indifference to danger, disdain for death, debauchery outside of war, absolute sobriety on a campaign, and ostentatious contempt for wealth made Europeans insecure. Therefore, they attributed a lack of civilization, barbarism, and savagery to them.

During World War II, as part of the Soviet Union, Ukrainian soldiers significantly contributed to the victory over Hitler's Germany.

In 2014, Russia occupied Crimea and eastern Ukrainian territories. Just like the Cossacks, Ukrainian non-government volunteer battalions of the people's militia together with regular Ukrainian units stopped the onslaught of Russians who intended to seize the entire territory of Ukraine.

On February 24, 2022, Russia launched a new full-scale war against Ukraine. The Ukrainian army, much weaker in terms of military strength, dealt a devastating blow to the aggressor.

"If it is true that Russia has lost 15% of its troops since the beginning of the war, then this is a world record for an invading army's losses", said Joseph Borrell, the Chairman of the European Parliament.

Before the beginning of the war, journalists interviewed five famous American military experts. Four of them predicted the defeat of Ukraine within three days. The fifth expert noted that, theoretically, a "miracle on the Dnipro River" was possible, and the Ukrainians would be able to defend Kyiv.

You can understand the experts' reasoning. Russia had four times the air force, aviation, missiles, and air defense equipment that Ukraine had; twenty times the number of guns; forty times the ammunition. Ukrainian artillery was limited to a radius of twenty-five kilometers, while Russian artillery could strike from a distance of 300 kilometers or more. Ukraine had no large warships, and Russia had shifted almost its entire fleet to the Black Sea. Putin had an enormous military budget, the factor of surprise, and a robust intelligence network in Ukraine and worldwide. Aid to Ukraine from the West and a "Lend-Lease" program took some time to begin. But the Ukrainians did the impossible: they began to grind the "second army of the world methodically", stopped it, and drove it back from Kyiv.

At That time, a joke circulated in Ukrainian social media

"Western military experts' comments on the Russian-Ukrainian war. Day 1: Ukraine loses in three days. Day 4: Ukraine is holding up because Russia has not yet brought real units into battle. Day 10: it's hopeless; the Ukrainians will lose anyway. The twentieth day: the Russians are about to regroup and take Kyiv. Day 30: Russia has achieved air superiority, and it will soon be over. Day 40: We don't understand what's going on. Day 50: Ukraine fights so well because we taught them well".

Vasyl Taras, a professor at the University of North Carolina-Greensboro, claims: "Ukrainians are showing unprecedented heroism. It is clear that they are fighting for their land, their family, and their home; their anger has accumulated since 2013. But still, we witness not isolated cases of daring attacks but mass heroism. And they fight very intelligently. The smallest units have autonomy and very cunning commanders. They lure, encircle, and twist in such a way that sometimes they take a disoriented enemy almost with their bare hands. This is surprising, given that most Ukrainian soldiers are non-professional military".

General Marchenko, the commander of the city of Mykolaiv's defense against Russian troops, noted: "Everything written in World War II literature about the Ukrainian soldier is true. He is cunning, skillful, stubborn, and steadfast. He was the anchor of the entire Soviet army. Now a Ukrainian soldier is like pure alcohol, undiluted by Muscovites, making the Ukrainian armed forces invincible".

Education and Science

During the time of Kyivan Rus, the education level on the territory of this state, according to the testimony of travelers of that time, was higher than in Western Europe. Having destroyed the state, the Mongol-Tatar invaders destroyed education along with cultural values.

The situation has improved significantly since the 15th century. Being part of Poland opened the opportunity for Ukrainians to study at Western European universities. Fluent in Latin — the lingua franca of that time — Ukrainian students fully took advantage of this opportunity. In 1481, Yuriy Kotermak from Drohobych was elected rector of the University of Bologna, then one of Europe's most prestigious educational institutions.

In the sixteenth to the seventeenth centuries, the educational level of the inhabitants of the Ukrainian territories was inferior to that of Western Europeans but far ahead of Muscovites. Unlike the Moscow nobility, the Ukrainian Cossack leader knew Latin and Polish, some knew Greek, and some German. It is no coincidence that the first institution of higher education in the Russian Empire, the Kyiv-Mohyla Academy, was founded in Kyiv. It gathered a galaxy of thinkers with European training within its walls and, for a long time, remained the center of education and free thinking for all Orthodox countries, including Russia, Serbia, Bosnia, Moldova, Bulgaria, Montenegro, Belarus, and Greece.

Graduates of the Academy founded most of the higher education institutions in the Russian Empire. The Ukrainian Kyrylo Razumovsky was the president of the Russian Academy of Sciences from 1746 to 1798 (over fifty years, which is an absolute record in world practice). He was the first Slav of the Orthodox faith to hold this position; leadership of Russian science before him was exclusively in the hands of Germans.

As part of Russia, Ukraine was rich in scientific achievements in agriculture and medicine. In 1908, Ilya Mechnikov from Kharkiv was awarded the Nobel Prize for discovering the importance of phagocytosis for the body, which became the basis for the development of immunology. He was awarded an honorary doctorate from Cambridge University and became a member of the French Academy of Medicine and the Swedish Medical Society.

In 1952, Zelman Waxman, a native of Nova Pryluka in Kyiv province was awarded the Nobel Prize for the discovery of streptomycin.

Volodymyr Vernadsky, the first president of the Ukrainian Academy of Sciences, became the founder of the doctrine of the noosphere, the planetary sphere of the mind. He claimed that humankind should perceive the universe as a unified living organism. At first, few people understood his concept, even the thinkers of the Sorbonne, where he taught for a long time. But thanks to Vernadsky, the integrity of all spheres of life on the planet is perceived as beyond dispute in our time.

Ihor Sikorsky (1889–1972), an outstanding aircraft designer from Kyiv, laid the traditions of world helicopter construction. To this day, 95% of all world models of helicopters are based on the design principles developed by Sikorsky.

In Soviet times, the sphere of scientific interests of Ukrainian research institutes included quantum field theory, probability theory, cybernetics, computing, atomic energy, the physics of super-high and super-low temperatures, the synthesis of heavy nitrogen, astronomy, and medicine.

Ukrainian scientists took an active part in space exploration. The Ukrainian Serhii Korolev was the chief designer of Soviet spaceships.

The super-heavy transport aircraft AN-124 Ruslan and the AN-225 Mriya, the brainchild of the Antonov Kyiv Design Bureau, set more than 200 world records for carrying capacity and flight range, surpassing their American and French counterparts.

However, in the sphere of education and science, Ukraine is increasingly losing its position. The level of teaching in schools and universities is decreasing; many subjects are studied haphazardly;

the quality of knowledge is deteriorating; the requirements for scholarly works are diminishing; and scholars are too lazy to master the English language. Much of what is happening in Ukraine today is also happening in other countries. Still, the training level of specialists in Ukraine is currently inferior to that of the world. No Ukrainian university is on the list of the best institutions in the world.

Culture

In the middle of the 15th century, thanks to close ties with Italy, the Renaissance began quite early in Poland. The Renaissance, which entered Ukraine through Poland, let Ukrainians have a taste of new traditions and trends earlier than other Central European nations. This influenced the formation of Ukrainian Renaissance culture. The West was open to Ukrainians, and Ukrainians were open to the West.

Kyiv retained its great potential in this process. The Age of the Enlightenment began there in the 17th century. This wave reached Muscovy much later.

Ukrainians adopted trends that did not bring their own worldview into contradiction with that of the West. The Ukrainian Baroque, a local style, emerged, influencing national architecture, painting, music, literature, and poetry. It became a reflection of Ukrainians' unique way of thinking: of the plethora of Western European styles, it was the extravagant, whimsical, decorative, and optimistic baroque that was the closest and most relatable for Ukrainians.

Thanks to Peter I, Russia also began to open to the West. The sovereign attracted shipbuilders, craftsmen, and architects from Europe, while public figures, scientists, and clergy from Ukraine brought education and culture to Russian society.

The absorption of Ukrainian talents by Muscovy and the suppression of everything Ukrainian significantly depleted Ukraine. However, despite all the efforts of the imperial authorities, Ukrainian culture continued to develop. Contacts between the inhabitants of the eastern and western Ukrainian territories never stopped, and this caused the emergence of a coherent cultural and mental space. While absorbing something foreign, Ukrainian culture preserved its own values. The symbiosis of the imported and native was organic in Ukraine and has not caused a divide between borrowed and local culture.

And yet, Ukrainian culture is traditionally reduced to its own ethnographic material and to the search for national identity. It fails to keep up with the times and the processes that concern humanity.

Architecture

Ukrainian architects could not afford to build palaces such as those in Versailles, but they inevitably instilled the spirit of optimism and the affirmation of life into their buildings. After all, the baroque style, which impresses the imagination with its effect, decorative scope, and violent dynamics, organically informed their worldview. The Ukrainian Baroque is a bold and, at the same time, naive desire "to make it beautiful", to make it "no worse than others".

Unconscious images of the folk mentality, which until the 17th century had a rather limited sphere of manifestation — in icon painting, embroidery, pysankas, decorative and applied art objects — received an immense field for realization with the beginning of the Renaissance in the Ukrainian lands. Ukrainian churches and architectural structures by the "Ukrainian Gaudí", Vladyslav Horodetsky (1863–1930), prove it.

Theater

It makes no sense to talk about milestones in the development of Ukrainian theater in this book. It is worth noting, though, that many classic Ukrainian plays have been in the repertoires of many theaters for over a hundred years.

Serhii Lyfar (Serge Lifar) (1905–1986) from Kyiv occupies a worthy place among the stars of the world theater. He was a soloist and director of the Paris Grand Opera, one of the best ballet companies in Europe. During his twenty-six years of creative activity, Lyfar staged over 200 ballets, trained a constellation of outstanding soloists, founded the Institute of Choreography, and established his own ballet school. The Department of Dance History and Theory at the Sorbonne was created for him.

The last couple of decades have not been the best of times for Ukrainian theater. On-stage performance groups are traditionally poor, fearful of experiment, exploit old-fashioned acting, and strive to please and flatter an undemanding audience. This is because the criterion for everything became selling tickets.

However, leading Ukrainian actors and directors continue to create "art without borders". The most famous European ballet troupes include Ukrainian dancers (e.g., Yana Salenko, prima ballerina of the Berlin State Ballet; groups with Ukrainian artists gave half of the performances of "Swan Lake" in Europe in the 2023 season); Ukrainian opera performers (Yuriy Samoilov, a soloist of the Frankfurt Opera; Oksana Lyniv, a conductor who worked in the opera houses of Munich, Graz, Vienna, and the Paris National Opera; Kyrylo Karabyts, a conductor and music director in Weimar) worked in the theaters of Geneva, Strasbourg, Nancy (France); and many other artists continue to perform on leading world stages.

Painting

Experiencing the Polish way of life in the sixteenth and seventeenth centuries, Ukrainian doyens began to follow European traditions. They became especially enamored of the trend of creating portraits. Ukrainian artists set off to study in Warsaw, Rome, and Vienna. Returning home, they brought Renaissance painting techniques to their works. This prompted the rapid development of the local painting scene and the emergence of a unique Ukrainian portrait style.

At a time when portraits had already become a full-fledged part of life in Ukraine, they did not yet exist in Russia. Dmytro Levytskyi (1735–1822) from Kyiv and Volodymyr Borovykovskyi (1757–1825) from Myrhorod were the founders of the Russian portrait genre. After moving to St. Petersburg, Levytskyi earned the title of academician and was appointed head of the Academy of Arts portrait class in 1771.

In the 19th century, a whole galaxy of talented painters appeared in Ukraine. They included Taras Shevchenko, Mykola Pymonenko, Mykola He, Mykola Yaroshenko, Oleksandr Murashko, Alexander Archipenko (Oleksandr Arkhypenko),

Oleksandra Ekster. Vassily Kandinsky grew up in Odesa, where he was certainly influenced by bright southern Ukrainian motifs.

Arkhyp Kuindzhi was born in Mariupol. His *Ukrainian Night* caused a considerable sensation at an exhibition in Paris in 1878. And the work *Moonlit Night on the Dnipro River*, in which the colors become phosphorescent, became a world sensation. Nicholas Roerich was Kuindzhi's student.

The outstanding painter Ilya Repin, famous for his Ukrainian-themed *Reply of the Zaporozhian Cossacks to the Sultan*, was born and grew up in the Kharkiv region.

Triumphs in Europe and the USA always greeted Casimir Malevich from Kyiv. His style became the basis of Suprematism, a new movement in art. And his *Black Square* still causes passionate disputes among art critics.

To understand the Ukrainian mentality, it is necessary to point out the peculiarities of the works of Ukrainian artists that distinguish them from those of Russian and European masters.

I addressed this question to Olena Kashuba-Volvach, a scholar at the Institute of Art History, Folklore and Ethnology of the Academy of Sciences of Ukraine. Here is what she said.

"Olena, what are the peculiarities of Ukrainian art?"

"*Take, for example, Archipenko. He is a Ukrainian artist and a native of Kyiv. In the first decade of the twentieth century, he moved to Paris, quickly embraced avant-garde approaches to his art, and felt very comfortable with them. He captivated the French themselves with his unusual and non-standard art*".

"What was it that appealed to the French?"

"*Western art was inspired by Roman antiquity. Archipenko, on the other hand, drew inspiration from the stone figures of Scythian women, which are everywhere in Ukraine. He took this form, refined it, and brought some original substance into the painting. We analyze form to its simplest elements. And what form could be simpler than Scythian stone sculptures? They are laconic and concise*".

"Perhaps Archipenko was not very familiar with antiquity?"

"*Without a doubt he knew it very well because he received a classical art education. But this Scythian woman took up residence 'in his brain'. In addition, he was the only sculptor of that time to paint his sculptures.*

At the beginning of the twentieth century, this was unheard of. Some historians remember that, in ancient Greece, all sculptures were painted and even dressed. But everyone else was convinced that the sculpture of Greece consisted of white marble statues. In reality, all Hellenic statuary was painted. For Archipenko, as a person from the south, color weighed considerably in the system of artistic expression".

"And for the French?"

"Not so much for the French. Braque and Picasso, and, in fact, all great artists of the beginning of the century, were more interested in form, its state, the transformation of one form into another, the ratio of space to volume, etc. And Archipenko brought color to the system of the European avant-garde. And in general, not only Archipenko but also all of Ukraine brought color to the global avant-garde. Moreover, the color appears in some dynamic forms".

"And what about color in Russia?"

"The Russian avant-garde, if we consider, let's say, Popova, Udaltsova, Larionov, is, in principle, more saturated with color than the French, but less so than the Ukrainian. Oleksandra Ekster (Alexandra Exter), for example, a Ukrainian artist who entered the ranks of both the Russian and French avant-garde, also distinguished herself by her use of color. Or take Oleksandr Bogomazov (Alexander Bogomazov). If you visit an exhibition with the works of various avant-garde artists, you can identify the Ukrainian roots of artists simply visually, by color".

"Is it brighter? More saturated?"

"They are both brighter and more saturated, overflowing with an unusual combination of colors; the works are very joyful and open. They are not washed out – this is a pure pigment, which, together with another pure pigment, produces a sound and strong impression. Neither Russian nor French art has these 'Ukrainian' combinations: yellow, blue, turquoise, lilac with ultramarine, pink with light green or bright blue".

"Thank you very much."

So, stylistic variety, a bright color spectrum, optimism, an unusual combination of colors, colorfulness, and naivety comprise the distinctive qualities of Ukrainian artists' artwork.

All this is present in the works of Kateryna Bilokur, about whom Pablo Picasso once said: "If we had an artist of this kind, we would have the entire world talk about her". We should note that Picasso usually spoke of other artists with disdain.

The works of Maria Primachenko, the master of naive art, are vivid illustrations of the Ukrainian worldview. Her paintings are an example of archetypal artistic expression. Based on the traditions of decorative folk painting, she created her own fantastic world inhabited by blue monkeys, flower-green crocodiles, and other fanciful creatures. The elements of ancient art are present in the images of animals. The tradition of drawing animals emphasizing the border of the head and torso harkens to Paleolithic times. The bull in Primachenko's paintings appears as a star-studded creature. Often her works include totem animals of the ancient Slavs: horses, bears, doves, swallows, storks, and snakes. These images lived in people's consciousness for centuries and entered the artist's work. After Marc Chagall saw Primachenko's canvases in Paris, whimsical creatures also began to appear in his works.

Modern artists also continue to develop Ukrainian painting traditions. In 2007, Ivan Marchuk from Kyiv was included in the list of the "Top 100 Living Geniuses" compiled by the British newspaper *The Daily Telegraph*.

Music

Ukrainians consider themselves one of the most musical of nations. This is for good reason: more than two hundred thousand Ukrainian folk songs have been recorded.

Some Ukrainian songs, such as the well-known "Carol of the Bells", are typical Indo-European mantras. Others date back to the times of Kyivan Rus.

Prominent European composers of the eighteenth to the nineteenth centuries were quite familiar with Ukrainian musical art. Beethoven used the motifs of the song "The Cossack Rode beyond the Danube" in his Piano Variations. Ferenc Liszt remade and set to music the Ukrainian folk song "The Winds are Blowing". Russian composers knew Ukrainian folklore better than Europeans. Pyotr Tchaikovsky, for example, who was proud of his Ukrainian roots, used Ukrainian folk themes in his Piano Concerto No. 1 in B-flat Minor, Op. 23, in the "Little Russian" (read: Ukrainian) Symphony

No. 2 and in many other works. Rimsky-Korsakov wrote his operas *May Night* and *The Night Before Christmas* based on the Ukrainian motifs from the short stories of Mykola Hohol (aka Nikolai Gogol).

The composers Maksym Berezovsky (1745–1777) and Dmytro Bortnyansky (1751–1825) laid the foundations of Ukrainian academic music. The name of Berezovsky, who wrote many instrumental and choral works for Italian orchestras, is engraved next to Mozart's name on the marble tablets of the Boulogne Philharmonic Academy. In their work, both Berezovsky and Bortnyansky drew inspiration from the melodic turns characteristic of Ukrainian songs. They brought polyphony to Orthodox religious musical culture, which had previously recognized only monophony. Having determined the further development of world choral singing, these two musicians influenced the works of European and Russian composers.

Sergei Prokofiev grew up in the village of Sontsivka, Donetsk region, and taught there for a long time.

Igor Stravinsky is a composer of Ukrainian origin. He changed the musical traditions of his time. The Stravinsky family from Volyn, Ukraine were descendants of Hetman Ivan Sulyma. It was in Ukraine, inspired by local folklore, that Stravinsky began to write his first works, which brought him world recognition. Fleeing from the Bolsheviks, the composer emigrated to the USA but always considered Ukraine his motherland.

Modern Ukrainian composers, including Valentyn Sylvestrov, Myroslav Skoryk, Yevhen Stankovych, and others, are also recognized worldwide.

According to producers' estimates, two-thirds of Russian pop stars are from Ukraine. Ukrainians won the Eurovision Song Contest in 2004, 2016, and 2022. In 2022, the British band Pink Floyd recorded the anthem of the military unit of the Ukrainian Army of 1917–1919, "Oh, the Red Viburnum in the Meadow" in Ukrainian, which in English was called "Hey Hey Rise Up!"

Literature

Like every other, Ukrainian literature emerged long before the appearance of writing. Folktales, fantastic stories, legends, and poems were passed down from generation to generation. The literature of Kyivan Rus had a significant influence on the development of Ukrainian writing.

A book by Yuriy Kotermak (aka Yuriy Drohobych), Doctor of Arts and Medicine, was the first printed text by a Ukrainian author. It was published in Latin in Rome as *Iudicium Pronosticon Anni MCCCCLXXXIII Currentis* (*Prognostic Estimation of the Year 1483*).

Ivan Kotlyarevsky (1769–1838) is considered the first classic of Ukrainian literature. His works show the unique and original distinctiveness of Ukrainian literature.

The works of the Ukrainian writer Ivan Bahrianyi (1906–1963) were published in the USA, Canada, England, Germany, Holland, France, and Australia. The total circulation of his books in English alone is over a million copies. In New York, he was given the symbolic keys to the city. In his honor, January 22 is annually celebrated as Ukrainian Day, and a blue and yellow Ukrainian flag is draped over New York's City Hall.

UNESCO declared 1990 as the year of the Ukrainian writer Vasyl Yeroshenko (1890–1952).

The real name of the classic of English literature, Joseph Conrad, is Joseph Kozhenovskyi. He was born in the Zhytomyr region and lived in Chernihiv, Odesa, and Lviv before emigrating.

Sholom-Aleichem was born and raised in Pereyaslav in the Khmelnytsky region of Ukraine. He knew Ukrainian folklore well and was fond of folk tales; in his works, there is a unique flavor of Jewish-Ukrainian life.

Polish science fiction writer Stanislaw Lem was born in Lviv, studied the Ukrainian language at the gymnasium, and mastered it perfectly.

When Ukraine was part of the Russian Empire, Moscow's censorship did great harm to Ukrainian literature. Only those works in which the theme of a complicated, unhappy life dominated were approved for publication. One thing united all these works, the sediment that remained, after reading, that everything was not as it should be with Ukrainians. But nobody knew a better way.

But the best examples of Ukrainian literature are optimistic. Like folk tales, Ukrainian prose is rich in vibrant artistic tropes such as similes, metaphors, hyperbole, and epithets. Fantasy and a healthy pathos abound in it. The unique metaphorical nature of the Ukrainian language makes this possible. In literature, as in life, Ukrainians have demonstrated the ability to shade the sad with joy and the sorrowful with color, while deeply feeling both. On Ukrainian soil, themes of time, hope, fate, and the meaning of life are colored not by moderation but by emotion; they passed not through the mind but through the heart.

Fantasy is one of the most influential genres of Ukrainian literature. Paganism and a rich demonology influenced the inner world of Ukrainians and Ukrainian literature. Fantasy was Mykola Hohol's favorite genre. Mikhail Bulgakov was the author of the cult novel *The Master and Margarita*. He was a native of Kyiv who subconsciously absorbed the demonic archetypes of the Ukrainian mentality along with the Faustian European tradition.

Andrei Kurkov is a modern Ukrainian writer whose works are among European bestsellers. He writes on the border of reality and surrealism. His novels have been translated into forty-one languages, with a total circulation of over four million copies.

The British Book Club included the collection of poems by the Kyiv poet Iryna Ratushynska, which was presented to the queen, in the list of the world's best books. Current Ukrainian authors Yuri Andrukhovych, Serhiy Zhadan, and Oksana Zabuzhko are well-represented in translations in multiple European languages, including English.

Love

Foreigners who visit Ukraine remark on the attractiveness of Ukrainian women. Geneticists claim that the more open a nation is, the genetically healthier it is. Located at a crossroads of nations and intermarrying representatives of different ethnic groups, Ukrainians formed their own powerful genotype, which contributes to physical perfection for survival in difficult times and to natural beauty.

The anthropological attractiveness of Ukrainians probably developed thanks to the folk tradition expressed in the saying, "Ne bery vid porody, a bery vid pryrody", which roughly translates as "don't marry for status but marry for love". The observant ancestors of Ukrainians understood that the "purer" a race is, the more it is confined to "chosen ones" and the physiologically weaker it is. In Ukrainian society, the decisive factor in selecting a husband or wife was not his or her social status and not the imposed will of parents, but love. In case of parental disagreement, young people often ran away from home and married secretly.

Girls were expected to be virgins when they married. And when the young couple was left alone on their first wedding night, a "group of supporters" sang shameful songs to them at their window. The same tradition existed in the Greek settlements of the Northern Black Sea region.

Mosaic of the Ukrainian Soul

It's time we summed up the actual nature of modern Ukrainian mentality. It makes no sense today to identify the inhabitants of Ukraine with the Scythians or the Zaporozhian Cossacks. The Russian and later the Soviet periods could not have passed without a trace.

And yet, in the 7,500-year-long history of this region, these were only a small episode. Ukrainians are separated from Kyivan Rus by forty generations, from the ancient Greeks by about eighty, and the nationsucal character has only passed through 200 from Trypillian great-great-grandfathers and great-great-grandmothers. So they are not that much.

Sometimes one can get the impression that the residents of Ukraine have two different mentalities: one stemming from democratic Cossack traditions, the other from a pro-Moscow legacy, with its peculiar morality and cult of the iron fist. In the mentality of any person, let alone an entire nation, diametrically opposed features are inevitably present. Forty-five million citizens cannot have the same hair color or the same "color" of thoughts.

But, despite these seemingly mutually exclusive features, the Ukrainian mentality comprises a rather holistic and unique structure.

It is not our intention to evaluate the psychological traits of Ukrainians on the "good-bad" scale. There is no such scale in psychology. However, the basic features of the Ukrainian mentality can be provisionally divided into three categories: "Pearls of a Distinctive Necklace", "Between East and West", and "Echoes of Forgotten Ailments".

Pearls of a Distinctive Necklace

A Tendency to a Settled Lifestyle

Since ancient times, Ukrainians have lived in their own fertile habitat. Except for periods of misfortune, wars, and man-made famines, Ukrainians and their ancestors always had enough food. This is, without a doubt, the main thing necessary for a normal existence. And this shaped the tendency of Ukrainians to a settled lifestyle. A Ukrainian does not want to move anywhere, but is happy where s/he is.

On the other hand, there is no country that would not accept Ukrainian emigrants. After the beginning of the Russo-Ukrainian war, more than six million Ukrainians were forced into exile abroad, mainly to the countries of the EU. However, despite the advantages of European life, not everyone intends to stay there forever, and most migrants want to return home.

It seems that Ukrainians have developed the archetype of a cat: they wander wherever they want, but always return to their own yard. In Russia, where dependence on the land is not as significant a factor, the archetype of another, no less decent domestic animal, the dog, with its aggressiveness and devotion to its owner, is more pronounced.

Business Efficiency

Residents of Ukrainian territories are mostly of village stock. A villager is a person who takes pride in their home. It cannot be otherwise. In Ukrainian proverbs and sayings, the terms "master of the house", "mistress of the house", and "house-proud child" are a compliment. Neat and well-kept estates with hedges, orchards, flower gardens, and livestock are traditional in Ukraine.

Rural work is a family matter. Poverty is undignified, and wealth is respected.

And what can we say about Ukrainian care of the home? Where else, apart from Ukraine, do people plant gardens under the windows of high-rise buildings in cities?

Versatility

Living in small villages, every master and mistress of the house had to be a Jack or Jill of all trades: build a house, bake bread, give birth, and brew some okovyta alcohol. Everyone was master cook and bottle washer.

This universality has remained in the Ukrainian character to this day. The ability to repair a car on their own, to do any repair without help, and cope with any ailment without a doctor is the norm for Ukrainians.

By the way, in Ukrainian medical universities, students are trained not to be narrow specialists but holistic doctors. In their ability to see an infirm person as a whole, Ukrainian doctors are significantly ahead of their Western colleagues.

Peacefulness

Peacefulness is an indispensable component of a villager's outlook. The desire to conquer other territories is meaningless when there is already enough fertile land. The paradigm "let's live in harmony" is paramount in the relationship of Ukrainians and their ancestors with the surrounding world.

Although the early Slavs led a pure life of banditry and were always eager to let Byzantium have it, the Zaporozhian Cossacks adopted their military tactics, but never looked at other people's possessions. Having "taken a stroll" in Constantinople, they returned to the Sich. The troops of Hetman Bohdan Khmelnytskyi triumphantly reached the borders of Poland, liberated their territory, but did not go any further.

In Ukraine, due to the lack of aggressiveness and the ability to solve internal problems with the use of reason rather than power, there were neither "hot spots" nor threats of terrorism before the invasion by Russian troops. During the Orange Revolution of 2004, the world did not see any footage of fights and bloodshed. During the terrible night of February 18–19, 2014, when units of the Berkut presidential guard fired point-blank at protesters on Kyiv's Independence Square (*Maidan Nezalezhnosti*), the leaders of the resistance called out: "Guys, we are conducting a peaceful demonstration! Offer no resistance!"

The peacefulness of Ukrainians manifests itself even in the game of its national soccer team: tactics are oriented toward defense, there is rather little aggression in acute situations and shots on goal. Ukrainian soccer players who try to "hold on" until the end, rather than win the match, sometimes resemble diarrhea patients who try to "hold on" until the end of treatment. Playing such a "peaceful" game, in 2006 at the World Championship, the

Ukrainian team somehow managed to get into the top eight, but in 2016 at the European Championship, it failed to score a single goal.

Even during Russia's war against Ukraine, Ukrainian media has often discussed peace negotiations with the aggressor rather than victory.

Courage

Ukrainian pacifism does not in the least mean "cowardice". Speaking in the Senate, Russian Tsar Peter I characterized the Ukrainians as follows: "The Little Russian people are very clever and very cunning: they are like a hardworking bee, they give the Russian state both the best common-sense honey and the best wax for the candle of Russian education. But they have a stinger".

Well, it is what it is. Ukrainians are like bees that fly around leisurely, collecting nectar and bringing what they have collected to the hive . . . They are peaceful and a bit lazy; but they don't bother anyone. Until someone crawls into their hive. Then, not sparing themselves, they sting the uninvited visitor.

In past ages, only courageous and bold people could afford to live not by the laws of the jungle but by the much harsher laws of the steppe, wild and open to every wind and all nomads. The ancestors of Ukrainians never hid in the forests or behind the thick walls of castles. They fearlessly went into battle with a stronger opponent; appeared where they were least expected; and confused enemies with their audacity. In the Sich, Cossacks accepted only courageous, bold, and fearless people.

The courage of Ukrainians fully revealed itself when Russian troops invaded Ukraine in 2022. Putin foolishly failed to consider the Ukrainians' love of freedom, bravery, and ability to self-organize. Unexpectedly for Moscow and the whole world, the Ukrainian armed forces rebuffed the Russian military machine.

Love of freedom

Such traits as the love of freedom, independence, and disobedience to foreigners were passed on to Ukrainians from previous generations. According to the chronicles, their ancestors did not allow anyone to enslave or conquer them.

Prince Danylo Halytsky did not bow to the dictates of the Tatar-Mongol Horde in the 13th century. After defeating several Horde khans and ensuring the support of Lithuania, he prevented the Tatarization of Ukrainian territories and found a way to maintain the order and traditional way of life that existed from Kyiv to the Carpathians unchanged. These lands practically knew no slavery, or knew it only in passing.

The Ukrainians did not submit to the Poles either. "The serfs refuse to perform any duties or remain obedient to their masters", the Polish nobles complained. "Naked and barefoot, on the lookout for something to steal, yet he is free and never at a loss for words; strict with enemies, but loyal to a friend; a child of nature without a 'tsar in his head'" — this is how Polish sources portray a Ukrainian.

Ilya Repin wrote about Ukrainians: "What a people! My head spins from their noisiness and boisterousness ... I live with them without rest; I can't part with them, what a cheerful people ... No one in the whole world feels freedom, equality, and brotherhood so profoundly!"

Free, proud, and satisfied with their stormy life, not controlled by anyone, in 1654, the Ukrainians nevertheless "took the bait" of the Moscow boyars, who pulled the wool over their eyes and fraudulently annexed Ukrainian lands to their territory.

The Ukrainian Insurgent Army fought fiercely against two monsters — Hitler's Germany and Stalin's Soviet Union. During World War II, Ukrainian partisans fought for the independence of Ukraine simultaneously on two fronts. In that situation, there was little hope for victory. The rebels did not win, but they did not surrender either.

In the 1960s and 1980s, a seemingly hopeless movement of moral resistance to the communist regime unfolded in Ukraine, again proving the Ukrainian repudiation of slavery and injustice with a strong sense of self-worth preserved through the centuries. The Revolution of Dignity of 2013–2014 and the war with Russia in 2022 bore witness to these traits.

Democracy

The paradigm of ancient Greek democracy is firmly "embedded" in the archetypes of the Ukrainian mentality. In contrast to European countries, where the traditions of royal dynasties prevailed for centuries, the East Slavic ethnic group always gravitated toward democratic or anarchic forms of government: popular assemblies always made important decisions among the early Slavs; the *viche* (public assembly) played a key role in Kyivan Rus.

After the collapse of Kyivan Rus, Cossack democracy took root in Ukraine; in it, the council dominated, and the hetman, chosen from among his own people, was besmirched from time to time so that he didn't put on airs. Actually, the same thing is happening now.

The first constitution drawn up by Hetman Pylyp Orlyk in 1710 reflected the concept of Ukrainian democracy. This system of laws, which appeared eighty years before the French Declaration of the Rights of Man and of the Citizen and sixty years before the American Declaration of Independence, was ahead of the trends of the French Revolution in both its relevance and high level of democratic ideas.

For almost 350 years, Ukraine was part of the Russian Empire and the Soviet Union. During this time, democracy in Ukraine was in a lethargic slumber. But its inviolable premises, such as the people's rule, fair elections, and the absence of authoritarian rule, have already awakened today.

Some representatives of the Ukrainian ruling elite still have the Tatar-Soviet belief that immorality in government is acceptable, and when you manage to climb to the state podium, you should take advantage of it and steal a lifetime's worth of money. This principle is rare in Western democracies. Ukraine is also in the process of eliminating it.

Spirituality

Grain farmers comprise the category of humankind that is organically closest to the earth. You don't need to explain to them that a church is a temple built by man, and Nature is a temple created by God. Being entirely dependent on the whims of Mother

Nature, peasant farmers, to whom the majority of the inhabitants of Ukraine belonged, were a priori religious. They profoundly, more intuitively than consciously, believed in a Higher Power that governs existence.

Whoever is belligerent is forced to be reserved. One who lives in harmony with the world and does not try to conquer anyone is open. All his windows and doors are open: a guest can easily enter, and God can always enter.

The world believes that the center of spirituality is in the Vatican. For Ukrainians, it is in the heart of every man.

Aptitude

The gene pool of people who consume products grown on fertile black soil contains a predisposition to good health, physical and mental endurance, and, last but not least, aptitude.

Aptitude is a fragile matter, and it reproduces poorly in captivity. The communities that lived on Ukrainian lands under the rule of others left little for the world. Instead, independent and free individuals enriched it with their achievements. World civilization is inconceivable without the heritage of Trypillia, the ancient culture of the Northern Black Sea region, Scythian gold, the jewelry masterpieces of Kyivan Rus, the Eastern Slavic chronicles, Ukrainian icons, myriad songs, and embroidery.

Ukrainian Orthodoxy never separated itself from the West and Catholicism by a solid wall nor did it prevent spiritual and cultural interpenetration. The Greek Catholic Church was in union with Rome, which also provided a link to Western religiosity and ideas. However, Ukrainian culture, absorbed by imperial Russia in the east and Polish-Austro-Hungarian culture in the west, resembled Cinderella. In the eighteenth to the twentieth centuries, we see Russified cities and Ukrainian-speaking villages. Hence the myth that Ukrainian means something provincial. The Russian colonial authorities strongly instilled and fixed this myth in the minds of the empire's inhabitants.

However, one can trace the basic archetype of culture in the mentality of all the ethnic groups of the Ukrainian *chernozem* (black soil). Life at the crossroads of different civilizations enriched their worldview with tolerance, flexibility, dynamism, and, as a result, the ability to create spiritual values.

Figurative Perception

Ukrainians' perception of reality is a stream of colorful slides. The figurativeness of Ukrainian thinking, in contrast to abstract and philosophical Russian thinking, is expressed in painting, poetry, and literature. Russian literature consists, first and foremost, of structure. It combines Russia's traditional pomposity, discernment, and the search for answers to "eternal" questions. Russian authors leisurely construct plots, work out details in the compositions, and invest them with mental play, profundity, and bold conclusions. What dominates here is not the visual canvas but the general idea and skillful placement of details.

Ukrainian literature has a powerful sense of visuality. It is almost always a picture. Ukrainian authors are not always adept at building a structure: they lack the ability to play with accents, rhythm, and intonations. The creative search of Ukrainian authors does not take place within the framework of a structure or in the manner of narration, but rather, in an atmosphere of spirit and imagery. They work not on the "philosopher's stone" of the work but on expressiveness, the illustrations placed on the canvas of the plot, and the cinematic depiction of life. It is no accident that one of the foremost genres of Ukrainian literature is fantasy.

"Ukrainian and Russian literature are different in their chemistry", as Eleonora Solovei, the Head of the Comparative Literature Department at the Shevchenko Institute of Literature, figuratively puts it. Similarly, Ukrainian and Russian mentalities are "chemically different".

Emotionality

Solar energy influences the formation of temperament and emotionality. In this sense, Ukrainians are subordinate to southern European peoples such as the Italians, Spaniards, and inhabitants of the Balkans, but ahead of more northerly nations.

All the same, Ukrainians are people of the South. It is difficult to call them phlegmatic. They are used to bright colors, saturated images, and deep emotions. Ukrainian artists prefer clean, bright colors in unusual combinations. Their canvases are characterized by dynamism, emotionality, and a wide variety of styles.

And in Ukrainian literature, everything traverses through the heart, colored not by reason but by emotionality.

Sentimentality

The geographical environment made a decisive impact on the formation of Ukrainians' worldview. Endless steppe landscape with an endless horizon lost in infinity, soft waves of golden ears of corn, clear quiet rivers, a hot but not scorching sun under the blue dome of the sky—all this gave rise to sentimentality, vulnerability, dreaminess, sensuality, passivity, lyricism, deep emotionality, and romanticism in the local people.

The Ukrainian language is similar to the Ukrainian temperament: both are soft, melodic, and song-like. This is the language of poetry, feelings, and love.

Mysticism

Proximity to the soil and dependence on the natural world also instilled another trait of Ukrainian mentality, mysticism. Ukrainians perceive nature and all its inhabitants as their own, native, and apprehensible.

For Europeans, with their love of order and desire to avoid chaos and unpredictability, the concept of "nature" is associated with a clear landscape, the straight lines of planted forest, and trimmed lawns. Gnomes, trolls, or werewolves have trouble surviving under such conditions.

The ancestors of Ukrainians venerated the forces of wild nature: they considered everything related to it and inhabiting it as sacred, including wood nymphs (*mavky*), wood sprites, vampires, mermaids (*rusalky*), spirits, and other mystical creatures with all their laws and whims. This formed some kind of intuitive feeling in Ukrainians that, in nature, both the possible and the impossible are intertwined. And not only in nature, but also in life. In the depths of their souls, Ukrainians remain pagans. Living two belief systems, they continue to celebrate pre-Christian holidays.

And *rusalka*-mermaids, forest spirits, and other pagan creatures occupy a unique place in Ukrainian folklore. They migrated from folklore to literature, where it became clear who the Konotop witch is, what Gogol's demon in the story "The Viy" looks like, what miracles happen in the evenings on the farm near Dykanka, and how Woland's satanic balls and the gatherings of Kyiv's witches take place in Bulgakov's *The Master and Margarita*.

Surrounded by computers and mobile phones, Ukrainians still protect children from the "evil eye", do not extend anything (especially not a handshake) across a threshold, know how to protect themselves from energy-stealing vampires, and trust horoscopes and dreams. In their notebooks, to be on the safe side, there are several phone numbers of psychics, fortune-tellers, and astrologers. European public transport does not greet passengers with images of saints. The driver's seat in almost every Ukrainian minibus is decorated with small icons and amulets.

Sincerity

Experts believe "cordocentrism" comprises the main direction of the Ukrainian school of philosophy. It means the dominance of the heart over the mind, emotionality over rationality, and feelings over logic. Philosophy is inseparable from the mentality of the thinkers and people of a given land.

In addition to traditional Ukrainian canons, the traditions of Ancient Greece, the philosophy of Byzantium and Kyivan Rus shifted the emphasis to the soul, which, in the Ukrainian perception of the world, takes root in the heart. Sincerity is the core of kindness, spirituality, love, and the source of cheerful thoughts and actions.

Hryhoriy Skovoroda (1722–1794) introduced the concept of sincerity into New European philosophy. In his teaching, he brought what his people have always lived by to the fore: the warmth of relationships, the vibrance of being, sincerity, naive hope, and the ability to compromise with external darkness.

After Skovoroda, Ukrainian philosophers repeatedly addressed the dilemma of the heart and the head, spirit and pragmatism, and wisdom and reason. The heart usually wins in the clash between feelings, emotional experiences, rationalism, and logic.

This somewhat contradicts Europe's worldview with its tendency to a rational interpretation of everything.

Openness

"Evergreen" nature, a mild climate, and fertile soil not only softened the national character of Ukrainians, made their soul docile and non-aggressive, but also instilled the trait of openness. Since the time of Kyivan Rus, and probably even earlier, there were no curtains on the windows in the people's homes in this territory — life flowed in full view of everyone.

The open space of the Ukrainian landscape, the small number of mountains, and the absence of territorial borders also made the population of this territory more open. It may have been precisely this national trait of openness that prevented Ukrainians from creating their own state for many centuries. Europeans, who traditionally lived in small territories surrounded by hills and forests, are a relatively reserved people. Protecting themselves from enemies, they have always surrounded their estates, cities and countries with stone walls and border barriers.

However, if the European community closed its doors to unwanted guests, it opened them to Ukrainians in 2022. Millions of Ukrainian refugees fleeing Russian shelling received shelter, protection and sincere aid in their time of need from European countries.

Baroque Thinking

The Baroque is festive, decorative, and doll-like, with swirls and the interplay of light and shadow. A baroque person is a romantic: friendly, benevolent, soft, but not persistent, not stubborn, and not purposeful. The train of thought of this fantasist and dreamer is challenging to gauge: no one can guess what s/he will do in the next moment.

Neither a Ukrainian Gothic nor a Ukrainian Empire style exists. Ukrainian craftsmen so designed monumental houses to give them an intimate, "chamber" impression.

The baroque worldview of Ukrainians penetrated literature, painting, and songwriting.

Baroque is the style of thinking of the Zaporozhian Cossacks, who won victories, not due to strength and military tactics, but thanks to actions that no one expected.

Liveliness, confusion, orientation to a broken line, non-standard moves, asymmetric responses, unpredictable decisions — all this can be traced both in Ukraine's economy and geopolitics. Almost all national leaders were representatives of the Ukrainian baroque culture, displaying the capricious ethics, subtle "Byzantine" intrigue, decorative appeal, and unpredictability typical of the baroque. From time to time, this causes misunderstandings between Ukrainians and their Western partners.

The European way of thinking is more structured. This allows the quicker acquisition of information, according to a template or scheme. The use of fixed clichés helps Westerners to clearly organize their ideas, expend less energy on thinking, and avoid clogging their heads with the search for answers to rhetorical questions. Ukrainians tend to discuss a given problem for a long time, while Europeans quickly seek to find solutions in the context of current tasks.

Intelligence, Astuteness, Craftiness

The penchant for non-standard decisions and unexpected actions did not form in Ukrainians by chance. Through natural selection, the need to survive in the environment of wild nomads, the primordial necessity to hide something, to adapt to someone, and not to expect anyone's help gave rise to such character traits as acumen, cunning, and craftiness in the ancestors of the Ukrainians. They had to think one thing, say another, and do something completely different. The ability to deceive the enemy, confuse him, and force him to fight under circumstances incomprehensible to him was the main weapon of previous generations of Ukrainians, particularly the Zaporozhian Cossacks.

Dmytro Bantysh-Kamenskyi, the Ukrainian historian of the 19th century, characterized his compatriots as follows: "A Ukrainian is sluggish and carefree. But he is cunning and tireless when, through this, he aims to achieve a desired goal. Kindness and simplicity are obviously defining features of his character, but they are often a consequence of cunning, which is the reflection of his mind".

Cunning and unconventional thinking are among the defining features of the modern Ukrainian mentality. A Ukrainian can easily find a loophole in the tax code or make the electric meter spin in the opposite direction. Ingenuity allows the Ukrainian military to confront an enemy five times in number during the Russo-Ukrainian war.

The English perceive the bulldog, a strong and stubborn animal, as their national symbol. The symbol of Russia is a bear; in China it is a dragon; in France it is a rooster; Germany has either an eagle or a German shepherd. What animal would symbolize Ukraine? Most likely, it would be the fox. This animal is cautious, cunning, and wise in its own way, but also insidious and devious. The fox cannot be trained, and in response to the same command, it performs a different trick every time.

Self-Will

To be the master of one's life, you need something more than cunning. Self-worth and self-will comprise that something. Without these traits, Ukrainians would simply not have survived. Or if they did survive, they would have lost their identity, dissolving in a stronger and more aggressive environment.

These features save them even today, just as they did in the past; Ukrainians do not allow them to be tamed and made submissive and meek. Their weapon has remained the same: inconsistency, "shifting" from side to side, multilateralism, and, last but not least, a readiness to give someone the finger at the most unexpected moment when an agreement cannot be reached.

The self-will of Ukrainians is a constant. If in Russia, "the master will come and judge us", then Ukrainians don't give a damn about the master, the tsar, or the president. Self-will is the main accusation against the Cossacks recorded in Polish documents of the sixteenth and seventeenth centuries.

An 1876 decree of the Russian imperial government forbade the publication of books in the Ukrainian language and the organization of theatrical performances. Nothing could have promoted the development of Ukrainian literature more than this decree, which initiated a turbulent flow of literary and dramatic works.

During the Ukrainian revolutions of 2004–5 and 2013–2014, another wave of disobedience shook Ukraine: a Ukrainian, sleeping without a care in his home, suddenly woke up, collected his entire household, brought it to Maidan Square in Kyiv, prepared to give someone the finger when the opportune moment came, and stirred up such a carnival row that it left even him surprised.

Self-will brings Ukrainians both benefits and problems. The refusal to recognize Russia's supremacy over Ukraine became the cause of the Russo-Ukrainian war. But it could not be otherwise. The absolute majority of Ukrainians do not under any circumstances recognize any foreign ruler over them. For Ukrainians, Putin is not a king, a demon, or a hero. For Ukrainians, Putin is a schmuck. How can you let a schmuck walk all over you?

A horse in a stall and a horse on the steppe are two different horses. The Ukrainian "horse" is not used to a rider or a stall.

Ability to Self-Organize

Ukrainians do not need a command from above to unite. During times of danger, volunteer points, volunteer battalions, barricades in the center of cities, or roadblocks appear as if out of nowhere. This happened during the Orange Revolution, the Revolution of Dignity, and the invasion of Ukraine in 2022 by Russian troops. City dwellers cooperate with each other, and, without any instructions or orders, protect their neighborhoods, patrol the streets, make rough and ready roadblocks, tie looters to poles, and return to a peaceful life once the danger passes.

It is worth noting that self-organization is characteristic only of the active segment of the Ukrainian population. The passive majority "supports" their country by sitting on the sofa and watching TV.

Optimism

Serhii Krymsky, Doctor of Philosophical Sciences, has taken note of an interesting point: "Every Christian temple must necessarily have a scene of the Last Judgment. But in the main temple of Kyivan Rus, this scene is absent! They say it has not been preserved. However, judging by the engravings and reconstructions, it was never there! Why? Because the ontological optimism permeating Ukrainian culture is also embedded in the archetypes of our mentality".

Without their eternal optimism, Ukrainians would not have survived. Many cheerful folk songs comprise a cure for boredom, a sour mood, gray everyday life, and a serious attitude toward life. Despite complex life challenges, the Ukrainian soul has little room for depression, malice, and fatalism.

In 2022, Western experts predicted that Kyiv would not survive the Russian troops' offensive against Kyiv. Conversely, the Ukrainians had no doubts about their victory. Kyiv held out. Having committed terrible crimes against the civilian population in Bucha, Borodyanka, and Irpin, the Russian terrorist forces retreated in disgrace.

Resistance to Stress

Stressful situations affect people in different ways. Different peoples also react differently to the same stressors. Living in constant danger, Ukrainians have developed a certain tolerance for global catastrophes. During the Chornobyl catastrophe, which found all of Europe in a panic, Kyiv, located 30 kilometers from Chornobyl, remained calm. There was no panic in Ukraine either during the Revolutions or during the Russian troops' offensive. Putin tried to create chaos in Ukraine by bombing and shelling the residential areas of almost all Ukrainian cities. His plan failed. People died from the occupiers' missiles, bombs, and bullets. But those who survived did not break. Psychologists had a lot of work, but there were no mass appeals.

The armed conflict has a negative impact on the military. Many of them may develop post-traumatic stress disorder. According to the Scientific Research Center for Humanitarian Issues of the Armed Forces of Ukraine, only 20–30% of the Ukrainian military personnel who suffered psychological traumas during combat missions can overcome their psychological problems without help. Having worked for three years as a psychotherapist with the personnel of the armed forces of Ukraine, the author of this book has the firm conviction that Ukrainian soldiers recover very quickly. And this is not only thanks to psychotherapy but also thanks to their habitual optimism.

Joy of Life

Optimism and cheerfulness are almost identical concepts. Both are directly linked with all aspects of Ukrainian ancestors' life. The bright colors of their ceramics attest to the cheerfulness of the Trypillians, and the aforementioned cheerful disposition of the ancient Slavs time and again appears in visiting travelers' records.

What did the Black Sea Greeks say about their neighbors? Let me remind you: "Hyperboreans were a happy people who learned harmony, did not know enmity, or diseases, did not need anything, lived in a surprisingly mild climate, and died only from being full of life".

All this has passed down to modern Ukrainians: traditionally undemanding in everyday life, Ukrainians decorate their surroundings with bright colors. Their houses are neat and freshly whitewashed, with a cherry orchard nearby and flowers in the flowerbeds. The dishes are simple but attractive. Joie de vivre characterizes Ukrainian folk embroidery, ceramics, painting, and music. Their national dress is a work of art, a decoration for any holiday or wedding.

Last but not least, Ukrainians cannot live without humor, and it reflects their cheerfulness and optimism.

A Well-Developed Sense of Humor

In Ukraine, no conversation, no repast at a table, no scholarly or political discussion ever happens without humor, jabs, and jokes. Humor is an inherent attribute of Ukrainian television, parliament, business life, and even court proceedings. Well, only those who know the taste of life, enjoy it, and can see its unexpected essence are capable of joking.

Ukrainian humor is not a unique phenomenon. Many of the plots of Ukrainian jokes resonate with those found throughout the world. But any kind of humor, whether it is English, French, German, or Italian, has its own characteristics. According to Olesya Brytsina, a senior researcher at the Institute of Art History, Folklore and Ethnology of the National Academy of Sciences of Ukraine, there is little destructive reflection and black sarcasm in Ukrainian humor; rather, good-naturedness, self-irony, and a life-affirming attitude prevail in it, making it unique.

The most famous object of Ukrainian jokes is not someone whom a Ukrainian arrogantly tries to make fun of, but himself: getting into different situations, he sometimes turns out to be smart, but sometimes looks stupid. Ukrainian social media have been full of humorous posts and anecdotes even during the war. Of course, they primarily mock the enemy.

Here are a few examples.
God:
"Today, I am creating Ukrainians. They will be beautiful, hard-working, intelligent people. I will give them the sea, mountains, and fertile land ..."
St. Peter:
"Aren't you, God, too generous to those Ukrainians?"
God:
"You don't know who their neighbors will be ..."
A Russian officer addresses a subordinate on a walkie-talkie:
"What is the situation near Kyiv?"
"We're boldly retreating!"
"And the Ukrainians?"
"They're running after us in shame!"
The Americans asked the Ukrainians what they would pay for Lend-Lease.
The Ukrainians replied: "Well, we will give you Siberia. Take it away".

The Reverence of Women

On both sides of the Dnipro River, respect for women has always existed. The people of Trypillia, the Proto-Slavs, and the Greeks venerated them. The social order of the Sarmatians was gynocratic. The Slavs were similar, and their women, as foreigners record, "were more intelligent than a person should be by nature". In Kyivan Rus, the legal status of women was more advanced than in European countries, while in families, it was a common phenomenon when "women own their husbands and rule over them".

The cult of women reached Ukraine. The daughter-in-law assumed leadership immediately once she was released from the care of her mother-in-law. Note that the head of the family was a woman, not a man. This is how the Ukrainian family differs from the Russian and some Western European counterparts. The results of sociological surveys showed that 62.4% of Ukrainian teenagers see the supremacy of their mothers in the family. In Russia, this figure only reaches 39.2%.

A woman's dependence on her husband is enshrined both in European legislation and in the Russian sixteenth-century *Domostroi* (set of household rules). Actually, in Russia, it was always considered normal to beat a woman. As they say in Russian, if he hits her, then he loves her.

There is nothing like that in Ukrainian folklore. In the popular imagination, a woman is a wife, a support, and a rudder. If the birth of a son was more desirable in other countries, Ukrainians were always happy to have a girl: she would spin, sew, clean, and wash shirts. A Ukrainian never endowed a woman with various mocking "feminine" features. A Cossack always tried to be a knight in her eyes.

In today's reality, we witness something different: a Ukrainian woman can receive disdainful treatment from men, and there are few women in parliament. However, this mentality is not Ukrainian but Soviet, a carbon copy of alien traditions.

Thanks to official positions in the state and business in Western countries, women play a more significant role in society than they do in Ukraine. However, in Ukraine, the role of women is important because of their influence on men.

Having read books on gender issues, Ukrainian women are now paying much more attention to their own careers and independence. They learn to "love themselves", strive for "autonomy", material independence from men, and go for the position of a president. And men, as before, believe that a woman should first be kind, wise, beautiful, a good mother and housewife, and that leadership qualities and willpower are the last things she needs.

Respect for the Family

Family values have always occupied a special place in the Ukrainian mentality. The family owned a plot of land, and several related families formed a farmstead or a small village.

Russian and European societies have similar family values. But if in most countries of Medieval Europe, the eldest son inherited all the property, Ukrainians distributed all the wealth equally among the children. This often led to insults and arguments since not everyone was satisfied with his or her received share. But the idea, characteristic of the Ukrainian mentality, that everyone in the family is equally entitled to both misfortune and good fortune comprises the very principle of property equality.

Legal norms known as Roman law still regulate the relations between members of European families. Modern marital contracts are a logical extension of this trend. High material well-being is a significant criterion of European family happiness. As sociological surveys show, love is the main criterion in choosing a life partner among young Ukrainians. According to the Institute of Social Research's data, 68% of Ukrainian men and 61% of women are satisfied with their families despite their low income level. Seventy percent of young families live with their parents, and 90% systematically receive financial assistance from their parents.

In 2013, the police in Kyiv brutally beat students who protested against the authorities. The next day, over a million people from all over Ukraine came to the capital, chanting, "they beat the children!" They carried out the Revolution of Dignity and subsequently overthrew the existing regime. Neither in Russia nor Belarus, did the brutal beating of students by the police ever cause a revolution.

It is customary in American and European societies to send elderly parents to a nursing home. In Ukraine, this is inconceivable.

Eroticism

Eroticism is the backbone of the mentality of all southern peoples. Northern societies are erotic, yet more restrained, which adds a particular flavor to their secret life.

Agricultural communities in Ukrainian territories have always linked the cult of Love with fertility; they saw a sacred connection between Mother Earth and Mother Woman. Trypillians were overtly passionate; the ancient Greeks of the Northern Black Sea were incorrigible erotomaniacs; the goddess of love often appears on the gold artifacts of the Scythians; and the Slavs had an easygoing attitude toward erotic life.

Ethnic groups that have been kept on the edge of survival for centuries tend to be especially sexually active. There has always been a population shortage in the wild Ukrainian steppe, constantly ravaged by nomads. Under these conditions, the birth rate and, accordingly, the level of what leads to the birth rate, have always been very high.

Folk tales, songs, and proverbs reveal the secret life of Ukrainians. The Ukrainian woman, with her authority, frankness, rich palettes of eroticism, is an archetypal phenomenon for Ukrainians. Even a witch in the Ukrainian imagination is not the archetypal hideous Russian Baba Yaga, not an insidious pest, but a cheerful and attractive woman. She is fashionable and intelligent, has stunning success with men who tend to suspect every woman of witchcraft, especially the one who bewitched him, and because of whom he has lost his mind.

And to this day, Ukrainians belong to ethnic groups who treat love and eros with natural ease. Such traits as emotionality, sincerity, and sensuality are characteristic of most Ukrainian women and compensate for their lack of refined manners or the inability to build their own career. Ukrainian women are friendly, modest, naive, and dreamy. The number of beautiful women in Ukraine amazes foreign tourists. Once after an overview on the main news, the TV host said goodbye to the audience with the words, "Let's make love!" And the same thing was written on advertising billboards in Kyiv: "The country lacks Nobel laureates! Let's make love!"

In Ukraine, literary works about the people's secret life are in demand and are regularly nominated for the state Shevchenko Prize. A conversation about "whether Ukrainian literature needs an orgasm" provokes a lively discussion in the press.

Mykola Hohol's conclusions seem right: "No, sirs, brothers, to love like a Cossack soul, to love not only with the mind or anything else, but with everything that God has given, all that is within you. Ah! No, no one else can love like that!"

Between East and West

Ukraine is between East and West not only geographically but also mentally. A pendulum-like swinging between different neighbors permeates the entire history of Ukraine.

The worldviews of the East and the West are opposed. Scholar Dmitry Lykhachev defined the West as the civilization of Matter and the East as the civilization of the Spirit. The Indian philosopher Osho called both the East and the West two different kinds of imbalances. The West, according to him, suffered from the "Yang" archetype. The male element is expressed as technocracy, competitiveness, energy — physical and financial advantage dominates it excessively. The long-suffering, conservative East suffers from the "Yin" archetype, in which passivity, inaction, and non-interference in the world structure occupy a central place.

However, the West is like the brain's rational left hemisphere and the East resembles the right imaginative hemisphere. The Western mental field, whose strengths are logic, structure, pragmatism, and clarity of movements can be defined as "mind/reason". With its meditative contemplation of life, the unconscious East is usually equated with wisdom. Right-handed "logicians" think more linearly, which is why their behavior is easier to calculate. Left-handed people are unpredictable.

Balancing between East and West, the Ukrainian psychotype was formed as a synthesis of various seemingly incompatible phenomena, which, however, were combined in their mentality with integrity and unity.

Introversion

An individual and the whole of society can follow an extroverted or introverted structure. Extroverted societies such as Sparta, Rome, the USA, Russia, or Germany are "masculine", strong, and strong-willed. Open to external influences, ready to absorb the innovations of world culture, they are characterized by a fiery nature, perseverance, purposefulness, a tendency to self-actualization, and a certain asceticism. Their distinctive features are a desire to seize other people's territories, selfishness, an inclination to risk, an openness to connection, and a need for movement.

Principally introverted "feminine" societies, to which Ukraine belongs, are more conservative. They revolve around their internal needs, ideals, culture, and values. This slows down their development and causes them to lag behind global trends. Introverted countries are not so much focused on creating something new as on preserving what has already been created. That is why reforms in such countries take time. People in such societies are calm, patient, and compliant. They are characterized by apathy, naivety, suggestibility, the need for an ally, moderation in action, and the need for external decoration. Feminine elegance also marks soft feminine culture. This is expressed in the baroque perception of life, beautiful clothes, exquisite meals, sentimentality, and the need for comfort in everyday life.

Moderation

The lack of the possibility for easy enrichment and the average size of its territory explain the moderation of the lifestyle of Ukrainians. The vast expanses of such countries as the USA, Russia, and China have brought into the mentality of their inhabitants bravado, maximalism, striving for a great goal, and the conviction that it is worth sacrificing a lot to achieve this goal.

Correspondingly, a country's small size can lead to the formulation among its inhabitants of such traits as modesty, thrift, and pettiness—not only in financial terms, but also mentally. To illustrate this, let's consider folk dances: in small countries, such as Hungary, the dance includes close movements maintaining a distance between partners and tapping one's feet in place. In larger countries, there is more enthusiasm. But even the Spanish flamenco or Brazilian samba cannot compete with the hopak, a Ukrainian folk dance, which reflects the vitality of the restless Cossack soul and does not accept any moderation of folk life.

Mercantilism — Unselfishness

The saying goes, "A Russian is poor but thinks he is rich; a European is rich but thinks he is poor". And what about the Ukrainian? They do not seek great wealth but do everything to avoid falling into poverty.

The ancestors of Ukrainians always had everything necessary for life. But it was unprofitable to accumulate surpluses because the bigger the farm, the sooner invaders would appear and take away hidden reserves. Perhaps for this reason, the character trait of mercantilism is less developed in Ukrainians than, say, in Europeans, but more than in Russians. Ukrainians value wealth. However, they do not respect millionaires and owners of luxurious estates but rather representatives of the middle class.

In Europe, a bank account is especially revered. A rich person enjoys more respect. While Orthodox culture has embraced the willingness to renounce everything material, carnal and earthly, in the mental field of Catholicism, and even more so in Protestantism, serving God does not exclude worldly pleasures, material well-being, and wealth.

Unlike a European, Ukrainians do not expect to be paid for everything they do. But they are also in no hurry to pay for someone's work. Uploading books, movies, music, and computer programs to the Internet without aiming to make a profit, they do not understand why they should pay for something that can be pirated and downloaded. Paying taxes is like a personal insult to them. To earn a large amount of interest at someone else's expense, a Ukrainian is willing to invest his savings in any fraudulent bank, only to lose everything later.

So, for all their "greed", Ukrainians still have a well-developed vein of selflessness. During the war with Russia, countries such as the USA, Great Britain, Poland, Canada, Estonia, the Czech Republic, Lithuania, Latvia, and others provided Ukraine with enormous support. For its part, Ukraine also helps friendly countries in any way it can. Having created a powerful volunteer movement, Ukrainians give their time, energy, and savings to gain victory. But not everyone does this, of course. There are also those who try to profit from war.

Cautiousness — Inertia

The living conditions in small villages, a lack of unity, and vulnerability in the face of conquerors developed the character trait of cautiousness in Ukrainians. Ukrainians will not do anything without carefully brainstorming over all the "pros" and "cons", will not quickly decide on any action, and will not rush headlong into a shady enterprise. They are not prone to sudden moves and decisive actions: caution has saved them from danger more than once. But it has also often harmed the development of society.

Ukraine has always lacked leaders ready to assume personal responsibility. This explains the absence of fundamental economic reforms in the thirty years since independence. Moreover, during this time, no one, neither the government nor the opposition, bothered to plan the development of society for the sake of the nation as a whole, and not just for personal promotion. And the people have no great expectations — they perceive political games as soccer (hooray! Our team scored!). The government is satisfied with this status, does not bother thinking too much about the economy, and behaves the way the "lower classes" perceive it. Excessive caution coupled with slowness, a typical feature of provincials, gives rise to inactivity, inertia, and a desire not to get involved in active games.

One of the rules of Ukrainian politicians is to refrain from making sudden movements. It is necessary to participate in intrigues but not cause them. This causes less than charismatic figures to often win political campaigns. Ukraine has not experienced the rule of destructive leaders, aggressors, or sadists. But it has not known avid creators either. Ukrainian aspiration for a parliamentary-presidential collective leadership is, on the one hand, a "celebration" of democracy, but, on the other, it is an effective means of avoiding personal responsibility.

But changes are happening. The war with Russia has forced Ukrainians to forget about their inertia and act cautiously, cheerfully, but decisively.

Passivity — Initiative

Historically, Ukrainians rarely had to prove themselves as firm and energetic to achieve their goals. They hardly ever appreciated the sense of statehood and duty, which must be performed in a disciplined, organized, and systematic manner. The peasant worldview, limiting its interests to one's own yard and plot of land, reacts to any social initiative, whether it be setting up a club, a library, or fixing a road, with the rhetorical question: "do I need this?" Villagers move to the city, take high positions up to and including the presidency, and bring the algorithm of caring only for their own little world to affairs of state. Everything else is "do I need this?"

But there is another side to this coin. In some countries, particularly Russia, everything is imposed forcibly from above at the behest of the ruler. In Ukraine, all "reorganization efforts" have always started from below, with the people themselves or their representatives in the *viche*, among the Cossacks or in the Verkhovna Rada (Ukrainian parliament). The events of the Revolution of Dignity and the war proved that the algorithm "do I need this?" is inherent only in a passive stratum of the population, while the active part of society is able to take responsibility for the further development of the State. In the Ukrainian army, field commanders are allowed to act according to the situation without waiting for orders from above.

Diligence — Laziness

Ukrainians cherish the myth that they are the most hard-working nation in the world. One thing is certain, their ancestors had to go to work at sunrise, including men, women, and even children. However, favorable natural conditions allowed them, to tell the truth, to work without breaking a sweat. The economic life of peasants in the Ukrainian territories was traditionally very "unobtrusive" — they grew and harvested no more than what they could use, with a little to sell. It seems that, even now, Ukrainians treat work like the ancient Greeks, in an easygoing way, understanding that one must work to survive, but one shouldn't overdo it. Sometimes one gets the impression that an "Italian strike" never ends in Ukraine—everyone is at work, but no one is doing anything.

Ukraine's production level has always been lower than in developed European countries. Recently, Chinese cars have become a quite decent commodity. In the past twenty years, Brazil created its own aircraft from scratch and is now far ahead of Ukraine in aircraft construction. Israel's hard work in the wilderness produces impressive harvests.

Therefore, the statement that Ukrainians are a hardworking nation remains a pleasant illusion.

However, Ukrainians still know how to work well. As an example, there are a large number of wealthy farms in Ukraine. We can cite many instances when a Ukrainian, once in dire conditions, performed miracles of hard work. Especially outside their own territory, after emigrating to the USA, Canada, Latin America, and receiving from the governments of those countries an allotment of uninhabited land, the future farmers day and night cleared the forests, plowed the unsuitable soil, and achieved an unprecedented harvest in the end.

During the present war, when Ukrainians end up in other countries, they immediately try to find a job there. About a quarter of the Ukrainians who left for Poland at the beginning of the full-scale invasion in 2022 refused financial aid just two months after arrival in the country hosting them and found jobs. "This is a phenomenon of global significance. This has never been the case with refugees anywhere else", said Paweł Szefernaker, the Polish Deputy Minister of Internal Affairs.

Unpretentiousness—Striving for Comfort

If we believe the Byzantine authors, the ancestors of Ukrainians always easily endured "heat, cold, rain, threadbare bodies, and poverty". Similarly, Scythians and Sarmatians were unpretentious. The inhabitants of Kyivan Rus used simple furniture and dishes, and the princes' palaces were not marked by European sophistication. Zaporozhian Cossacks were indifferent to their living conditions.

To some extent, this has passed down to modern Ukrainians. They will patiently endure all adversities and will do without hot water and air conditioning. In general, the Orthodox worldview does not embrace concern for personal comfort. If in Catholic churches parishioners sit during the service, in Orthodox churches, there is nowhere to sit, even for the sick and infirm.

But there is another side to the coin. A tillerman, whose world is his farm, house, and family, organizes his life so that everything is comfortable and "close at hand." In Ukrainian yards, everything is neat and convenient.

After the outbreak of the war, Europeans were surprised that migrants from Ukraine did not look like most refugees. They were neat, manicured, dressed in quality clothes, with comfortable shoes, and had iPhones in their hands. It is the norm for Ukrainians to live in their own homes, buy expensive things, go on vacation abroad, and not save money. They are used to living in comfort.

The neatness of Ukrainian homes, with a neat yard, domestic animals, and a cherry orchard near the house, provoked the fury of the Russian invaders. They fired at the manor houses from their tanks for no reason, just out of envy. And they left inscriptions on the ruins: "Who allowed you to live so well"?

Individualism — Collectivism

Ukrainians tend to believe that they are incurable individualists. At first glance, things appear to be this way. Living on a farm far from "civilization", Ukrainians were forced to rely only on themselves, to achieve well-being only through their own efforts. "Being one's own boss" is the life philosophy of a Ukrainian who could not imagine existence without his own farm. Private interests in Ukraine have always been more important than collective interests. Communal agricultural production, copied from Russia, where everything is "ours", did not take root in Ukraine. In Ukraine alone is the insulation of high-rise buildings the business of each individual apartment owner, who insulates only his premises from the outside of the building.

However, a European is much more individualistic than a Ukrainian. Living in a crowded space taught him to isolate himself from his neighbors and be different.

For a Ukrainian, "my house" is not "my fortress", as in Europe. But not everyone is allowed in his or her house: a person from a small family, small teams, a small circle of acquaintances and friends. In the West, it is customary to meet friends in restaurants — everyone orders and pays for themselves. In Ukraine, people often meet at someone's home.

Although individualism is one of the defining archetypes of the European mentality, Western democracy has successfully made politicians take care of society before their own interests. The entire history of Ukraine shows that the leaders in power were mainly concerned about their own interests. Echoes of this "tradition" have remained to this day.

History also shows that during World War II, while in German concentration camps, Ukrainians kept separate from others and did not really seek to establish any contact with each other. In modern Europe, most Ukrainian refugees, displaced persons, or emigrants do not participate in peaceful rallies to help Ukraine and often communicate with each other not in Ukrainian but in some other language.

In striving to isolate themselves from their own kind, Ukrainians lose in many ways. However, having absorbed the influences of the East and West, they are, to a good degree, the carriers of both individualism and communalism. Sociologists view the specifically Ukrainian brand of individualism as a guarantee of the success of prospective market transformations and the Westernization of the Ukrainian economy.

Sociability — A Closed Nature

All that has been said about the sociability or introversion of a Ukrainian can be applied to the discussion of individualism versus collectivism. In this regard, s/he is also "in the middle" between the East and the West: s/he makes contact more quickly than a European but is more withdrawn than a Russian. Let's say, in the carriages of Russian trains, passengers quickly get to know each other. In Ukraine, people usually communicate only with their immediate neighbors in train cars, and even then, without giving their names. And in Europe, even neighbors in a compartment talk discreetly among themselves.

Every year, Ukrainians communicate with each other less and less, preferring television and computers.

However, meetings with friends are still an integral part of Ukrainian life. The whole village gathers at a village wedding without an invitation. As a rule, the Ukrainian gathering lasts until late at night; a Georgian one lasts three days; and a European one lasts only two to three hours.

Kindness — Unkindness

The natural environment shaped the Ukrainian into a gentle and good-natured person. In his or her society, there was never a belief that life was about winning a place under the sun. S/he always lived under the sun. Since the time of Herodotus, the inhabitants of the forest-steppe north of the Black Sea were happy to provide shelter to their neighbors who were "attacked by snakes". Byzantine authors also left an excellent recollection about the ancestors of Ukrainians: "they are not bad and not at all malicious ... They are kind to those who come to them and enjoy their hospitality as if they were old friends".

And modern Ukrainians are relatively forgiving. In their archetypes, the concept of revenge is almost absent, and there is a lack of hatred for those peoples who have wronged them. Having survived the atrocities of Hitler's fascism, Ukrainians did not harbor evil against Germans; and the Poles, historical enemies of Ukrainians, are their best friends now.

The softness and kindness of the Ukrainians both help and harm them. Suffering from Russia's military terror, Ukrainians hate Putin, yet a significant segment of the population treats the Russians who support the atrocities of their "tsar" without contempt as if they were oligophrenic individuals who do not understand what is going on. "In response", the Russians destroy the Ukrainians with twice the brutality.

Patriotism — Tolerance

A vital feature of the English, French, and American character, which can be traced in literature since the times of Shakespeare, Victor Hugo, and Jack London, is a deep, almost reflexive patriotism. Patriotism consolidates the nation. On the other hand, the higher the degree of patriotism, the lower the ability to objectively self-reflect and the greater the chance of succumbing to national paranoia.

Ukrainians have never had a developed state of their own. And the one that has existed since 1991 does not give rise to much admiration among many of its own residents. A few years ago, one could hardly call a significant part of the population of Ukraine patriotic. But the Ukrainians were never bothered by insecurities, as if they were better, smarter, "cooler" than others. Their worldview contains no notion that, as they say, ours are always the good guys, and "others" are always heathens.

Despite the complex historical development, or perhaps precisely because of it, the national spirit of Ukrainians has shown remarkable resilience. Unlike Bavarians, Moravians, or Provençals, who almost dissolved into the mentality of their more numerous neighbors, Ukrainians managed to maintain their identity. National patriotism grew incredibly after the Russian military attack. Over a million Ukrainians who worked abroad returned to defend their country in the war. If until recently, girls tried to marry foreigners, now many of them are looking for a "real Ukrainian guy".

Despite these examples, a Ukrainian cannot be called a nationalist: less than 5% of the population voted for a political party that promoted "national ideas", and that party did not even win enough votes to become part of the Parliament; in the 2019 presidential elections, 73% of Ukrainians voted for Volodymyr Zelensky, a Jew.

Yet, as before, a certain part of the population of Ukraine has a blurry concept of patriotism. While "loving Ukraine", they do not love anything Ukrainian, demonstrate tolerance for the "Russian world", attend the churches of the Moscow Patriarchate, and sing songs in the occupiers' language. But if you say something insulting about Ukraine even to such an "uncertain patriot", there is no guarantee that he will not slap you in the face.

Politeness — Straightforwardness

Few people, except Ukrainians themselves, will claim that a Ukrainian is sincere and straightforward. S/he marches to his own drummer; s/he thinks one thing, says another, and does something completely different. Well, s/he learned to be like that while surrounded by not always friendly neighbors.

Compared with a Ukrainian, a Russian is more straightforward. S/he persistently pushes his or her own agenda and cannot understand why the Ukrainians mess with his or her head, are evasive, and say neither "yes" nor "no".

However, even a Ukrainian rarely understands why a Russian behaves rudely and uses profanity. Elderly people recall that some fifty years ago, in a Ukrainian village, "Muscovite swearing" was perceived as foreign, even among men. Of course, foul language has been an integral part of military vocabulary and the curses of some of Ukraine's loud-mouthed neighbors. However, during the revolution on the Maidan, a small part of Kyiv where several thousand paramilitary men were stationed during the resistance movement, the general atmosphere was remarkably civil. "Thank you", "please", and "you are welcome" echoed again and again. And there was no Russian vulgarity expressed among them.

But Ukrainian politeness still cedes place to European politeness. A Ukrainian finds it surprising that in France, even the bus driver says "Bonjour" to everyone who enters the bus. A Ukrainian would not immediately guess that, rather than "good afternoon", it meant "please present your ticket". He is not used to the fact that in Europe, it is customary to communicate using polite automatic cues, a habit preserved from sophisticated court etiquette when the forms of conversation or business negotiations were built on an extensive system of conventions that require knowledge not only of what you want to say but also how, when, and in what form.

Yet is Ukrainian politeness really inferior to European? Here is a brief story from the life of wartime Kyiv in 2022, told by Yuriy Kovalskyi, the editor-in-chief of the literary magazine *Raiduha* (*Rainbow*):

"Queues have returned to Kyiv from the distant past. The one in front of the pharmacy especially terrified me. It was fifty meters long, or even more. I stamped my feet in it for about ten minutes. "The hell with it!" —I gave up. And in the evening, I reproached myself: "What could I do without my medicine?!" The next day I hurried there early. The queue turned out to be even longer. But I courageously entered it. I previously stood in line for the never-ending deficit of goods under Soviet rule. You might say I returned to my youth.

But I quickly realized that this was a completely different queue. It was nothing like those nervous and belligerent lines where you could hear: 'No more than one per one pair of hands!', 'Where the hell are you going!', 'You weren't standing here!' Now it was a kind of a family queue of close people who cared about each other. Someone told an older woman to go home to warm up:

'Why don't you come back in an hour, no sooner?'
'But I will forget who I was behind'.
'Don't worry, we'll let you know'.

Someone ran to look for the man, whose turn was already approaching, but had wandered off somewhere. Several of those who left our queue to buy bread and sausage returned and reported:

'They are giving away free cucumbers, tomatoes, and persimmons from a car. We took some, you go get some'.

A woman left later than the others. She returned with only a bunch of cilantro.

'What, there was nothing else?' they asked her sympathetically.

'Yes, I was late ... They said they might bring some more tomorrow. But they don't know for sure'.

'Take some of mine', someone handed her a few tomatoes.

'What are you saying!'

'Take them! I have enough'.

'And take some from me', someone else was already sharing their cucumbers.

It's my turn. And a long wait among such group of people doesn't bother me anymore".

"Backwardness" — High Intellectual Capacity

Intelligence is a property of each individual but not of a nation as a whole. To claim that some people are more intellectual and some "didn't make it" means taking the stance of the author of *Mein Kampf* or the idiots in the Ku Klux Klan.

However, intelligence is not only an innate quality. It also depends on the influence of the surrounding environment. Ukrainian history, it would seem, was not conducive to forming a community of high intellect: literature appeared late among Ukrainians; the economy was always lagging; and science never offered any particularly special achievements. Examples of the expression of Ukrainian intellectual production among world-class masterpieces can easily be counted on the fingers of one hand.

Ukrainians have not given much to the world in this respect. But it was they who formed Russia in their time. Actually, the Russian Empire emerged as a great power only after Ukraine became part of it. In the seventeenth to the eighteenth centuries, Ukrainian intellect simply colonized Muscovy in what historians have called a south Slavic influence. Before that, the backward state of Muscovy had no educational institution equal to that of the Kyiv-Mohyla Academy, and there were no teachers who knew Latin and Greek, history, ancient literature, and theology. Peter I remarked: "Our priests do not know literacy that much ... I wish they... were sent to study in the schools of Kyiv ...".

When, in the first half of the 17th century, it was decided to carry out church reform in Muscovy, there was nowhere to acquire "intellect" from except Kyiv. And Muscovy took everything they could from Ukraine. There was a period in the history of the Kyiv-Mohyla Academy when its graduates were not allowed to work in Ukraine. It was a colossal brain drain, including public figures, scientists, clergy, all those who brought education and culture to Russia. As Professor Ohienko has written, the Ukrainian influence on Muscovy, whether Russians want to admit it or not, was evident in architecture, painting, clothing, songs, music, traditions, literature, and even the Muscovite language itself. This may be why it is so unbearably bitter for modern Russia to admit that they lost Ukraine.

In 2022, Europeans were impressed by Ukrainian refugees' high level of education. They did not expect that about 50% of Ukrainians have university degrees when in Germany the figure is only 21%. Many Ukrainians (though still fewer than Germans, Swiss, and Scandinavians) speak English fluently, have excellent computer skills, and are familiar with graphic design, management, marketing, and programming. This presented a striking contrast compared with other immigrants. According to NATO instructors, Ukrainian gunners need less time to learn how to use the latest high-precision weaponry than gunners from other countries.

Charisma

"No man is a prophet in his homeland" is a universal archetype. However, it has taken root in the Ukrainian mentality. The provincial psycho-culture sees dazzling individuality as a source of evil and strives to eliminate it. This is probably the reason why active Ukrainians had more chance of achieving success not in their homeland but outside of it. Nevertheless, Ukraine has birthed a constellation of charismatic personalities.

Ivan Mazepa (1687–1709), hetman of the Zaporozhian Army, became a hero in the works by Byron, Pushkin, Hugo, and Voltaire. Three operas are dedicated to him. Liszt created a symphony in his honor. And Tchaikovsky wrote several musical compositions based on him. Delacroix, Repin, and Vernet painted his portrait.

Alexander Bezborodko (1747–1799), the son of a Zaporozhian Cossack, managed Russia's foreign policy during the reign of Catherine II, later became state chancellor, and had the title of count of the Holy Roman Empire conferred on him. His career was not the result of the favoritism customary at the imperial court — he won all his titles thanks to his unique memory, hard work, knowledge, sharp mind, and, last but not least, charisma. In his palace near St. Petersburg, he assembled a unique collection of paintings by European artists, which later became part of the Hermitage Museum.

Field Marshal Ivan Paskevich was the most talented commander in the Russian Empire for nearly thirty years. The troops under his command were victorious in four wars: against Persia,

Turkey, Poland, and Hungary. Only after his death, Russian historians discovered, to their surprise, that the man whose name served as a symbol of Russia's military glory was Ukrainian on his father's side and Belarusian on his mother's.

Yuriy Kulchytsky, a Zaporozhian Cossack, and a hero of the European-Turkish war of 1683 founded the first coffee house in Vienna. At first, few people drank that coffee because of its bitter taste. People visited the café not for its coffee but to see the legendary hero. When Kulchytsky started adding sugar and a little milk to the coffee, his establishment could no longer fit everyone, and he had to look for several more locations. Thanks to a charismatic Ukrainian, the tradition of coffee drinking spread throughout Europe.

Lev Bronshtein, better known as Leon Trotsky, a native of the what is today the Kirovohrad region, did everything to turn the world upside down. By the way, he almost succeeded.

A resident of Kyiv, Golda Meir, was the prime minister of Israel from 1969 to 1974. She led her country through its most challenging times.

The Soviet leaders Nikita Khrushchev, Leonid Brezhnev, and Mikhail Gorbachev all had Ukrainian roots.

Modern Ukrainians do not lack charisma: among them are the soccer players Oleh Blokhin and Andriy Shevchenko; world boxing champions Volodymyr and Vitali Klitschko; Presidents Volodymyr Zelensky and Petro Poroshenko. . . .

There are just too many to mention them all!

Echoes of Forgotten Ailments

The previous chapters of this book might give the impression that a Ukrainian resembles an angel: cheerful, intelligent, emotional, if only moderately hardworking, but s/he sings well. It appears that it is not Ukrainians who should apply to be part of the EU, but on the contrary, the European community should persuade Ukrainians to join this commonwealth.

However, while sincerely accepting Ukrainian refugees, Europe is in no hurry to grant Ukraine EU membership. There are, of course, reasons for this: Ukrainian corruption, economic instability, low GDP, and, last but not least, the war.

But it is not just that. Raised on the archetypes of Ancient Rome, it is not easy for Europe to include Ukrainians in its community because Ukrainians are a modernized version of Hellenic revelers with fully mastered socio-psychological traits. An aesthete indulging in merrymaking, a supporter of long conversations, and helpless when it comes to making important decisions, a Ukrainian presents a challenge for Europe, a challenge to predictability, stability, and boredom.

Well, let's consider the "other side of the moon" — those features of Ukrainians of which they should hardly be proud.

Provincialism

Ukraine is a provincial country. The fact that it is located within Europe does not change anything since provinciality is not only a geographical concept but also a mental one.

No one is in any hurry in the provinces. Everything happens by inertia there, as if by itself. The speed of thinking is also slowed down. The rate of speech can be an indicator: the Italians, British, French, Spaniards, and Americans speak much faster than Ukrainians. Unlike Paris, New York, and London, Kyiv is a leisurely, cozy, and calm place, where life proceeds according to the principle "more haste, less speed".

In general, Ukrainian provincialism is not too different from the provincialism of the Austrians, Finns, Canadians, Swiss, Hungarians, or other leisurely peoples. Why, then, is the economy in those countries flexible and dynamic? Because in those countries, people do not pretend to work, they actually work hard.

It would be wrong to consider the concept of provinciality as an entirely negative phenomenon. It also forms such qualities as openness, sincerity, good-naturedness, friendliness, and sentimentality. The provincial's highest values are stable work, family well-being, and the comfort of their little world. These values are generally similar in Ukraine and in the West.

And how about Russia? A Russian wants to live in a world where his country dominates over others and is sincerely indignant when s/he sees someone living for their own sake. Russia's colonization of Ukraine led to Ukraine's loss of appreciation of its own uniqueness and significance for the world. This doomed the country to a provincial path of development. The bearers of such a worldview created a society "fixated" on itself and devoid of globalism.

But times are changing. Ukraine has felt its importance to the world, and the world has felt Ukraine's role in the fight against chaos and darkness.

Conservatism

The structure of a provincial society includes features such as stubbornness, lack of trust, irony, and rejection of everything new. Is that good or bad? Of course, it is bad in some ways, although we are determined not to evaluate anything on this scale. It so happens that in agrarian societies, efforts are not focused on searching for something new but on preserving what already exists. A conservative approach is always more intrinsic to a closed natural economy where only what is necessary for the life of the family is produced.

We can give many examples to show that the inability to keep up with the development of humanity brought nothing but harm to Ukrainians. On the other hand, conservatism helped Ukraine survive and maintain its identity, preserving its language, culture, and view of life.

Ukrainians' way of thinking remained conservative and essentially pre-Christian-pagan, with its respect for nature, as well as its propensity for magic and sorcery. Even the names of the months, which have nothing to do with generally accepted ones, have remained pre-Christian and not based on the Latin.

The Inability for Strategic Planning

For a stable existence, a country needs to carefully calculate the sequence of actions to ensure economic efficiency for its present and future. It is apparent that both the current and previous leadership of Ukraine never prioritized this logic and only had current affairs on their agenda. Hence Ukraine has the worst economic conditions among European countries.

One might think that Ukrainian politicians were not interested in any changes at all. They try to preserve what exists, which ensures them a place in the sun. If you ask Ukrainian deputies, ministers, or cultural figures their thoughts, not about the current problems in their field, but about the future of Ukraine in the broader context of world civilization, they may not understand what you want from them.

Both the Ukrainian government and Ukrainian society have little concern for strategic planning. National television offers no discussion about how Ukrainians would like to see their country in five, ten, or twenty-five years. Anyone who starts a conversation about it hears in response: "Hold on, we will talk about that later, right now we should be solving urgent issues". It seems that Ukrainians are not particularly interested in thinking beyond the affairs of the day, seeing everything globally, and calmly calculating how to move forward.

Low Self-Esteem

Ukrainians' inability to plan strategically is not an accident. For centuries, Ukrainians were concerned not about the quality of life but about survival, perseverance, and endurance in the face of adversity. This also led to developing low self-esteem.

To a large extent, small salaries and pensions aid in maintaining this quality. A poor man cannot be confident. Timidity, obsessive reflections about one's personality, and other inferiority complex symptoms characterize such a man.

Ukrainians are a unique nation. They don't give a damn about their talents. Only a tiny segment of the population has heard anything about Yuri Kondratyuk, whose name is engraved in gold in the International Space Hall of Fame. Few have any idea about six fellow countrymen who won the Nobel Prize. Not many can name even one Ukrainian listed in the Guinness Book of Records.

Günter Grass wrote a novel about the Odesa submarine commander Oleksandr Marinesko, glorifying the brave sailor before the whole world. By order of Winston Churchill, a monument was erected to him in Britain during his lifetime. In Ukraine, there were only isolated articles about him in the press and a few programs on television.

Serhiy Parajanov's film *Shadows of Forgotten Ancestors* won twenty-eight prizes at film festivals in twenty-one countries. However, following worldwide triumph, the copyright holders of this film at the Dovzhenko Film Studio in Kyiv burned all copies.

Oleh Blokhin, one of the best football players in Europe and the winner of the UEFA Golden Ball of 1975 had trouble finding a job in Ukraine for a long time. When the Ukrainian national team under his leadership reached the finals of the World Cup in 2005, it was supposed to become a sensation, a national holiday, and the number one news on all Ukrainian TV channels. Indeed, this event became the number one news item on the BBC. In Ukraine, a mention of it appeared at the end of a news release. And President Yushchenko conveyed congratulations to the team and the coach via a third party.

Is the inferiority complex a specifically Ukrainian phenomenon? Certainly not. Only it manifests itself differently in other nationalities. Even if he knows English, a Frenchman will most likely respond to a tourist in French. A Japanese man secretly adds poison to canned goods. English football fans prove their "superiority" by fighting with the fans of other teams. The Russians rejoice when their missiles hit theaters, maternity hospitals, and train stations in Ukraine. These examples (the list could go on and on) are indicators of the same inferiority complex.

Ukraine participates in space flights. It maintains a good reputation in metallurgical and chemical production, heavy engineering, and the production of large transport aircraft. The country leads in the production of high-quality natural food products. However, because of their modesty, delicacy, and tendency to self-indulgence, Ukrainians still habitually perceive themselves as provincials.

The Russo-Ukrainian war changed the attitude of Ukrainians to themselves in many ways and, surprisingly, raised their self-esteem. During the war, a joke circulated in Ukrainian social media: "It's hard to be Ukrainian. In addition to protecting their territory, they also had to think about how to overthrow the dictatorial regimes in Russia and Belarus, how to ensure that Americans do not get disappointed in their president, that nothing disturbed the sleep of Europeans, and they needed to find a way to export their grain to the world market so that, God forbid, Africans do not starve".

Echoes of Communist Upbringing

Sociological surveys provide accurate data about the number of Ukrainians, Russians, and Tatars living in Ukraine . . . But no survey can say how many "Soviet" and "non-Soviet" people lived in Ukraine in the first-quarter of the 21st century.

During the Stalinist repressions in the Soviet Union, a course was taken to destroy the best strata of the population: wealthy peasants, the clergy, the intelligentsia, and all those who did not want to uproot mental traits that failed to conform to the type *Homo Sovieticus*. The regime persecuted proactive citizens who critically perceived reality, thus threatening the authorities. This "Darwinian" selection allowed the survival of only those who managed to adapt to the demands of communist schizophrenia in this witch hunt. A Soviet individual considered denunciations, embezzlement, immorality, and drunkenness to be the norm of life.

The experiments of that time inflicted a tangible blow on all the nationalities that were part of the Soviet Union and eroded in its citizens a sense of responsibility for their future and the future of the state. People who continue to be defined by the archetypes of the Soviet man still cannot adequately perceive the realities of life. They expect "justice", the authorities' extraordinary attention to them, general equality, and the implementation of other ideological mantras of communism.

A resident of a totalitarian state constantly creates secrets, hides something, and tries to "deceive" the state. Ukrainian businesspeople, of course, need European markets. However, many are ignorant about the rules of conducting business according to the Western model rather than the Soviet one. They find the introduction of civilized norms of life unacceptable as it destroys the system of relationships familiar to them, one grounded not in compliance to rules but in corruption.

The Soviet period was more than the horror of the "Evil Empire". After all, the citizens of the USSR could afford a carefree attitude about their future. However, there was no escape from duplicitous morality, sloppiness, cronyism, general rudeness, disrespect for people, and full-blown alcoholism.

Soviet psycho-culture embraced the microcosm of the communal apartment, comfortable for children with their urge to socialize, free candy, and waiting for cartoons on the TV. The childhood of some parts of the Ukrainian population was delayed for too long. It is surprising that both the elderly and young people, for some reason, try to live according to the barracks-style socialist norms and strive to instill these norms into the adult life of the new state. They nurture "Soviet" traits in every possible way, fundamentally contradicting the Ukrainian mentality. These include helplessness, the habit of not being self-sufficient, and reliance on some babysitter in the person of some good president who will come and change the light bulb in the hallway.

After all, the Ukrainian mentality is the topic of this book. And the shadow of the Iron Curtain is something both imposed and ephemeral. In 2021, decommunization occurred in Ukraine: communist monuments were dismantled, and streets were renamed. Decommunization also marked the Ukrainians' perception of surrounding reality.

Naivety, Infantility

Ukraine was always abundant in fertile land. This explains the lack of competitive struggle for the distribution of earthly goods from the life credo of the agricultural tribes that lived in the Ukrainian territories. When aggression does not condition survival, a person becomes kind and friendly, yet, at the same time, naïve and trusting. Sensitive and soft with his or her feminine soul, delicate taste, and aesthetic rejection of evil, a Ukrainian would perhaps be the happiest person in the world if humanity consisted only of like-minded people. Childishly perceiving life, s/he believes in beauty, truth, and nobility.

However, the world is not made this way. And once Ukrainians' natural candor collides with the realities of the "law of the jungle", painful discomfort ensues. Instead of resolving the situation in their favor, they simply try to ignore it. Like inconsistent children not used to choosing a clear line of behavior, they will weigh things for a long time, contemplate, consider options, combine them, and examine issues from different angles. They do all this with the sole purpose of not making any decisions at all. Even knowing the adverse consequences, they nonchalantly build castles in the air, procrastinate until the last moment, and then lift their arms in surprise: oh, how did this happen? Lost in daydreaming, they would rather be disadvantaged than leave their fairy tale for the space of cruel civilization—God willing, somehow, it will all work out.

This archetype—"somehow it will all work out"—occupies one of the critical places in the Ukrainian mentality. The blind hope inherent in the Slavic worldview was in Ukrainians transformed into an algorithm eulogized by the classics of national literature, such as Lesya Ukrainka's "Contra spem spero"—"I hope against hope". Hoping everything will somehow work out, a Ukrainian escapes into his or her world, avoiding solving pressing problems.

This is exactly what happened on the eve of the invasion of Russian troops into Ukraine: the West repeatedly warned the leadership of Ukraine about Moscow's plans but heard a childish answer in response: "Don't exaggerate; this won't happen".

Such thinking does not fit into the context of global norms, as serious difficulties have repeatedly marked the relations of Ukrainians with the West. Passivity and introversion are transformed in a Ukrainian into the avoidance of solving one's own problems. Social inertia, conservatism, reluctance to take risks, and the desire for isolation become severe obstacles to individual and state development.

During the war, Ukrainians found common ground with the West, realizing that they should rely on themselves first. Fewer and fewer Ukrainians cherish the infantile hope that should Ukraine, as it is, join the EU, all problems would suddenly disappear.

Carelessness

The ancestors of Ukrainians always lacked the patience to perform their work well. And today, no matter what a Ukrainian does, it rarely meets world standards. No wonder that there is a popular joke in Ukraine that the Japanese, they say, prefer children to anyone in Ukraine. Everything that Ukrainians do with their hands turns out badly.

The entire system of modern Ukrainian education is traditionally oriented to raising dilletantes. As in Soviet times, an outstanding student is considered what they call in Ukrainian a "white crow" (odd duck). A "normal" student pretends to be learning. And then goofs off at work, working according to the principle "I work according to my paycheck". But therein lies a paradox: even when someone is ready to pay a Ukrainian according to Western standards, they will still work as they did before. They cannot do otherwise. Any Ukrainian construction worker can write a doctoral thesis on how to make repairs. Only s/he will not be able to do a repair properly. Even more, given a promised timeframe, the difference between three months and three years is insignificant for him or her. This is true not only for construction workers but also for politicians, policemen, and soccer players . . .

Are Ukrainians ready to pay such a price for their equal presence in the EU and start working in a European manner? They are. Many changes have taken place over the past decades. Currently, the quality of Ukrainian food products is in many respects superior to European ones; the system of private medicine is no worse than in European countries (and in some places even better); every tenth captain employed in EU long-distance shipping companies is a Ukrainian. The Ukrainian Nova Poshta mail service has no parallel in other countries for the speed of work and low prices of their services. The Ukrainian-made Neptune missile system sank what was considered unsinkable: the flagship of the Russian fleet, the cruiser *Moskva*. More than a million Ukrainians working at factories in Poland, Hungary, and the Czech Republic perform their work well.

A Closed Nature among One's Group

The closed nature of the structure of a clan of relatives characterizes the East. One cannot choose relatives. However, one can choose buddies, friends, and godparents for kids. Nepotism is an ancient Ukrainian tradition in both the narrow and broad sense of the word. In the Ukrainian worldview, even an incompetent friend is better than someone promising but not from among one's own friends—it is customary to distribute positions and cushy jobs in Ukraine through an acquaintance. After the Revolution of Dignity in 2014, a number of highly professional foreigners were invited into Ukrainian government service, yet they did not last long in their positions.

Those who have cushy jobs or are in power will inevitably get together in a micro group of like-minded individuals. They usually do not care how hypothetical "others" live. All their actions are primarily aimed at satisfying the interests of the members of their group and their microcosmic world. In Ukraine, these rules of the game apply in every sphere, including business, production, and everyday life. Even in the artistic field of opera: instead of top performers, who are abundant in Ukraine, mediocre young women appear on stage "through connections". Consequently, in the National Opera, the viewer sees a product stuck in the past somewhere around the launch of the first artificial satellite. Performers who do not want to build their careers through nepotism have no choice but to look for creative self-realization abroad. Many, such as Olga Bezsmertna (Olha Bessmertna), have done so.

Lack of Purposefulness

A Ukrainian is not used to working for the future, whether in personal life or the government. By and large, s/he rarely tries to finish what s/he started. In this sense, his or her worldview is closer to the Eastern one, which gravitates toward self-sufficient contemplation, than to the Western one, which is based on rational action.

Purposeful activity does not characterize a Ukrainian intellectual either: universal thinkers, they accumulate a wealth of knowledge from various fields. But their universal nature does not benefit society as it lacks a sense of reality and practical meaning. Sooner or later, their thoughts become intellectual chewing gum, incompatible with the dynamics of the time. Their experience and knowledge are directed toward discussions "of everything and anything", fruitless "roundtables", and useless TV debates. Their innovative ideas find response only in a narrow circle of friends. Self-absorbed, they wait for recognition all their life without making any efforts toward self-realization and suffer from a lack of popularity and a "loser complex". Ukrainian reasoning works well in extraordinary and problematic situations. But where routine work is required, it lacks drama and is bored without a fairy tale.

Disrespect for the Law, Anarchy

Physics is the only sphere of life in Ukraine where laws are still enforced.
An anecdote

Disrespect for the law is also rooted in national historical algorithms. Unlike in Europe, where since the time of the Roman Empire, the attitude toward the law has been "Dura lex sed lex" (the law is cruel, but it is the law), in Ukrainian lands, the concept of legality has never been respected. Arbitrariness was the basis of the life of the Cimmerians, Scythians, and Sarmatians. The Northern Black Sea Hellenes shared a similar lack of respect for the law; the Kyivan-Byzantine psycho-culture lionized the criminal. The Zaporozhian Cossacks had their own unwritten code of honor.

In the Soviet Union, the communist elite always tried to adapt the "law" to its needs. After once communicating with law enforcement agencies, the citizens of the USSR inferred that it was better to stay away from those agencies. Under such conditions, people believed that breaking the law was not shameful but even prestigious. After all, the law, in society's view, is the food of bureaucrats, swindlers, and bribe-takers.

To some extent, similar sentiments exist in Ukraine even now. For Europeans, lawlessness immediately raises a red flag. Ukrainians are often indifferent to it. As before, they consider non-compliance with the law to be the "norm": they park on the sidewalks, use "pirated" computer programs, and know how to find a way to "approach" judges. Hardly a single enterprise in

Ukraine conducts business in full compliance with the law. In the context of the rampant corruption that has marked recent years, not a single high corrupt official has been brought to justice. In Ukraine, the feminist protest group Femida works like commercial fishing on the Discovery channel: catch — show — release.

Ukraine applied to join the European Union. The EU requested that Ukraine reorganize its economic and judicial systems according to European practices. Hopefully, this will fundamentally change the situation.

However, the situation already started changing even without the influence of the EU. In April 2022, when a certain number of enterprises were not working because of the war, tax collection plan exceeded the previous norm in Ukraine. This happened due to the cancellation of several senseless audits and regulations that pressured businesses.

Inconsistency, a Striving to "Serve Two Masters"

We have already mentioned the inconsistency and cunning of the Ukrainian character and the reasons that explain these characteristics — they were necessary to deceive the invaders. "They are extremely treacherous and unfaithful in keeping an agreement; if they decide something together, they immediately violate the terms of what has been agreed upon", Mauricius wrote about the Eastern Slavs.

Slavic chaos, Scythian treachery, and Byzantine intrigue organically ended up in the Ukrainian mental soil, adding some nuances.

The desire to serve two masters at the same time or to dance at two different weddings at the same time characterizes Ukrainians. As the Ukrainian folk saying goes, the fox with just one entrance to its den is unfortunate.

Lack of Curiosity

The most important places in the world are filled with Chinese tourists. There is no question about the Europeans', Americans', or Japanese mobility. A Ukrainian has a sluggish disposition. This is not because of a half-empty wallet. The reason is that travel is separate from the nation's worldview, which is tied to the land. And that's why a Ukrainian, like an old fox who can't be lured out of the forest, doesn't travel much and doesn't understand why tourists flock to its "forest".

It is difficult to surprise a Ukrainian. S/he is not very interested in what does not concern him/her or his/her "house". Ukrainian mass media are focused only on local events. During a European book exhibition, an entire room may be packed for a meeting with some Albanian or Bosnian writer, of whose existence no one had any idea. People wonder what s/he would say. But a Ukrainian is as indifferent to what any Nobel laureate will say as to who will win the elections in Paraguay.

Lack of Attention to Health

Thanks to the mild climate and organic produce, the health of Ukrainians is relatively good. Death under sixty is often caused not by diseases but by accidents, poisoning, or injuries. This is not surprising: Ukrainians rarely use seat belts, are indifferent to workplace safety regulations, get back on their feet after an illness, and smoke excessively.

However, Ukrainians' disdain for health occupies an intermediate position between the attitude of Europeans and Russians to their physical well-being: in Europe, where it is simply shameful to show indifference to one's health, the mortality in the 24–64 age group in 2003 was 350 per 100,000; in Ukraine, it was 890; in Russia, it was 1,200.

Amorous Adventurism

With their archetypal polygamy, Eastern Slavs developed a very tolerant attitude to adultery. Erotic fervor has been prominent throughout the entire history of Ukraine.

This was not accidental. The lack of men due to military campaigns meant that a woman could not always find the love of her life and was forced to settle down with someone. However, she would often look for a better suitor on the side who, in her opinion, was a more worthy representative of the opposite sex.

The Bolsheviks' axiom that wives should be shared did not arise out of nowhere; it appeared on fertile mental soil and took root in the subconscious of Russians and Ukrainians. Ukrainian women keep their wedding rings in their jewelry boxes, and if they wear them, they don't wear them on the left hand "closer to the heart", as is customary all over the world, but, for some reason, on the right hand. And, frankly speaking, to a Ukrainian Casanova, a wedding ring is not a deterrent; quite the opposite.

While in the Western world, a married woman is addressed as Frau-Madame-Mrs. followed by her husband's last name, and an unmarried woman is addressed as Fräulein-Mademoiselle-Miss, the Polish-Ukrainian address "*Pani*" (Ms. or Mrs.) ignores a woman's marital status altogether, and this form of address can be used both for married and unmarried women.

When a European woman marries, she sometimes loses not only her maiden name but also her first name. For example, in Hungary, if a certain Zhuzha becomes the wife of Kovacs Sandor, then from that time on, she is Kovacs Sandorne, and the name of Zhuzha disappears both from her passport and in any reference to her. The same system not so long ago (Madame Charles de Gaulle) also existed in France. The American pop star Tina Turner, who lives in Switzerland, is addressed by the local residents, who are well aware of who she is, by her husband's last name as "Frau Schultz".

There is more flexibility in Ukrainian customs. If you ask a Ukrainian woman if she has a married friend who has never had a lover, she will most likely answer: "Well ... Yes, I do have one!"

Russian Mentality and How It Differs from the Ukrainian

Suppose we follow a generally accepted formula and single out two traits in each nationality. In that case, it may turn out that the Englishman is proud and tenacious, the Italian is pious and talkative, the Frenchman is refined and capricious, the German is punctual and thrifty, and the Ukrainian is kind-hearted and cunning. And what attributes characterize a Russian, then?

In this book, I have not attempted to provide a comprehensive answer to the nature of the Russian mentality. My emphasis is on the differences between Russians and Ukrainians, which are significant. In describing these differences, I aim to avoid the temptation to judge what is negative and what is positive. After all, there is no "good-bad" scale in psychology. Even such Russian traits as assertiveness, aggressiveness, cruelty, and imperial thinking would be erroneously interpreted as "bad". Perhaps these traits, unlike Ukrainian naivety and romanticism, allowed the Russians to create a huge state, conquer Siberia, defeat the armies of Charles XII, the Ottoman Empire, and Napoleon, and create geniuses of literature and art.

Russians cherish the myth that finding the key to their character is impossible. How many authoritative voices have declared that the Russian soul is a great unsolved mystery. That is, the Russian people are different from everyone else.

But indeed, they are different from everyone else! Just like the Americans, English, Italians, Japanese, or any other nation. And the assertion that the Russian people cannot be measured with a "common *arshin*" (an old unit of measure), in Fyodor Tiutchev's four-line poem,[19] is nothing other than a mantra of Russian propaganda.

In the 21st century, Russians have come under the powerful attack of Kremlin propaganda. Adopting the narratives of Hitler's Germany, Putin's Russia turned into an aggressive fascist state. However, it is not worth considering the mentality of the population of this country only from the point of view of the influence of the barbaric Nazi ideology. The German nation is not a reflection of Hitler's thoughts. Similarly, the Russian nation is not a reflection of Putin's thoughts.

Let's consider what is attractive and what is less attractive in the "mysterious" Russian soul.

Nation, Territory, Nature

There are many theories about the origins of the Russian people. That's why many things remain unclear. Most scholars believe that

---

19 "You can't understand Russia rationally,/You can't measure it with a common measure:/It has a special character –/In Russia you can only believe" (1866).

while the tribes of Eastern Slavs formed the basis of the Ukrainian nation, the northern tribes that inhabited the lands from the Urals to the Baltic Sea in the tenth to the thirteenth centuries became the basis of the Russian nation. In his book *Historical Portraits*, the Russian historian Vasyly Klyuchevsky (1841–1911) writes: "Finnish tribes settled among the forests and swamps of central and northern Russia at a time when there was no evidence of the presence of Slavs there. The influence of these tribes comprises the ethnographic core of the question about the origin of the Great Russian tribe which was formed from a mixture of Slavic and Finnish elements. . . . Our Russian physiognomy does not quite accurately reproduce Slavic features and is most likely attributed to Finnish influence".

The maturation of the community that we know as Russians began with the emergence of the Moscow principality in 1263, which was never part of Kyivan Rus. Due to the climatic features of the region, this principality was created at the discretion of emigrants from the lands of Kyiv, who, having absorbed a considerable amount of Finnish blood, acquired, as the Ukrainian historian Mykhailo Hrushevsky claims, a number of qualities, such as lethargy, lack of initiative, and submissiveness to violence.

Peter the Great significantly strengthened the state and "opened a window to Europe". In 1721, he ordered Muscovy to be renamed "Russia". "However, what happened was not what the haughty Peter wanted: Elegant and strong, Russia did not join the banquet of great powers. But, pulled by Peter I by its hair, bathed in blood, and maddened by horror and despair, it appeared before its new relatives as pitiful and unequal—as a slave. And no matter how much the Russian cannons thundered menacingly, it so happened that the great country, stretching from the Vistula to the Great Wall of China, was enslaved and humiliated in front of the whole world", wrote the Russian writer Aleksei Tolstoy in his book *Peter I*.

Most of the territory of Russia comprises forests, swamps, the taiga (coniferous forests), and barren tundra. This area is not suitable for agriculture. And from the land where something can grow, the yield is poor. Low cloud cover, heavy precipitation, and the darkening engendered by thick forest do not foster the formation of cheerfulness among the local inhabitants. Instead, they give rise to melancholy, suspicion, a sense of threat and fear. "Sad, harsh, monotonous nature could not [...] develop in man a sense of beauty, a desire to beautify their life, to raise it above everyday mundane monotony", wrote Russian historian and rector of Moscow University Sergei Solovyov (1820–1879). "The very landscape of Russia itself," Professor of History Alexander Yanov at the University of California wrote, "marked the Russian soul with its monotony. The endless gray plain, the endless stretch of changing waters, and the gray, gloomy northern sky do not promote inner individuality, and the song of Volga fishermen or barge haulers is monotonous, colorless, and sad, like nature. The emptiness of space flows into the emptiness of a human being".

Foreign tourists are struck by the wall of gloomy and joyless Russian faces they encounter on the streets and public transportation. Foreigners who visit Russia for an extended period become much gloomier than they were before.

The Cult of the Tsar

In the Russian mentality, one of the fundamental features is the cult of the tsar. The faith of the illiterate people in God, the tsar, and the state has been absorbed with mother's milk since ancient times; it is not imposed; it is inherent, all-pervasive.

The cult of the ruler is an inherently Eastern tradition. The Moscow princes were vassals of the Mongol-Tatar khans for almost five hundred years and adopted from them a manner of behavior based on the despotic centralization of power in the hands of a single person. Starting from the 13th century, Tatar ways were introduced everywhere in Moscow lands, including the administration, courts, ways of collecting tribute, and dealings with ordinary people. Any attempts to build life on the initiative of the people were brutally suppressed. "The persecution of everything independent, everything that was not Russified started a long time ago; it became the political essence of Muscovy many hundreds of years ago. It penetrated the blood of the Great Russian statesman and was always particularly visible at an everyday level", writes Volodymyr Bilinsky in his book *The Moksel Country, or Muskovy*.

The nature of the Horde has taken over the soul of a Muscovite to a great extent, and entered the flesh and blood of all too many Russians. Such traits as personal devotion to the sovereign, avoidance of dissent, encouragement of denunciations, and the desire for military expansion have always been a part of the Russian mentality.

Despite the loyalty to the sovereign, in Russia, the government and the people have always opposed each other. Expecting goodness, help, and support from their ruler, Russians usually associated the injustice around them with the sovereign. The people lived expecting both the next handout and the next swindle. Russian humorist Viktor Shenderovych remarked: "When the government turned its face to a person, that person screamed in terror".

And until now, a Russian "screams in terror" while continuing the tradition of supporting his or her "tsar", regardless of the latter's idiotic actions.

Russia has either a strong authoritarian government or none at all. The president has no problems with parliamentarians: the latter will unanimously vote for any of his whims. State policymaking in Russia consists of off-the-record agreements between the ruler and a handful of his confidants. Or just the perverted will of a single paranoid person such as Lenin, Stalin, or Putin.

The Archetype of the Iron Fist — Aggressiveness and Cruelty

As in the Mongol-Tatar Horde, cruelty has always characterized power in Russia. Horrified by state atrocities, the people still recognized the right of the state to be that way, too. According to them, you can't run a home, a community, or a state without ruthlessness (*krutost'*).

Polish historian Kazimierz Waliszewski (1849–1935) described Ivan the Terrible's capture of Novgorod as follows: "On Friday, January 6, Ivan himself arrived with his son and the Streltsy [the units of Russian guardsmen from the sixteenth to the early eighteenth centuries]. He ordered them to beat all the monks with sticks until they died ... In the following days, the terror reached terrifying proportions ... Citizens were brought in by the hundreds, tortured, burned on a small fire in various sophisticated ways, then almost all were sentenced to death by drowning ... Babies were tied to their mothers and drowned. The Oprichniks stood with spears on boats and watched, ensuring that no one escaped ... In all, 60,000 people died ... And when Ivan had no one left to kill, he turned his rage on inanimate objects. With particular cruelty, he attacked the monastery first ... All the shops in the city and the surrounding area, including houses, were looted and completely destroyed".

The violence of the rulers is an imprint of the customs that have been an integral part of Russian life for centuries. Ruthlessness, cruelty, and the boundless right of the strong comprise archetypes that formed a collective consciousness with little room left for philanthropy and forgiveness. Even holidays in the Russian hinterland necessarily include fist fights.

Unjustified violence is prominent in all Russian literature: an axe to the head for cash? This is "normal" for Russians.

Speaking about the 20th century, the Russian writer Maxim Gorky noted: "Russian cruelty has not changed; its very forms have remained the same. A chronicler wrote at the beginning of the 17th century about the torture of his era: they put gunpowder in the mouth and set it on fire; alternatively, they put it in a man's rectum. In 1918–1919, the same practice was used on the Don River and in the Urals: they blew up unfortunate men by inserting dynamite into their buttocks ... If this cruelty were only a manifestation of the perverse psychology of some individuals, it would not be worth talking about as it would be a topic for psychiatry, not morality. But I am talking about the collective enjoyment of suffering. Who is crueler — the Red armies or the White? They are equally cruel because they are both Russians".

Aggressiveness is still one of the leading Russian state principles. Mutilated Ukrainians in Bucha; tortured and then raped teenage girls in Borodyanka; tortured babies in Irpin . . . This happens everywhere where the so-called "Russian World" goes. "Kill the Ukrainian fascists!" Russian mothers instruct their sons in captured cellphone conversations. And the sons obediently kill.

"They drove into the village and immediately rushed to the yards", recalls a woman, who did not wish to disclose her name, about the behavior of Russian soldiers in the Ukrainian village they captured in 2022:

"They shot at the windows. Windows were falling like church bells. When they broke into the house, I shouted that we were Russians, that we were waiting for them, that we were believers of the Moscow Patriarchate, that my mother belonged to the church parish, and that the priest knew her.

They shot my mother immediately. They pulled me by the hair. They wanted to eat, drink, and have sex.

It lasted for five days. I wanted to die, but I couldn't because I was tied up. Besides me, there were two neighbors and another girl. She once was a beautiful blonde. Now she has one open wound and hematomas. But it didn't bother them.

These were not the Buryats. They had typical Muscovite traits and were proud of being from Moscow. There was a major, two lieutenants, and three soldiers.

That girl begged them to kill her. She was silent, she begged with her eyes. She could not speak. And she died that night. And I couldn't...

And death was near. It spoke to me. Death. And it said that it was not mine... And they said that I was not Russian but a fucking Banderite.[20] There was a photo of my daughter and granddaughter on the mantelpiece. They asked where the husband and son-in-law were. I did not say that my son-in-law was in the Armed Forces. But my neighbor said that and promised to show where rich people lived and those with military family members... She did that. And she was shot.

They robbed the house and everything that they could take along. They covered us with feces and left us raped and tied up.

I survived. But I'm not alive. Everything died in me. I feel dirty. Because that's how it is. My self died in me. The person who believed in goodness.

---

20 The English word for followers of Bandera.

I can't listen to the Russian language. It makes me sick. My parents are from Russia. They came to Ukraine as teachers in the 1960s. Mother was a Russian teacher. A Russian officer killed her.

He took pictures of my things in my house and consulted with his wife over the phone what he should take. He packed my dresses, makeup, pajamas, and underwear in a suitcase. He packed mother's wedding ring, rings, and earrings. He took my daughter's clothes and granddaughter's dolls . . .

They are not people. Inhumans. Degenerates. Freaks.

There are murderers and rapists in all countries of the world. But to normalize terror as state policy with the support of almost the entire population is a large-scale civilizational perversion. The Russians are now doing what they do best—being savages. During Soviet leader Mikhail Gorbachev's time, they pretended to be civilized. But Putin let them off their leash and allowed them to reveal their essential nature".

Statehood — Patriotism — Lack of Individual

Freedom "Russians need to put Cupid on their coat of arms".
"Why is that?"
"They are also naked, armed, and thrust themselves
upon everyone with their love".
Anecdote

One of the essential differences between Russian and Ukrainian mentalities is that Russians have been living in their own country for several centuries, while Ukrainians never had one. For a Russian, it is important "to have a great state".

But "statehood" is the state's right, or its rulers', to dominate a society in which a human being is a cog, a worm, a dung beetle. The Russian authorities never left their people alone. All the time they interfered in their lives and, using forceful methods, imposed on them the complex of an "eternal debtor". Suppressing the individual, it had ultimate control over its people. All strata of the population became dependent on it. If Kyivan Rus knew free merchants and craftsmen, then in the Moscow principality, it was hard to find a member of a free profession; people had various obligations before the state, and in case of need, they were forcibly transferred from one place to another.

Since the 16th century, serfdom gradually died out in Europe. In the Russian Empire, it only grew stronger. The enslavement of one's own citizens made it possible to create a powerful empire on a poor economic basis. The impoverished state, which was growing without end or limit, could develop only thanks to joint superpowers, forced labor, and terrible, senseless sacrifices. "[Alexander] Herzen said that Peter I was the first free person in Russia. You could not argue with him. The trouble is that Peter was the only free person in Russia; all the others, from the field marshal to the peasant, were, in fact, slaves", writes A. Gudzenko in the book *Russian Mentality*.

Russia is no different today.

Imperial Thinking — Breadth of Soul

Belonging to a great state is a compelling feeling. There haven't been too many empires in world history — Ancient Rome, Byzantium, the Golden Horde, Great Britain during the Great Colonization, the Ottoman Empire, the United States of America, and dozens more. Russia can be added to this list.

Imperialism as a phenomenon radically transforms the world. Unlike an ordinary country, an empire demands special internal tensions and spiritual maximalism from the national elite and every one of its citizens. Empire is a rejection of provincial thinking in favor of a sense of responsibility for the fate of the whole world.

Since the time of Peter I, Russia has claimed the title of a state with higher values than other countries. The essence of one of the Russian myths, which has since entered official ideology, is that Russia has a unique path. It believed itself to be the "third Rome", called to bring salvation to the world, to give answers to the most important questions of a humankind stuck in self-interest, to be a spiritual and cultural guide, a mediator between God and those who are bogged down in the impoverishment and worthlessness of existence. Not a group of intellectuals alone, but the entire country shared these ambitions.

On the one hand, such an approach is quite creative—what would Russian writers, composers, and artists have achieved without such "missionary work"? But on the other hand, the desire to save humanity expressed by the members of a society that adopted the customs of the Tatar-Mongol Horde is alarming.

In 1654 Muscovy began to colonize Ukraine. The policy of boyar-controlled Moscow was not much different from the policy typical of colonizers, and it was carried out through humiliation and with contempt for the non-Russian peoples that were part of it. Russians firmly knew that they were not some Little Russians (their pejorative term for Ukrainians) but Great Russians! And their language is great and powerful! And their soul! And thoughts! Being bullied by their own rulers, they considered it their duty to show the inhabitants of the territorial outskirts how, in their opinion, they should live. Colonizers always brought their language and traditions to their conquered territories. Russia was no exception, and having eviscerated Ukrainian culture, it brought its own to replace it.

"Imperial thinking" and "breadth of soul" are not identical concepts, but they are quite close. Both are related to the immeasurable expanses of the state—a Russian, forced to overcome vast distances, has to make both physical and spiritual efforts. S/he is prone to solving grand tasks. Careless in small matters, s/he will "move mountains" in big ones. S/he is unsatisfied with Western values such as a house, family, career, and bank account. S/he seeks to serve something grand, be it approaching the Kingdom of God, the exploration of space, or world communist revolution.

A Russian has a special relationship with time: s/he does not appreciate it, does not save it, and does not understand the meaning of the phrase "punctuality is a hallmark of kings". Self-discipline is not compatible with the rampage of his passions. Let's take it to the limits! If you drink, then drink hard! If you steal, then steal something big! If you beat someone up, then do your best! Only it does not apply to work.

Russians attach an exclusively positive meaning to the phrase "breadth of soul". However, the state, generosity, and scope of their impulses time and again lead to the imposition of their tastes, interests, and desires.

Russian rulers traditionally managed the country's economy according to the laws of the "breadth of soul": money spent on political projects exceeded budget funds allocated for education or health care by several times. "A soul with breadth should be narrowed down", one of the characters in Fyodor Dostoevsky's novel *The Brothers Karamazov* concludes.

And the "broad" Russian individual narrowed him-/herself down. Mykola Hohol (Nikolai Gogol) wrote a novel that caused a stir in Russia. Here is what he wrote: "The reason *Dead Souls* terrified Russia and made such a stir inside it was not that the novel revealed any of its wounds or internal diseases, and not because it offered terrible pictures of invincible evil and suffering of the innocent ... But the vulgarity of it all together petrified the readers. A Russian man was terrified by his own insignificance more than all other of his faults and shortcomings".

The entire civilized world also "narrowed Russian down": devastating economic sanctions were imposed on it for military aggression against Ukraine; sports teams were disqualified from participating in international championships; Russia was even expelled from the Eurovision Song Contest.

Selflessness vs. Corruption

Russians can tell you that the secret of their soul is its power of selflessness. Helping a neighbor, a Russian does not expect to profit from someone else's grief. To the contrary, s/he often acts to his or her own detriment. "To give away your last shirt" is a purely Russian phenomenon. A Ukrainian will also give away his "shirt", but he will always have another one.

And yet, sincerely helping a neighbor in trouble, a Russian, without thinking, would burn down his house if fortune would smile upon him.

Bribery is a universal phenomenon. It exists in many countries. But in Russia, this phenomenon has acquired an almost sacred meaning. The embezzlement of the state budget by a handful of oligarchs close to the president is a model for other Russians, who also steal everything they can get their hands on.

Corruption also exists in Ukraine. However, in trying to join the European Union, Ukraine is forced to undergo "training" by the EU to eliminate this defect. Maybe sooner or later, the civilized world will "train" Russia as well?

Morality and Disrespect for the Law

Catherine II, who ruled the Russian Empire from 1762 to 1796, uniquely shaped the Russian mentality. She instilled in Russia the idea that for a state career, it is less important to have intelligence or talent than to please the royal person in charge. Catherine was perfectly aware of the frauds perpetrated by her entourage, but she did not even try to deal with it. Emboldened by such leniency, her relatives stole with renewed enthusiasm, and the entire country followed their example. The empress corrupted not simply a dozen or so of her favorites but the entire Russian people, from lackeys to senators.

Along with the conviction that there is no sin in embezzling state property, another principle became customary in the Russian Empire: the judge always judges unjustly because he judges "justly" only when he receives a bribe. And the bigger the bribe, the "more righteously" will he judge.

There are two main characters in Russian fairy tales. The first is a fool and a "lucky guy" who embodies the happy deadbeat. The second is a thief. Even children's fairy tales claim that there is no sin in stealing from the rich. The main character of a modern Russian television series is a bandit for whom the Russian people show an overwhelming fondness. Criminal concepts have penetrated business, parliament, the fabric of relations between people, and, in fact, the very nature of Russian thinking. To this day, Russia is a country where an individual enjoys no guarantees, where the police are a semi-governmental and semi-private corporation of extortionists, and where deceiving a business partner is not shameful but a virtue.

Nobility vs. Contempt for Man

In past centuries, the nobility comprised a powerful stratum of Russian society. This added many positive features to the outlook of the entire nation. Noble families raised their children based on aristocratic ideals. Lofty values such as honor, bravery, enlightenment, and a heightened sense of self-worth formed such character traits as nobility, pride, and determination in boys, and sophistication, romanticism, and loyalty in girls.

On the other hand, such upbringing also instilled swagger, arrogance, inflated self-esteem, an exaggerated perception of one's worth, and contempt for representatives of the lower classes. Russian society was traditionally divided into strata that hated each other. The upper classes showed contempt for the lower classes, and the lower classes hated not only the upper classes, but even their own geniuses. For example, in 1918, peasants burned down the estate of their national poet Alexander Pushkin. They burned it while dancing and singing, not intending to rob it—it was akin to a celebration for them.

Contempt for the individual is still one of the sad features of the Russian mentality. Ivan the Terrible and Peter the Great destroyed thousands of their own citizens; Lenin, Stalin, and Zhukov killed millions ("women will bring more into the world"). And it is these individuals, not Gorbachev or Yeltsin, who are considered "heroes" in Russia. Putin is also "doing his best" to follow his violent predecessors—in the first ten days of the war with Ukraine, more Russian soldiers were killed than in several years of war in Afghanistan. He destroys mainly Russian-speaking cities in Ukraine such as Kharkiv, Mariupol, Mykolaiv, and Odesa with bombs and rockets. He needs victims precisely among "his own". This is what the Muscovite tradition is. Such is their mentality.

In fact, all Russian literature romanticizes a person incapable of living and working but capable of dying beautifully ("just look how he dies!") as a model of morality and spirituality.

Hospitality vs. Lack of Kindness

Hospitality is a traditional Russian trait. Guests are warmly welcomed there. This friendliness is sincere and comes from the heart.

It is not about window dressing or the fear of being "ashamed" in front of a guest, especially in front of a foreigner, about whom, by and large, a Russian doesn't really care. Disobedience to foreigners, just like hospitality, is as genuinely a Russian trait.

Are Russians nationalists? Nine out of ten will say: no, we are not nationalists, we are patriots. However, throughout Russian history, Russians have proven that treating representatives of other nationalities as inferior is by no means uncommon to them. This is the nationalism that Africans, Asians, and inhabitants of the Caucasus feel on their skin in Russia today.

In 2006, the human rights organization Amnesty International published a report, the title of which speaks for itself: "Rabid Racism and Xenophobia in Russian Society". According to a poll conducted by the Russian Levada Center in November 2005, 60% of Russian citizens supported xenophobic slogans in one way or another. Chechens, Romani, Azerbaijanis, Arabs, Americans, Jews, Estonians, Germans, and Japanese were considered "the worst" nations by Russian citizens at that time. In 2008, Georgians were declared the "most dangerous enemies". After 2014, the Ukrainians, of course, became public enemy number one, and after 2022 they were joined by the British, Poles, and Lithuanians.

Xenophobia exists not only in Russia. Covertly or openly, it also exists in European countries. However, anyone can travel peacefully in Europe as no one will react with hostility to a different language or skin color. You can't say the same about Russia.

Although, it also happens that a foreigner in Russia can be treated even better than a fellow Russian. After all, a Russian sees a decent and honest person in a foreigner, especially from the West, incapable of the mischief that is so common among his or her own people.

Culture vs. Ignorance

For centuries, Muscovy remained an underdeveloped wilderness. There were practically no schools, so usual for Kyiv and European lands, in the country. According to James Billington, director of the U.S. Library of Congress and the author of the book *Russia in Search of Itself*, until the middle of the 18th century, there was no national art, literature, or science in Russia. For a long time, everything new in Muscovy was produced by foreigners or people with an admixture of foreign blood. But the Russians consider them all to be Russians. The ability to accept everything great into their spiritual organism is one of the prominent features of Russian culture and mentality.

Subsequently, Russia offered the world a whole galaxy of talented and creative personalities such as Mikhail Lomonosov, Leo Tolstoy, Fyodor Dostoevsky, Ivan Turgenev, Anton Chekhov, Vladimir Nabokov, Sergei Rachmaninoff, Modest Mussorgsky, Pyotr Tchaikovsky; if this list were to be extended, it would take more than one page. From a backward wasteland, Russia gradually turned into a country that entered the vanguard of world art. The dynamism of the intellectual life of Moscow, St. Petersburg, and even regional centers is every bit as impressive as Russia's constant ability to include creative personalities from other countries.

However, all this has nothing to do with the cultural level of ordinary Russians, which traditionally remains low. For example, the Russian balalaika, a folk musical instrument, has three strings, and the Ukrainian bandura has as many as sixty-five.

Entrepreneurial Dexterity vs. Laziness

A Russian man is a conglomerate of contradictions. He is woven of dramatically opposite and mutually exclusive qualities. Practically all the heroes of the classics of Russian literature are ambiguous individuals. The contrary possibilities in the soul of a Russian person were and remain a source of creative energy for writers who know life firsthand.

The ambiguous Russian nature also includes such seemingly opposite traits as entrepreneurial dexterity and laziness.

In noble families, the focus on business acumen was not part of children's education. The main values did not include hard work, but rather a noble nature, intelligence, and honor. However, these are not tools for success. They are values. A nobleman learned his hereditary privilege — an aversion to labor — from early childhood. He disdained to engage in crafts, industrial activities, or trade; instead, he devoted all his time to hunting, cards, and formal balls.

Honest earnings have never been appreciated in Russia. Those who sought to achieve something were treated with contempt. In the countryside, a gallant worker was despised more than a lazy person, and to prevent him corrupting others with his "contagion" of labor, people were always ready to destroy his farm.

A Russian person often wants to do something extraordinary: swim across the ocean, plant apple trees on Mars, invent a perpetuum mobile. However, few are willing to sow grain, stand at a work table, repair roads, and do anything that lies "outside the laws of a broad soul".

However, Russians are historically active and productive people. The myth of Russian laziness is not always well-founded. In the 1860s, the first wave of Russian capitalism arose. It was an era of primitive pirate capital accumulation. The purchase of land, the construction and development of railways caused a great stir and led to the making of massive fortunes.

The second wave marked the years between the revolution of 1905 and World War I. According to many indicators, these were the most favorable years in the life of Russia. During this time, industry strengthened, and agriculture was reformed. In terms of the level of scientific activity and the quality of the training of specialists, Moscow and St. Petersburg universities reached the level of leading European institutions.

The level of entrepreneurship is relatively high in modern Russia as well. But it is hampered by incredible corruption, a habit of defrauding and deceiving one's business partners, disrespect for hard work, and, last but not least, easy enrichment through the sale of oil. This is what the modern economy of Russia is based on—"a gas station with a nuclear bomb".

Haste—Categorical thinking—Determination

> *There are two problems in Russia: fools and roads. And*
> *Ukraine has three problems: fools, roads, and Russia.*
> Anecdote

Reckless haste characterizes the Russian man. He wants immediate gratification. The most important thing is to have everything in abundance and with no effort. He does not like lengthy negotiations weighing the pros and cons; he makes decisions in one fell swoop, without deliberation. And his passion for argument and rejection of any opinion other than his own have long been a characteristic feature of Russians. Everyone yells, and never listens to others, during discussions on Russian TV channels.

Decisiveness and purposefulness manifest themselves in character traits such as determination and self-confidence. Tracking the origins of self-confidence in different peoples, Leo Tolstoy remarked that education explained self-confidence in Germans; faith in their own charm explains it in the French; pride in their state in the English; and temperament in the Italians. For Russians, the writer found the following explanation: "A Russian is self-assured simply because he knows nothing and does not want to know anything".

The Russian's assertiveness and haste play a part in his stubbornness. But in the event of loss, he is ready to destroy everything he can get his hands on, as often happens after soccer matches, or after the defeat of Russian troops near Kyiv in 2022. While retreating, Russian soldiers tortured and shot hundreds of civilians, mostly women and children.

Unpredictability — Curiosity — Unpretentiousness

A Russian's propensity to extremes is evident in his or her unpredictability: a Russian will captivate with hospitality, generosity, and selflessness while at the same time striking with brutality and rudeness.

A Russian does not recognize general canons either in business or everyday life. He has his own rules. He is inquisitive and seeks to discover new lands and acquire new impressions; the Russian language resonates in the most remote corners of the planet. Russians' curiosity of is evidenced not only in their passion for travel but also in their powerful scientific promise: eighteen Russians are among Nobel Prize laureates.

A Russian is unpretentious in everyday life and not picky about food — he can eat whatever he finds. Russian national cuisine is quite primitive, almost non-existent: potatoes, buckwheat porridge, pancakes, cabbage soup, pies, dumplings . . . Any restaurant delicacies are the products of the imagination of gourmet chefs rather than the people.

Humor — Camaraderie — Drunkenness

As a rule, a Russian is an extrovert — he cannot stand a reserved lifestyle; it is difficult for him to adapt to loneliness; he is happy to meet new people. Unlike a Westerner, he does not visit psychotherapists that much. Why? friends replace them: "pouring out his soul" and "crying on someone's shoulder" is commonplace.

But this medal has another side: the habit of imposing one's problems on others. Foreigners, admiring the openness of the Russian soul, note Russians' lack of tact and observance of generally accepted personal space. They are also struck by Russians' coupling of their mission with "God's Providence", pretentiousness, a desire to be in the foreground, and high ambitions, combined with a broad but categorical and infantile personality. compared with organized, disciplined, and punctual Europeans, who have achieved much in their life, a Russian with his carelessness, lack of responsibility, and unpredictability resembles a big foolish child.

On the other hand, a Russian is a skeptic and scoffer, a talker, and a cynic. Jokes, puns, and witty remarks always accompany everything from business negotiations to the funerals of general secretaries.

Similarly, everything in Russia is necessarily accompanied by alcohol. Peter I established the tradition of drinking — participation in multi-day royal drinking feasts comprised one of the most important duties of his subordinates. Pleasing the sovereign, high-ranking individuals of all ranks cemented this tradition in the collectives entrusted to them. Even in the army: drunkenness is a vice in an officer worldwide, but in Russia, it is the norm. After all, a Russian can rest, work, and even fight with nothing more than a bottle in his pocket.

Love

A Russian woman is a national treasure. She is beautiful, sweet, friendly, and ready to follow her chosen one to Siberia, space, or even the Hawaiian islands. Her openness of soul shaped her charming, subtle, and sensitive nature.

Russian love songs are no less diverse than Ukrainian ones. However, complaints from a young woman who is being forced to marry, or reproaches from a husband to an unloved wife are much more common in Russian songs. From reproaches, a man moves to action: "if he beats her, that means he loves her" — this is what Russian women concluded, and this is what the representatives of all Russian society agreed upon. Receiving rude treatment and abuse from the authorities, Russians copy this pattern in family relationships.

Conclusion

Let's avoid generalizations about the Russian character. What we have considered here is only the tip of the iceberg. It would take an entire book to depict the entire iceberg.

They say that Russians live according to concepts close to Murphy's law. Perhaps this is true. However, we are talking about a nation that, living in difficult natural conditions, managed to create a huge state that plays an important role in the world. We are talking about the people who, in World War II, in an unimaginably short period of time, transferred industry to the Urals, provided Soviet troops with weapons, and, together with the nations that were part of the USSR, along with the United States and Britain, won victory over fascism.

Now Russia is trying to turn the course of history in the opposite direction. In 2014 and later in 2022, full of contempt for democracy and grounded in hatred and envy of everything civilized, the "Russian World" invaded Ukraine. The vast majority of the Russian population supported the actions of its paranoid president. In essence, Russia unleashed World War III. This is not only a World War but also a war of worlds with fundamentally different value systems.

In his column for *The New York Times* of May 19, 2022, American historian and Yale University professor Timothy Snyder noted:

"We should all say it. Russia is Fascist. [. . .]

The war against Ukraine is not only a return to the traditional fascist battleground but also a return to traditional fascist language and practice. [. . .] The fascist leader has to be defeated, which means that those who oppose fascism have to do what is necessary to defeat him. [. . .] If Russia wins in Ukraine, it won't be just the destruction of a democracy by force, though that is bad enough. It will be a demoralization for democracies everywhere. [. . .] If Ukraine does not win, we can expect decades of darkness".

Ukrainians, whose mentality is based on democracy, freedom, and defiance of foreign invaders, stopped the onslaught of Russian troops. All civilized countries have risen up against Russia. The unity of Ukraine and the West guards the existence of the Free World, whose antithesis is the "Russian World".

Winds of New Times

Let's return to the topic of Ukrainian mentality.

Has much changed in the worldview of Ukrainians in the 21st century?

It certainly has. Moreover, the process has been striking. Ukraine has undergone colossal changes over the past thirty years. Like a quiet village waking from a lethargic sleep, it began to build fountains, banks, and supermarkets on the sites of Lenin monuments . . . Having freed themselves from communist illusions, Ukrainians, on the one hand, rushed to the fairway of world civilization and, on the other, returned to their original values. Along with the ruins of the Soviet empire, unfulfilled hopes, the anticipation of a bright free future, poverty and drunkenness remained in the past. However, the eternal Ukrainian problems, including lack of economic reforms, corruption, political instability, and Russian aggression, have not disappeared. On the way to joining the European Union, Ukraine remains almost where it was two decades ago.

And yet the process is underway. Today in Ukraine, there is much less class envy toward those who have achieved material stability and success in life. Freedom of speech is an immutable reality with an inviolable authority. The Ukraine of the 21st century — in terms of service quality, the development of private businesses, food quality, restaurant service, attractiveness of the interiors of public places, bureaucratic efficiency, simplicity of bank transactions, quality of the beauty industry, quality of private medicine, and the general feeling of security and hospitality—appears to be much better than ever.

Unprecedented conditions such as the Revolution of Dignity and the War with Russia revealed many features of the Ukrainian mentality. Unforeseen circumstances, which threatened a national catastrophe, brought to the surface the traits instilled in Ukrainians since ancient times—disobedience, determination, and dignity. The Ukrainian army turned out to be one of the strongest in the world and the Ukrainian government, usually sluggish in peacetime, showed incredible efficiency in the most challenging conditions.

Ukrainians have "grown up". Once tax inspectors were removed, taxes were paid. Once the truth was told about the number of people killed in the war, there was no hysteria. Once firearms were distributed to the population, the number of occupiers decreased, and the level of crime in the country declined.

The Ukraine of the past and the Ukraine of the present appear to be different countries. Therefore, it is not surprising that, until now, the world had no idea about Ukraine; now it has united with it in the fight against world evil.

How Ukrainians See Themselves

To understand Ukrainians' perception of themselves, it is worth comparing the data of polls conducted in 1996 and 2016. Any sociological poll is subjective and hardly reflects the entire range of opinions of the country's residents. However, certain conclusions can be drawn.

In 1996, Ukrainians most frequently positively noted such traits as hospitality, kindness, generosity, hard work, sociability, intelligence, a good sense of humor, and mastering the household. They registered greed, cunning, laziness, indifference, and stupidity among their negative traits.

In 2016, hard work, optimism, tolerance, cheerfulness, love of freedom, perseverance, and dignity came to the fore.

Analysis of this data with percentage comparison would suggest that Ukrainians believe that, in twenty years, their hard work has tripled (really?); the same can be said about optimism, love of freedom, and sense of humor (although it is doubtful that there were any issues with the latter before). Hospitality remained unchanged. Although, according to the respondents, Ukrainian generosity decreased (respondents seem to be ignorant of the massive volunteer support of the army); tolerance and kindness also decreased substantially.

The Ukrainians' subjective attitude toward themselves makes sense, just like anyone's attitude toward themselves. And what do foreigners say about Ukrainians?

The View of Foreigners

Dietmar Stüdemann, Ambassador Extraordinary and Plenipotentiary of Germany to Ukraine from 2000 to 2006

"When I recall the five years I spent in Ukraine, it seems to me that everything was spinning as if in a fast-paced movie. If for a long time Ukraine was content stating that it was not Russia, starting in November–December of 2004, the entire world community realized this as well. Despite all the challenges and turning points of its development, despite the deadlocked situations that repeatedly arose in its path, Ukraine has great potential, which indicates its ability to develop independently in all fields. And as the awareness of the inseparability between the state and society grows in Ukraine, so does my satisfaction with the fact that it is moving in the right direction".

Yuval Noah Harari, author of the international bestseller Sapiens: A Brief History of Humankind.

"Ukraine now resembles a power plant that provides energy to most of the world. People worldwide admire Ukrainians. At the same time, they learn their own lessons from what is happening in Ukraine.

Europe has united in a way that was inconceivable some three months ago. Finland and Sweden are joining NATO and sending weapons to Ukraine. Switzerland is imposing sanctions. Giant corporations are withdrawing their investments from Russia. Much is happening because everyone can see that Ukraine is fighting with its bare hands against Russian tanks. They think, 'I can also do something to improve the situation'.

The whole world admires the courage of the Ukrainian people, who are fighting not only for their freedom but also for the protection of HUMAN achievements. The future of all of us largely depends on Ukraine".

Natalia Yaresko, an American of Ukrainian origin, a graduate of Harvard

The entrepreneurial spirit of Ukrainians is inexhaustible. If it were different, business would not have been able to survive for the last 10–15 years. In Ukraine, there are two main obstacles — corruption and bureaucracy. But an economic breakthrough is possible. Was Ireland or Finland much better or more powerful than Ukraine?

There are industries where Ukraine has strong development. Art is one example. Ukraine is the homeland of outstanding personalities who have influenced artistic trends both in music and in the visual arts. Modern Ukraine has a fantastic, diverse, rich, and highly professional culture. I wish you had seen the eyes of my eight-year-old daughter when she was talking about the Kyiv Puppet Theater! And this is after she had visited both Disneyland and Disney World.

Alla Kovnir, a Russian actress

What impresses me the most about Ukrainians is their politeness. When they recognize me in the streets of Kyiv or in a village near Poltava, where I sometimes spend time at my grandmother's house, people smile at me, may come up and ask permission to take a picture with me. If they recognize me in Moscow, all I hear is either, "you look better on TV" or "where's your dog?"

Tatiana Maikova, import manager, Russia

I see many similarities between the Ukrainians and the French. Both are gourmets. For a Frenchman, the main compliment for any house, city, or resort is "they have great food there". And for Ukrainians, the basis of hospitality is to provide an exquisite food experience.

Kishichiro Amae, Ambassador Extraordinary and
Plenipotentiary of Japan to Ukraine

Many Japanese still consider themselves samurai by blood. Although we lost in World War II, we made progress in economic development. Ukrainians are close to samurai. They have a Cossack spirit. Both samurai and Cossacks embody independence, respect for ancestors, protection of society, hatred of discrimination, and fear of dishonor.

Katerina Makarevich, Russian journalist

In 2015, Katerina Makarevich emigrated from Russia to Ukraine for political reasons. She discusses the Ukrainian mentality after one year of living in Kyiv.

Ukrainians have a distinctive mentality. When I first moved to Kyiv, many Russians who had emigrated here before told me: "You'll warm up here". At first, I didn't really understand what they meant, but now I can articulate it.

Warming up is when you walk down the street, and people look not at your feet but into your eyes. It's like a dialogue through eye contact as if they are asking you: "How are you?"

Warming up is when you are in a hurry, and an older woman walking in front of you lets you pass. Respect for your time from a complete stranger is priceless!

Warming up is when you notice someone holding the subway door for you. It seems like a small thing, but other people's care for you informs how you treat them.

Warming up is when you realize that you hear the words "thank you" much more often than before.

Warming up is when you realize that the accidental death of a boy shot by the police during a chase became the topic of public discussion. There is a "flip of stereotypes" when you see that the police initiate a conversation interested in the public's opinion about whether it is appropriate to limit police authority to use weapons. And you can't help thinking: "How fantastic is that! They want to understand and be inclusive of society! A citizen's point of view is important to them!"

Well, I can say I feel warm in Kyiv.

One of the main features of the Ukrainian mentality is kindness. In this sense, Ukrainians are indeed a unique nation. They remain open, hospitable, and somewhat idealistic after so many trials and disappointments. They are like that because they believe in the best in people.

However, Ukrainians clearly understand the difference between normal and adequate people, who respect the country's territorial integrity, and those who, let's say, have television screens instead of brains.

The Ukrainian people are indeed inherently non-aggressive. During my entire stay in Kyiv, I never felt any prejudice against me.

Ukrainians are friendly and hospitable. However, whether they let you into their circle depends on you. I was lucky — in just six months, I acquired a wide circle of the most diverse acquaintances, such as I could not have dreamt of when living in Moscow. In Russia, the vertical operates not only in power but also in socializing.

The habit of extensive communication is one of the main features of Ukrainians. It's always a long-distance marathon. People always care about you in Kyiv. There really is a special bond between people here on an energy level.

This is in contrast to Moscow, when you shut up in your conversation with friends, not daring to touch on the topic of politics, or when you lower your voice when passing a policeman, or when you can't resist proving something ridiculous to colleagues at work because it is customary to always prove something to someone. With Ukrainians, I enjoy the right to be myself. What is so strange here, as it would seem? But when you have past experience, then you are surprised and happy about what, for Kyivans, are the most ordinary things.

Ukrainians know how to listen. In Moscow, I often used to catch myself thinking that people were constantly talking to themselves, allowing you to insert a few words here and there. Everything is categorical there. In Ukraine, I noticed that such words as "in fact" and "I know" have almost disappeared from my lexicon. Instead, I began to use "it seems to me", "I think", and "in my opinion" more often. I developed another habit: I stopped drawing conclusions if they seemed too simplistic.

Ukraine is a mystical country. Here, the basis is not logic or reason but the heart's wisdom. I was not able to feel it right away. Kyiv is where the heart begins to beat in tune with its true nature. Sometimes it seems that something irrational is happening, but in reality, there is a different logic behind it.

During a few months of living in Ukraine, comparatively quite a short period of time, I made so many internal discoveries that it cannot even be compared with five years of experience during my stay in Moscow. Moscow is masculine, indifferent, and rational, while Kyiv is feminine, sympathetic, and wise. This is an entirely different, more profound perception of life.

Ukraine has definitely made me wiser. I found myself in an environment of such mental geniuses, where innovation is the norm. Here are guys who make copters, Ukrainian Bill Gateses, developing microcircuits for giants in the field of electronics, a geek program developer who designed a coffee machine that cleans water ten times better than ordinary ones. Young artists are creating the kind of paintings of which Salvador Dalí would be jealous! Dozens of projects that make your head spin! I walked around with my eyes wide open because all this was so cool! This is where the future is being born, and I see it.

Compared with Moscow, Kyiv's rhythm is more moderate. In Russia, when asked "How is Moscow?" people usually answer: "It's still standing!" And when my acquaintance from Moscow asked me: "How is Kyiv?" I realized I couldn't answer the way I used to answer about Moscow. The answer came naturally to me: "Kyiv is alive!" So, there is a dynamic in Kyiv, which is life!

I will also mention a few things to avoid the misconception that I am idealizing Ukrainians.

Like any nation, Ukrainians are not devoid of insecurities. The main one is the "younger brother" complex. I feel there is a tendency to overcoming it, but it is a long process.

Ukrainians do not always keep their word; they do not really like to take responsibility; they will readily transfer it to others. I experienced this many times. Everything seems to be agreed upon, and then all kinds of excuses appear, such as, it's not time yet, let's do this and that first, and then we'll see . . .

Another issue is that Ukrainians, like children, still believe in a fairy tale about a beautiful life. One of the main attributes of this fairy tale is the importance of having a considerable amount of money. One guy from Luhansk admitted to me that before the start of hostilities, when he watched Russian news on TV, he believed that if Russia appeared, everything would improve. After all, he shared the illusion that Russia is a country of wealthy people living satisfied lives. The Russians came and brought destruction, hunger, and death instead of a fairy tale . . . The fairy tale exists only on TV. I have also heard stories from many Crimeans about how the residents of Crimea, looking at Russian tourists throwing around money and having a great time, thought that everyone in Russia lived like this. So, they wanted the same thing for themselves. Rubles and Russian pensions arrived, and with that came the Russian mentality. Here it is, the dream of a beautiful life that played a cruel joke on them.

When I moved to Kyiv, I noticed you could often see SUVs and jeeps on the roads. That was surprising because the city is full of narrow streets, and the lack of parking makes it inconvenient to use large cars. I remember my first thought was: "How can that be? And they complain that the country is poor". In fact, everything turned out to be quite different. My friends explained to me that it is not that Ukrainians love big cars, but that an expensive foreign car, preferably a jeep, gives its owner a sense of significance and importance, especially when a person is not rich in terms of status.

Well, in Ukraine, the material component is critical in interpersonal relations. Here, many adhere to the principle "you scratch my back, and I'll scratch yours". If in everyday life it seems innocent, at the state level, no politician or official would exert their influence without profit for themselves. This might be why Ukrainians have such a bad attitude toward the authorities. But that attitude usually begins with fascination. Idealization passes quickly. And, regarding the speed with which the transition from fascination to disillusionment with the authorities occurs, Ukrainians probably occupy the leading position.

An interesting feature of the Ukrainian worldview is that you often find two parts of the same meme in the Ukrainian media: "betrayal" and "victory". This clearly underscores the peculiarity of the Ukrainian mentality, where everything is either black or white. Fifty shades of gray are for other nationalities, but you are either respected or ignored here.

Ukrainians are well aware of the difference between the concepts of "state" and "country". A country is a nation, people. And the state is power, officials. If in Russia, most citizens equate Russia with the Russian president, such a belief is nonsense for Ukrainians. For Ukrainians, "authority" is only hired managers who are allowed to manage the state, not the people, for a certain period of time. And at this point, Russians, who think criticizing the state means betraying the Motherland, are entirely at a loss.

Russian and Ukrainian worldviews also differ in their attitudes toward their heroes. In Ukraine, national heroes are people no different from you, but they surpass you in terms of honesty, justice, courage, or dignity. Russians don't have heroes; they have idols. Bowing before an idol is not self-development but awareness of one's insignificance before their greatness. People who bow before idols do nothing to emulate them; they just believe in them. The presence of heroes should lead to the evolution of one's own personality, and the aspiration to become one. And here we see why Russia is stuck in stagnation—why change yourself and the surrounding reality if there is someone who will do everything for you? Perhaps this is the main reason you feel staleness in Russia and hope in Ukraine.

Ukraine is a free country. I admit, before moving here, I was skeptical of such claims. The upside-down world of Russia, where slavery is called freedom, lies are called truth, and war is called peace, deprived me of faith that such big words can have precisely the meaning invested in them originally. But the longer I live in Kyiv, the more convinced I am that Ukraine is truly a place of freedom. Inner freedom. Despite everything. Many of my Moscow acquaintances say that I have changed. I look different, and I am different. Now I can say with confidence what the reason is. This is the very inner freedom that you feel surrounded by similarly free people. I will never be able to explain to Russians what it feels like to live in a country where there is a war, yet in which it is much easier to breathe, live with more freedom and think much more globally because where there is freedom there is honesty. And where there is honesty there is openness. And where there is openness there is respect for others. In a country where respect is the norm, you feel free a priori. And when there is inner freedom — you want to live!

Once, while walking with friends in the central square of Kyiv, *Maidan Nezalezhnosti*, I noticed an inscription made with chalk on the wall of a building. For some reason, though it was just a brief expression, it was very empowering. The phrase was: "Do not be afraid!" This would seem to be a simple phrase, but it is part of this air of freedom, and you automatically begin to believe it is not there by chance.

There is an Odesan proverb: "Wash your feet first, and then do a pedicure". So, according to this saying, Ukrainians are now washing their feet, washing off the entire burden of the Soviet era. It is difficult, and it is probably even frightening for those who are used to living by the old rules. But if anyone still doubts that Ukraine is Europe, I know for sure: it is.

Epilogue

I have only partly described the world that we call the Ukrainian mentality. Previously, little was known about it. Even we Ukrainians have not really understood it. We did not think we had such strength, courage, and will to continue to strive for freedom. All this lay under the ruins of history waiting to explode as a new star that appeared among the other stars in the earth's sky.

In 2022, a new expression appeared in the English Urban Dictionary after the beginning of the Russo-Ukrainian war—"to be Ukrained". It means resisting the aggressors and humiliating them before the world. Russia has enough military power to destroy Ukrainian cities. But it has proved too weak to overcome the Ukrainian spirit.

During the Russian military invasion, Ukraine became a catalyst for the restoration of the planet. Previously, there was an agreement among world analysts that, with every passing year, Europe and the USA would lose their position in the world, and China would rise in dominance. Ukraine's heroic resistance to global evil brought the Western world out of hibernation: democratic nations pulled themselves up by their bootstraps and joined the effort to bring the planet in line with the principles of a developed civilization. Europe has become younger before our eyes. NATO has experienced a rebirth.

Looking at the situation in Ukraine, other countries rejected the idea that you can be friends with the perpetrators of evil on a massive scale. It became clear that evil must be destroyed, so that no one can repeat what Hitler did in the 20th century and what his senseless reincarnation Putin is doing in the twenty-first.

The Ukrainian experience has shown that a gigantic army, armed to the teeth, can be just as easily destroyed as any other. The people's will to be free is stronger than fighter jets, tanks, and missiles. The cartel of dictators who dream of absolute rule in the 21st century is undergoing a severe crisis. The reason for this is Ukraine's awakening of the West. Tens of thousands of human lives have been the price of this awakening. However, these sacrifices are not in vain.

Ukraine is located between the forty-fourth and the fifty-second parallels. This is the most favorable belt on the planet. Austria, Bavaria, Hungary, the Czech Republic, Luxembourg, France, Northern Italy, Switzerland, Belgium, England, parts of Canada, and the USA are in the same "oxygen zone". That is not bad company!

The ancestors of Ukrainians—the people of Trypillia and the inhabitants of Kyivan Rus—proved that by relying on reason, tireless work, and using the resources of an incredibly rich land, it was possible to build a mighty civilization on the land that is now called Ukraine. The Zaporozhian Cossacks walked through Europe as brave hunters. Ukrainians stopped the onslaught of darkness in 2022. A free society, stepping over the burdens of the moss-covered world, living contrary to the standards of that world, proved its right to be different from everyone else.

The unique character of the Ukrainian mentality as a civilizational phenomenon is based on the following: transcending stereotypes and clichés to preserve freedom, harmony, and beauty in the world.

Ukrainians have their own mentality, with their own archetypes, honed over the ages. And now the prophetic words of Carl Jung have come true: *Like riverbeds, archetypes dry up when the water leaves them. But they are replenished with a raging full-water stream when the time comes.*

Therefore, world, fear not! We are on guard. If you suddenly feel insecure, we will support you. After all, we are one family. And may harmony reign in this family.

Ukrainian Voices

Collected by Andreas Umland

1   *Mychailo Wynnyckyj*
    Ukraine's Maidan, Russia's War
    A Chronicle and Analysis of the Revolution of Dignity
    With a foreword by Serhii Plokhy
    ISBN 978-3-8382-1327-9

2   *Olexander Hryb*
    Understanding Contemporary Ukrainian and Russian Nationalism
    The Post-Soviet Cossack Revival and Ukraine's National Security
    With a foreword by Vitali Vitaliev
    ISBN 978-3-8382-1377-4

3   *Marko Bojcun*
    Towards a Political Economy of Ukraine
    Selected Essays 1990–2015
    With a foreword by John-Paul Himka
    ISBN 978-3-8382-1368-2

4   *Volodymyr Yermolenko (ed.)*
    Ukraine in Histories and Stories
    Essays by Ukrainian Intellectuals
    With a preface by Peter Pomerantsev
    ISBN 978-3-8382-1456-6

5   *Mykola Riabchuk*
    At the Fence of Metternich's Garden
    Essays on Europe, Ukraine, and Europeanization
    ISBN 978-3-8382-1484-9

6   *Marta Dyczok*
    Ukraine Calling
    A Kaleidoscope from Hromadske Radio 2016–2019
    With a foreword by Andriy Kulykov
    ISBN 978-3-8382-1472-6

7   *Olexander Scherba*
     Ukraine vs. Darkness
     Undiplomatic Thoughts
     With a foreword by Adrian Karatnycky
     ISBN 978-3-8382-1501-3

8   *Olesya Yaremchuk*
     Our Others
     Stories of Ukrainian Diversity
     With a foreword by Ostap Slyvynsky
     Translated from the Ukrainian by Zenia Tompkins and Hanna Leliv
     ISBN 978-3-8382-1475-7

9   *Nataliya Gumenyuk*
     Die verlorene Insel
     Geschichten von der besetzten Krim
     Mit einem Vorwort von Alice Bota
     Aus dem Ukrainischen übersetzt von Johann Zajaczkowski
     ISBN 978-3-8382-1499-3

10   *Olena Stiazhkina*
     Zero Point Ukraine
     Four Essays on World War II
     Translated from the Ukrainian by Svitlana Kulinska
     ISBN 978-3-8382-1550-1

11   *Oleksii Sinchenko, Dmytro Stus, Leonid Finberg (compilers)*
     Ukrainian Dissidents
     An Anthology of Texts
     ISBN 978-3-8382-1551-8

12   *John-Paul Himka*
     Ukrainian Nationalists and the Holocaust
     OUN and UPA's Participation in the Destruction of Ukrainian Jewry, 1941–1944
     ISBN 978-3-8382-1548-8

13   *Andrey Demartino*
     False Mirrors
     The Weaponization of Social Media in Russia's Operation to Annex Crimea
     With a foreword by Oleksiy Danilov
     ISBN 978-3-8382-1533-4

14 *Svitlana Biedarieva (ed.)*
    Contemporary Ukrainian and Baltic Art
    Political and Social Perspectives, 1991–2021
    ISBN 978-3-8382-1526-6

15 *Olesya Khromeychuk*
    A Loss
    The Story of a Dead Soldier Told by His Sister
    With a foreword by Andrey Kurkov
    ISBN 978-3-8382-1570-9

16 *Marieluise Beck (Hg.)*
    Ukraine verstehen
    Auf den Spuren von Terror und Gewalt
    Mit einem Vorwort von Dmytro Kuleba
    ISBN 978-3-8382-1653-9

17 *Stanislav Aseyev*
    Heller Weg
    Geschichte eines Konzentrationslagers im Donbass 2017–2019
    Aus dem Russischen übersetzt von
    Martina Steis und Charis Haska
    ISBN 978-3-8382-1620-1

18 *Mykola Davydiuk*
    Wie funktioniert Putins Propaganda?
    Anmerkungen zum Informationskrieg des Kremls
    Aus dem Ukrainischen übersetzt von Christian Weise
    ISBN 978-3-8382-1628-7

19 *Olesya Yaremchuk*
    Unsere Anderen
    Geschichten ukrainischer Vielfalt
    Aus dem Ukrainischen übersetzt von Christian Weise
    ISBN 978-3-8382-1635-5

20 *Oleksandr Mykhed*
    „Dein Blut wird die Kohle tränken"
    Über die Ostukraine
    Aus dem Ukrainischen übersetzt von Simon Muschick
    und Dario Planert
    ISBN 978-3-8382-1648-5

21 *Vakhtang Kipiani (Hg.)*
    Der Zweite Weltkrieg in der Ukraine
    Geschichte und Lebensgeschichten
    Aus dem Ukrainischen übersetzt von Margarita Grinko
    ISBN 978-3-8382-1622-5

22 *Vakhtang Kipiani (ed.)*
    World War II, Uncontrived and Unredacted
    Testimonies from Ukraine
    Translated from the Ukrainian by Zenia Tompkins and Daisy Gibbons
    ISBN 978-3-8382-1621-8

23 *Dmytro Stus*
    Vasyl Stus
    Life in Creativity
    Translated from the Ukrainian by Ludmila Bachurina
    ISBN 978-3-8382-1631-7

24 *Vitalii Ogiienko (ed.)*
    The Holodomor and the Origins of the Soviet Man
    Reading the Testimony of Anastasia Lysyvets
    With forewords by Natalka Bilotserkivets and Serhy Yekelchyk
    Translated from the Ukrainian by Alla Parkhomenko and Alexander J. Motyl
    ISBN 978-3-8382-1616-4

25 *Vladislav Davidzon*
    Jewish-Ukrainian Relations and the Birth of a Political Nation
    Selected Writings 2013-2021
    With a foreword by Bernard-Henri Lévy
    ISBN 978-3-8382-1509-9

26 *Serhy Yekelchyk*
    Writing the Nation
    The Ukrainian Historical Profession in Independent Ukraine and the Diaspora
    ISBN 978-3-8382-1695-9

27 *Ildi Eperjesi, Oleksandr Kachura*
    Shreds of War
    Fates from the Donbas Frontline 2014-2019
    With a foreword by Olexiy Haran
    ISBN 978-3-8382-1680-5

28 *Oleksandr Melnyk*
    World War II as an Identity Project
    Historicism, Legitimacy Contests, and the (Re-)Construction of
    Political Communities in Ukraine, 1939–1946
    With a foreword by David R. Marples
    ISBN 978-3-8382-1704-8

29 *Olesya Khromeychuk*
    Ein Verlust
    Die Geschichte eines gefallenen ukrainischen Soldaten,
    erzählt von seiner Schwester
    Mit einem Vorwort von Andrej Kurkow
    Aus dem Englischen übersetzt von Lily Sophie
    ISBN 978-3-8382-1770-3

30 *Tamara Martsenyuk, Tetiana Kostiuchenko (eds.)*
    Russia's War in Ukraine 2022
    Personal Experiences of Ukrainian Scholars
    ISBN 978-3-8382-1757-4

31 *Ildikó Eperjesi, Oleksandr Kachura*
    Shreds of War. Vol. 2
    Fates from Crimea 2015–2022
    With an interview of Oleh Sentsov
    ISBN 978-3-8382-1780-2

32 *Yuriy Lukanov, Tetiana Pechonchik (eds.)*
    The Press: How Russia destroyed Media Freedom in
    Crimea
    With a foreword by Taras Kuzio
    ISBN 978-3-8382-1784-0

33 *Megan Buskey*
    Ukraine Is Not Dead Yet
    A Family Story of Exile and Return
    ISBN 978-3-8382-1691-1

34 *Vira Ageyeva*
    Behind the Scenes of the Empire
    Essays on Cultural Relationships between Ukraine and Russia
    With a foreword by Oksana Zabuzhko
    ISBN 978-3-8382-1748-2

35 *Marieluise Beck (ed.)*
    Understanding Ukraine
    Tracing the Roots of Terror and Violence
    With a foreword by Dmytro Kuleba
    ISBN 978-3-8382-1773-4

36 *Olesya Khromeychuk*
    A Loss
    The Story of a Dead Soldier Told by His Sister, 2nd edn.
    With a foreword by Philippe Sands
    With a preface by Andrii Kurkov
    ISBN 978-3-8382-1870-0

37 *Taras Kuzio, Stefan Jajecznyk-Kelman*
    Fascism and Genocide
    Russia's War Against Ukrainians
    ISBN 978-3-8382-1791-8

38 *Alina Nychyk*
    Ukraine Vis-à-Vis Russia and the EU
    Misperceptions of Foreign Challenges in Times of War, 2014–2015
    With a foreword by Paul D'Anieri
    ISBN 978-3-8382-1767-3

39 *Sasha Dovzhyk (ed.)*
    Ukraine Lab
    Global Security, Environment, Disinformation Through the Prism of Ukraine
    With a foreword by Rory Finnin
    ISBN 978-3-8382-1805-2

40 *Serhiy Kvit*
    Media, History, and Education
    Three Ways to Ukrainian Independence
    With a preface by Diane Francis
    ISBN 978-3-8382-1807-6

41 *Anna Romandash*
    Women of Ukraine
    Reportages from the War and Beyond
    ISBN 978-3-8382-1819-9

42 *Dominika Rank*
    Matzewe in meinem Garten
    Abenteuer eines jüdischen Heritage-Touristen in der Ukraine
    ISBN 978-3-8382-1810-6

43 *Myroslaw Marynowytsch*
    Das Universum hinter dem Stacheldraht
    Memoiren eines sowjet-ukrainischen Dissidenten
    Mit einem Vorwort von Timothy Snyder und einem Nachwort
    von Max Hartmann
    ISBN 978-3-8382-1806-9

44 *Konstantin Sigow*
    Für Deine und meine Freiheit
    Europäische Revolutions- und Kriegserfahrungen im heutigen
    Kyjiw
    Mit einem Vorwort von Karl Schlögel
    Herausgegeben von Regula M. Zwahlen
    ISBN 978-3-8382-1755-0

45 *Kateryna Pylypchuk*
    The War that Changed Us
    Ukrainian Novellas, Poems, and Essays from 2022
    With a foreword by Victor Yushchenko
    Paperback ISBN 978-3-8382-1859-5
    Hardcover ISBN 978-3-8382-1860-1

46 *Kyrylo Tkachenko*
    Rechte Tür Links
    Radikale Linke in Deutschland, die Revolution und der Krieg in
    der Ukraine, 2013-2018
    ISBN 978-3-8382-1711-6

47 *Alexander Strashny*
    The Ukrainian Mentality
    An Ethno-Psychological, Historical and Comparative Exploration
    With a foreword by Antonina Lovochkina
    ISBN 978-3-8382-1886-1

48 *Alona Shestopalova*
    Pandora's TV Box
    How Russian TV Turned Ukraine into an Enemy Which has to be
    Fought
    ISBN 978-3-8382-1884-7

49 *Iaroslav Petik*
    Politics and Society in the Ukrainian People's Republic
    (1917–1921) and Contemporary Ukraine (2013–2022)
    A Comparative Analysis
    With a foreword by Oleksiy Tolochko
    ISBN 978-3-8382-1817-5

50   *Serhii Plokhii*
      Der Mann mit der Giftpistole
      ISBN 978-3-8382-1789-5

51   *Vakhtang Kipiani*
      Ukrainische Dissidenten unter der Sowjetmacht
      Im Kampf um Wahrheit und Freiheit
      ISBN 978-3-8382-1890-8

52   *Dmytro Shestakov*
      When Businesses Test Hypotheses
      A Four-Step Approach to Risk Management for Innovative Startups
      With a foreword by Anthony J. Tether
      ISBN 978-3-8382-1883-0

53   *Larissa Babij*
      A Kind of Refugee
      The Story of an American Who Refused to Leave Ukraine
      With a foreword by Vladislav Davidzon
      ISBN 978-3-8382-1898-4

54   *Julia Davis*
      In Their Own Words
      How Russian Propagandists Reveal Putin's Intentions
      ISBN 978-3-8382-1909-7

55   *Sonya Atlanova, Oleksandr Klymenko*
      Icons on Ammo Boxes
      Painting Life on the Remnants of Russia's War in Donbas, 2014-21
      Translated by Anastasya Knyazhytska
      ISBN 978-3-8382-1892-2

56   *Leonid Ushkalov*
      Catching an Elusive Bird
      The Life of Hryhorii Skovoroda
      ISBN 978-3-8382-1894-6

57   *Vakhtang Kipiani*
      Ein Land weiblichen Geschlechts
      Ukrainische Frauenschicksale im 20. und 21. Jahrhundert
      ISBN 978-3-8382-1891-5

58   *Petro Rychlo*
      „Zerrissne Saiten einer überlauten Harfe ..."
      Deutschjüdische Dichter der Bukowina
      ISBN 978-3-8382-1893-9

Book series "Ukrainian Voices"

Collector
Andreas Umland, National University of Kyiv-Mohyla Academy

Editorial Board
Lesia Bidochko, National University of Kyiv-Mohyla Academy
Svitlana Biedarieva, George Washington University, DC, USA
Ivan Gomza, Kyiv School of Economics, Ukraine
Natalie Jaresko, Aspen Institute, Kyiv/Washington
Olena Lennon, University of New Haven, West Haven, USA
Kateryna Yushchenko, First Lady of Ukraine 2005-2010, Kyiv
Oleksandr Zabirko, University of Regensburg, Germany

Advisory Board
Iuliia Bentia, National Academy of Arts of Ukraine, Kyiv
Natalya Belitser, Pylyp Orlyk Institute for Democracy, Kyiv
Oleksandra Bienert, Humboldt University of Berlin, Germany
Sergiy Bilenky, Canadian Institute of Ukrainian Studies, Toronto
Tymofii Brik, Kyiv School of Economics, Ukraine
Olga Brusylovska, Mechnikov National University, Odesa
Mariana Budjeryn, Harvard University, Cambridge, USA
Volodymyr Bugrov, Shevchenko National University, Kyiv
Olga Burlyuk, University of Amsterdam, The Netherlands
Yevhen Bystrytsky, NAS Institute of Philosophy, Kyiv
Andrii Danylenko, Pace University, New York, USA
Vladislav Davidzon, Atlantic Council, Washington/Paris
Mykola Davydiuk, Think Tank "Polityka," Kyiv
Andrii Demartino, National Security and Defense Council, Kyiv
Vadym Denisenko, Ukrainian Institute for the Future, Kyiv
Oleksandr Donii, Center for Political Values Studies, Kyiv
Volodymyr Dubovyk, Mechnikov National University, Odesa
Volodymyr Dubrovskiy, CASE Ukraine, Kyiv
Diana Dutsyk, National University of Kyiv-Mohyla Academy
Marta Dyczok, Western University, Ontario, Canada
Yevhen Fedchenko, National University of Kyiv-Mohyla Academy
Sofiya Filonenko, State Pedagogical University of Berdyansk
Oleksandr Fisun, Karazin National University, Kharkiv
Oksana Forostyna, Webjournal "Ukraina Moderna," Kyiv
Roman Goncharenko, Broadcaster "Deutsche Welle," Bonn
George Grabowicz, Harvard University, Cambridge, USA
Gelinada Grinchenko, Karazin National University, Kharkiv
Kateryna Härtel, Federal Union of European Nationalities, Brussels
Nataliia Hendel, University of Geneva, Switzerland
Anton Herashchenko, Kyiv School of Public Administration
John-Paul Himka, University of Alberta, Edmonton
Ola Hnatiuk, National University of Kyiv-Mohyla Academy
Oleksandr Holubov, Broadcaster "Deutsche Welle," Bonn
Yaroslav Hrytsak, Ukrainian Catholic University, Lviv
Oleksandra Humenna, National University of Kyiv-Mohyla Academy
Tamara Hundorova, NAS Institute of Literature, Kyiv
Oksana Huss, University of Bologna, Italy
Oleksandra Iwaniuk, University of Warsaw, Poland
Mykola Kapitonenko, Shevchenko National University, Kyiv
Georgiy Kasianov, Marie Curie-Skłodowska University, Lublin
Vakhtang Kebuladze, Shevchenko National University, Kyiv
Natalia Khanenko-Friesen, University of Alberta, Edmonton
Victoria Khiterer, Millersville University of Pennsylvania, USA
Oksana Kis, NAS Institute of Ethnology, Lviv
Pavlo Klimkin, Center for National Resilience and Development, Kyiv
Oleksandra Kolomiiets, Center for Economic Strategy, Kyiv
Sergiy Korsunsky, Kobe Gakuin University, Japan

Nadiia Koval, Kyiv School of Economics, Ukraine
Volodymyr Kravchenko, University of Alberta, Edmonton
Oleksiy Kresin, NAS Koretskiy Institute of State and Law, Kyiv
Anatoliy Kruglashov, Fedkovych National University, Chernivtsi
Andrey Kurkov, PEN Ukraine, Kyiv
Ostap Kushnir, Lazarski University, Warsaw
Taras Kuzio, National University of Kyiv-Mohyla Academy
Serhii Kvit, National University of Kyiv-Mohyla Academy
Yuliya Ladygina, The Pennsylvania State University, USA
Yevhen Mahda, Institute of World Policy, Kyiv
Victoria Malko, California State University, Fresno, USA
Yulia Marushevska, Security and Defense Center (SAND), Kyiv
Myroslav Marynovych, Ukrainian Catholic University, Lviv
Oleksandra Matviichuk, Center for Civil Liberties, Kyiv
Mykhailo Minakov, Kennan Institute, Washington, USA
Anton Moiseienko, The Australian National University, Canberra
Alexander Motyl, Rutgers University-Newark, USA
Vlad Mykhnenko, University of Oxford, United Kingdom
Vitalii Ogiienko, Ukrainian Institute of National Remembrance, Kyiv
Olga Onuch, University of Manchester, United Kingdom
Olesya Ostrovska, Museum "Mystetskyi Arsenal," Kyiv
Anna Osypchuk, National University of Kyiv-Mohyla Academy
Oleksandr Pankieiev, University of Alberta, Edmonton
Oleksiy Panych, Publishing House "Dukh i Litera," Kyiv
Valerii Pekar, Kyiv-Mohyla Business School, Ukraine
Yohanan Petrovsky-Shtern, Northwestern University, Chicago
Serhii Plokhy, Harvard University, Cambridge, USA
Andrii Portnov, Viadrina University, Frankfurt-Oder, Germany
Maryna Rabinovych, Kyiv School of Economics, Ukraine
Valentyna Romanova, Institute of Developing Economies, Tokyo
Natalya Ryabinska, Collegium Civitas, Warsaw, Poland
Darya Tsymbalyk, University of Oxford, United Kingdom
Vsevolod Samokhvalov, University of Liege, Belgium
Orest Semotiuk, Franko National University, Lviv
Viktoriya Sereda, NAS Institute of Ethnology, Lviv
Anton Shekhovtsov, University of Vienna, Austria
Andriy Shevchenko, Media Center Ukraine, Kyiv
Oxana Shevel, Tufts University, Medford, USA
Pavlo Shopin, National Pedagogical Dragomanov University, Kyiv
Karina Shyrokykh, Stockholm University, Sweden
Nadja Simon, freelance interpreter, Cologne, Germany
Olena Snigova, NAS Institute for Economics and Forecasting, Kyiv
Ilona Solohub, Analytical Platform "VoxUkraine," Kyiv
Iryna Solonenko, LibMod - Center for Liberal Modernity, Berlin
Galyna Solovei, National University of Kyiv-Mohyla Academy
Sergiy Stelmakh, NAS Institute of World History, Kyiv
Olena Stiazhkina, NAS Institute of the History of Ukraine, Kyiv
Dmitri Stratievski, Osteuropa Zentrum (OEZB), Berlin
Dmytro Stus, National Taras Shevchenko Museum, Kyiv
Frank Sysyn, University of Toronto, Canada
Olha Tokariuk, Center for European Policy Analysis, Washington
Olena Tregub, Independent Anti-Corruption Commission, Kyiv
Hlib Vyshlinsky, Centre for Economic Strategy, Kyiv
Mychailo Wynnyckyj, National University of Kyiv-Mohyla Academy
Yelyzaveta Yasko, NGO "Yellow Blue Strategy," Kyiv
Serhy Yekelchyk, University of Victoria, Canada
Victor Yushchenko, President of Ukraine 2005-2010, Kyiv
Oleksandr Zaitsev, Ukrainian Catholic University, Lviv
Kateryna Zarembo, National University of Kyiv-Mohyla Academy
Yaroslav Zhalilo, National Institute for Strategic Studies, Kyiv
Sergei Zhuk, Ball State University at Muncie, USA
Alina Zubkovych, Nordic Ukraine Forum, Stockholm
Liudmyla Zubrytska, National University of Kyiv-Mohyla Academy

Friends of the Series

Ana Maria Abulescu, University of Bucharest, Romania
Łukasz Adamski, Centrum Mieroszewskiego, Warsaw
Marieluise Beck, LibMod—Center for Liberal Modernity, Berlin
Marc Berensen, King's College London, United Kingdom
Johannes Bohnen, BOHNEN Public Affairs, Berlin
Karsten Brüggemann, University of Tallinn, Estonia
Ulf Brunnbauer, Leibniz Institute (IOS), Regensburg
Martin Dietze, German-Ukrainian Culture Society, Hamburg
Gergana Dimova, Florida State University, Tallahassee/London
Caroline von Gall, Goethe University, Frankfurt-Main
Zaur Gasimov, Rhenish Friedrich Wilhelm University, Bonn
Armand Gosu, University of Bucharest, Romania
Thomas Grant, University of Cambridge, United Kingdom
Gustav Gressel, European Council on Foreign Relations, Berlin
Rebecca Harms, European Centre for Press & Media Freedom, Leipzig
André Härtel, Stiftung Wissenschaft und Politik, Berlin/Brussels
Marcel Van Herpen, The Cicero Foundation, Maastricht
Richard Herzinger, freelance analyst, Berlin
Mieste Hotopp-Riecke, ICATAT, Magdeburg
Nico Lange, Munich Security Conference, Berlin
Martin Malek, freelance analyst, Vienna
Ingo Mannteufel, Broadcaster "Deutsche Welle," Bonn
Carlo Masala, Bundeswehr University, Munich
Wolfgang Mueller, University of Vienna, Austria
Dietmar Neutatz, Albert Ludwigs University, Freiburg
Torsten Oppelland, Friedrich Schiller University, Jena
Niccolò Pianciola, University of Padua, Italy
Gerald Praschl, German-Ukrainian Forum (DUF), Berlin
Felix Riefer, Think Tank Ideenagentur-Ost, Düsseldorf
Stefan Rohdewald, University of Leipzig, Germany
Sebastian Schäffer, Institute for the Danube Region (IDM), Vienna
Felix Schimansky-Geier, Friedrich Schiller University, Jena
Ulrich Schneckener, University of Osnabrück, Germany
Winfried Schneider-Deters, freelance analyst, Heidelberg/Kyiv
Gerhard Simon, University of Cologne, Germany
Kai Struve, Martin Luther University, Halle/Wittenberg
David Stulik, European Values Center for Security Policy, Prague
Andrzej Szeptycki, University of Warsaw, Poland
Philipp Ther, University of Vienna, Austria
Stefan Troebst, University of Leipzig, Germany

[Please send address requests for changes, corrections, and additions to this list to andreas.umland@stanforalumni.org.]

ibidem.eu